CRUISERS IN ACTION

Cruisers in Action
1939-1945

PETER C. SMITH

and

JOHN R. DOMINY

WILLIAM KIMBER · LONDON

First Published in 1981 by
WILLIAM KIMBER & CO. LIMITED
Godolphin House, 22a Queen Anne's Gate,
London, SW1H 9AE

Typeset by Robcroft
and printed and bound in Great Britain by
The Garden City Press Limited,
Letchworth, Hertfordshire, SG6 1JS

Contents

List of Illustrations

List of Drawings
by
John R. Dominy

List of Tables

Introduction

Warships are by their very nature and function dramatic examples of man's handiwork and, although the purpose for which they are constructed is that of waging war in the most efficient way then envisaged, they often result in creations of a special beauty as well as fear. The cruisers of the Royal Navy were among the most classical of warship types in the age of steam as the drawings and illustrations contained in this volume will show. The history of the cruiser is a long and diffuse one, for this warship type has the most diverse classification in naval terminology. In particular the cruiser is a uniquely British type of warship reflecting, as it did, the long and vulnerable sea highways of the Empire and the need to protect them. Whereas other nations could copy British types and assign special functions to them, cruisers in Royal Navy service although often designed to have particular merits always had to have a more spacious specification built into their plans.

In attempting to tell the story of the British cruiser in its last days of warfare we have tried to cover aspects of every facet of its many functions. To detail the individual histories of each ship and to describe every action in minute detail, with illustration showing every change in configuration and armament would have been a task which would have delighted us both. This would have been a mammoth work and publishing economics force us to compromise. This volume therefore contains details of the most interesting of the actions, many little-known, and the drawings cover many new aspects of the appearance of these lovely vessels, now alas, but a fading memory.

We would like to emphasise several points. This is *not* a technical history; such books are already prolific, and easily available. Nonetheless the basic background of the type is contained in the first two chapters, which will give the younger reader a basic guide for further detailed study. Armament changes were constant, and ships of the same class hardly ever were completed, and certainly never remained, with exactly the same armament. Therefore only general guides are given in the text, and the drawings show the ships at specific points in their careers. Plans were not always available showing the alterations made in wartime, but from minute study of those that are available together with photographs, the drawings reflect as accurately as is possible such changes in individual ships; many are thus absolutely new and should prove a boon to the model maker and ship enthusiast alike. The different functions of the cruiser are split up into eight *general* chapters for convenience of layout, but naturally the chapters overlap at various points. All operations described have been checked with official records as far as possible.

PETER C. SMITH,
Needingworth

JOHN R. DOMINY,
Aston-on-Trent

July 1981

CHAPTER ONE

British Cruisers: Development up to 1939

Historically, the cruiser type of warship in Royal Navy service has always been the most diffuse in characteristics and scope. Because of its gradual development throughout the latter half of the nineteenth century and the many and various concepts of warfare which the general classification was to embrace, the cruiser remained for much of the 1900's the most versatile and all-embracing of warships. In 1939 the world's fleets were still, in the main, built around the battleship. It was the most powerfully armed and armoured warship which could be constructed and came down in direct line of descent from the ships-of-the-line of Nelson's time. These vessels would decide the ultimate victory in a set-piece naval action. Although the ships had grown enormously, and the limits of their guns reached beyond the horizon for twenty miles or more, the basic concept of ship-to-ship slugging matches between such mastodons still remained the same. This mighty arbiter of the fate of nations had become so expensive with its growth that few nations could afford to build them, or had the massive expertise to do so, and this, coupled with the various limitation treaties imposed by war-weary governments after the Great War, had meant that by 1939 they comprised but a small proportion of the ships of all navies. In 1939 Great Britain had but twelve battleships and three battle-cruisers, the USA fifteen battleships, Japan nine and other nations even fewer. All were constructing new battleships to replace the old ships but the actual numbers would never exceed this figure by very much.

The dominance of the battleship in the scheme of things was already being challenged, as it had been so often in the past, by the alternatives of air-power and the submarine torpedo. Air power at sea was a new, and as yet unknown factor. Its advocates were strident in their demands that the aircraft carrier was the capital ship of the future, and they were to be proven briefly correct, but in 1939 there was no hard and fast evidence that this claim was any more valid than had been those of the torpedo boat and the submarine in earlier years, and these had proven quite incapable of taking away the battleship's crown. So aircraft carriers existed in the major fleets, but always in smaller numbers than battleships, and their role was divided between scouting duties, providing fighter protection and laying on torpedo- and dive-bomber attacks to weaken the enemy fleet prior to the main artillery duel which would decide the issue.

Although the development of the self-propelled underwater torpedo had continued apace, and had seemed an awesome weapon in theory, its deployment in time of war had proven something of a disappointment to its advocates. It exploited the weakness of the battleship by being able to pierce the ship's hull at its most vulnerable point, below the water line, under the main armour plating which kept out the heaviest shells; in practice however the ability to deliver the torpedo within close enough range to be effective in its execution had been insoluble. Surface torpedo-carrying vessels, the torpedo boat and a host of small craft of a similar nature, proved to be too unseaworthy to carry the torpedo outside coastal waters. With the development of the big gun and the adoption of long-range blockade their role became so limited as to render them extinct almost by World War I. To achieve a better platform to carry the torpedo to the enemy battle fleet at sea the torpedo boat was expanded into the destroyer and whole flotillas of such craft would accompany the main fleets to sea for this purpose. But again their size made their superior speed useless in anything of a seaway; quick firing guns made the approach of such lightly built craft almost suicidal in daylight and, in those pre-radar days, night attacks were very much hit-and-miss and rarely achieved anything concrete. The destroyer, although a powerful weapon and, if aggressively used, a limitation on the battleship, had not realised the hopes of their protagonists in this respect.

The submarine had even more potential, but once again the theory had not kept pace with the hardware. Submarines in the First World War were far too imprecise to achieve anything like what had been claimed for them, and, although development was continuing, they still lacked speed and staying power to drive battleships from the sea. What they did achieve was to put a new emphasis on the old policy of blockade. With the indiscrimate use of the submarine against merchant shipping the old power of Great Britain, the ability to starve its opponents into submission, was dramatically reversed. To cope with this threat ships to hunt submarines became as essential a part of a modern fleet as the more traditional types. Destroyers took over this role in addition to their usual one, and, because the threat was so great, specialised escort vessels had to be constructed by the hundred to counter the problem.

So, by the late 1930's most fleets included varying numbers of ships of the following types: *the battleship*, still the rock on which all others fell back upon in trouble; *the aircraft carrier*, with its varying roles, still something of a Cinderella but having enormous potential with the pell-mell development of aviation; *the destroyer*, escorter of fleets, potential threat to enemy fleets and anti-submarine ship *par excellence*; *the submarine* itself, a somewhat isolated and separate type of warship by its very nature, looked upon in Britain and Japan as a type to threaten enemy battlefleets, but in Germany, Italy and France as a commerce destroyer; and the various cheap *escort vessels*, known by a wide variety of names, sloop, corvette, torpedo boat, destroyer escort, but all really simply an anti-submarine platform for the protection of shipping. These were the main types, and they were supplemented by various specialised craft in small numbers, minelayers, minesweepers, boom defence, motor torpedo boats and the like.

The cruiser was different from all these. Its ancestors could be claimed to be the fast frigates, the corvettes and even, in Britain's case, the old 'second class' battleships, so wide was the range of functions it was supposed to perform and so mixed the experimentation over almost a century. Because of this hotch-potch of types, functions and duties it is not surprising that the cruiser, in theory the cheaper-to-build heavy warship filling the gap between the battleship and the destroyer, should embrace a wider latitude of sizes, armaments and speeds than any other type of warship.

The old arguments had produced almost as many classifications of the cruiser as there were ships to carry them: armoured and protected; broadside, first, second and third class, scouts, cruiser-minelayers, torpedo cruiser. The list at the beginning of the century was endless. The special conditions of the First World War had produced another refinement on these, the light cruiser, of high speed and capable of leading massed flotillas into action. By 1919 the word cruiser was almost without meaning, embracing as it did ships whose nominal displacement varied from 2,135 (*Pelorus*) to 14,600 (*Minotaur*) and where armament ranged from 4-inch to 9·2-inch. Certainly, new construction was indicative of a greater measure of homogeneity where displacement was to a more limited range of 3,500 (*Arethusa*) to 5,440 (*Birmingham*) and the new classes of wartime construction fell broadly within this range. Similarly, during the same period, there was a measure of standardisation in armament although it was not until the later war years that the policy of a mixed armament of 6-inch and 4-inch weapons for surface attack, was finally abandoned. Admittedly, there were the exceptions in the form of *Courageous* and *Glorious* with their battleship armament on a hull protected to light cruiser standards and although they were still described as cruisers until earmarked for conversion to aircraft carriers, they were accepted in practice as being something unique.

Many of these ships were obsolete by the end of the Great War and were soon struck from the lists, but under construction in Great Britain were the ships of the so-called *Improved Birmingham* class armed with 7·5-inch guns, and the 'E' class with 6-inch guns, high speed and no less than twelve, later increased to sixteen, torpedo tubes. Clearly the diversification was to be as great as ever.

It was due to the various international treaties that pre-occupied the Naval Powers during the 1920's and 1930's, that some rationalisation of these types came about, thus simplifying the issue. These treaties were far-ranging in their effects on British cruiser construction and proved a mill-stone against which the Admiralty was to struggle throughout the immediate pre-war years.

The main treaties were the Washington Conference and subsequent Naval Limitations Treaty of 1921-22, the Geneva Conference of 1927 and the London Naval Conference of 1939-40. The Second London Naval Conference of 1935-36 only handicapped her naval planners still further.

The potential armaments' race which initiated the American call for some form of limitation of naval armaments in 1921 was mainly concerned with battleship building, both in numbers and size. Most of the Conference was devoted to settling this thorny issue, but restrictions of cruisers were proposed as well. The Americans produced a set of figures out of the hat, as they had done for battleships and other types which proposed the total tonnage allowances for cruisers for the three principal naval powers (Great Britain, USA and Japan) as 450,000 tons apiece for the first two and 270,000 for Japan.

Not surprisingly this produced some indignation on this side of the Atlantic. To throw away her centuries-old dominance in sea power in terms of battleships took some swallowing, although

Governmental pressure and economics eventually ruled the day here. Yet with Great Britain's world-wide commitments and the vulnerability of her Mercantile Marine to armed surface raiders in the event of another war, the artificial restriction of her cruiser types, one of whose main functions was to patrol the trade routes against such raiders, was clearly intolerable. Even the politicians, ever-blind to defence needs, saw this point. Balfour himself pointed out that cruisers, as a type, should be treated from limitation viewpoints as special case. As the Admiralty argued, and the British Cabinet initially agreed, the needs of the USA and Great Britain in this respect bore no comparison at all. The British therefore countered with a proposal that even if such a limitation were necessary our own ratio should be correspondingly higher, volunteering tonnages of 450,000 for the Royal Navy, 300,000 for the USA and 250,000 for Japan as a more realistic yardstick.

Both Great Britain and America however were in accord on a limitation of the actual upper limit for cruisers as such, both coming independently to the conclusion that 10,000 tons displacement and 8-inch guns were the desirable maximums to work to, and this point was agreed. But no restrictions on the total number of ships was decided upon. In fact it quickly became clear that Great Britain had no great need for ships of this size at all, but, because other nations quickly embarked upon construction programmes for cruisers of the maximum size Britain had little choice but to follow suit. Thus came about the *County* class ships. Endless trouble was encountered with the new 8-inch gun designed for these vessels, for the Royal Navy already had highly-efficient alternatives. Although this was a wasteful policy in view of the limited funds available it was not fatal, providing we could also build sufficient smaller cruisers to suit our real needs. This was to prove not to be the case.

The Admiralty, responding to Japanese plans to build 10,000-ton 8-inch ships, put forward the *County* class as our reply and at once ran into trouble with the Treasury. A crisis followed which was only partly resolved by the threat of First Lord and the First Sea Lord (Bridgeman and Earl Beatty) to resign in 1925. But while Britain was being side-tracked on an issue which was somewhat irrelevant to her true needs, fresh proposals concerning cruisers came up at the Geneva Conference. This was brought about by America's suspicion of British intentions about the big cruisers. They now wanted to extend the 5:5:3 ratio imposed on battleship building for the three major powers to include cruisers as well, especially 8-inch cruisers. Britain countered with a proposal that the upper limit for cruisers be reduced to 7,500 tons and guns to 6·1-inches, which would amply suit our needs and our pocket.

The Admiralty again stressed the peculiar needs of Great Britain in this type of vessel to protect our trade routes and insisted that the *minimum* number required was seventy, twenty-five for fleet work and forty-five for trade defence. Unfortunately this figure was again to re-appear to haunt them in subsequent negotiations, and was never in fact to be achieved. The Americans would not hear of such a thing and further proposed a total tonnage restriction in ships of the cruiser type to only 250,000-300,000 tons and on this impasse the conference foundered. It was now a question of essential numbers of ships for Britain and a question of prestige for America, who would not accept 'a position of inferiority in any category of vessels', regardless of whether they needed them or not. The Americans would not accept cruisers armed with 6-inch guns and wanted parity; the British did not want 8-inch gun ships especially, but needed the quantity. There seemed no compromise.

In 1930, with a Labour Government in office in Great Britain and President Hoover in power in America, another attempt was made to cut down on armaments. This led to the London Conference and subsequent Naval Treaty of 1930, as a result of which all the earlier heroic attempts to hold out for a reasonable number of ships to defend the trade routes of the Empire went by the board. Initially the British re-iterated the need for at least seventy cruisers, the Americans demanded twenty-five 8-inch cruisers and neither side was any further forward. MacDonald and Hoover met in October; MacDonald had intimated that he would reduce the 'absolute minimum' cruisers needed to fifty! Not surprisingly agreement was quickly reached. The extent to which MacDonald had given way to US pressure is obvious from the final tonnage figures agreed to:

Heavy Cruisers (with guns larger than 6.1-inches): Britain; 146,800; USA: 180,000; Japan: 108,000
Light Cruisers (with guns of 6.1-inches or less): Britain; 192,000; USA: 143,500; Japan: 100,450

The Americans also won the right to build eighteen heavy cruisers against Britain's fifteen and Japan's twelve. Moreover although a higher proportion of British cruisers were over-age and obsolete than either of the other powers, a clause in the treaty prevented her from replacing these old ships with new vessels at anything like the speed necessary; the limitation was not more than 91,000 tons before the end of 1936, or only three small ships a year. Lord Chatfield's description of the outcome of this conference, as 'capitulation by the Admiralty to political *force majeure*', can be seen to be perfectly valid, and a high price was to be extracted for this sell-out in less than a decade.

Having thus been bound both numerically and quantitively by the will of the United States the Admiralty had to decide, in the face of continued hostility from the Treasury at home, how it could best provide for the needs of the nation's defences in an increasingly hostile world. It was a problem that cruiser building in particular was hard hit by.

Britain was now committed to building her fifteen heavy cruisers, with 8-inch guns. What tonnage was left over would need to be spread carefully to get even the new minimum numbers she needed. Moreover the question of air power was encroaching on all warship design and had to be taken into account. Increased AA weaponry could only come at the expense of other factors: reduction in armour protection, less main calibre weapons carried, speed and the like.

It was conveniently ignored, both by her foreign rivals and her own politicians, that the cruisers which survived for Britain in the mid-1920's contained a far larger proportion of ships that had seen hard war service and were therefore worn out, but these new treaties limited her ability to even replace these. In 1919 the Royal Navy had an overwhelming lead in all types of warship and possessed no less than 120 cruisers of all types. Even when the already obsolete vessels had gone to the breakers she still had this superiority, but whereas new vessels joining the fleet were confined to the limited remnants of wartime programmes embracing the 'C', 'D', 'E' and *Improved Birmingham* classes, twenty-one vessels in all, the Americans and Japanese were busy building *new* ships of these types, like the *Omaha* class of ten ships armed with twelve 6-inch guns, which far outclassed existing British types.

The continued pruning beyond safe bounds of the Naval Estimates by successive post-war Governments continued to bite, causing further scrappings and cancellations, and the appearance as early as August 1929 of the notorious 'Ten Year Rule', under which no major war was envisaged until that time had elapsed gave the already violently hostile Treasury a stick with which to beat the Admiralty still further as the 1920's progressed. To maintain even a semblance of the required cruiser strength during this period the Admiralty, under the outstanding leadership of Admiral Beatty, had to fight a two-front war. At times it is hard to see which was the bitterest enemy, the United States 'Navy-Second-to-None' Lobby or our own House of Parliament and the linked idealists with their woolly ideas of 'Collective Security'.

Thus under the 1919-20 Estimates of the 21 light cruisers which were ordered and under construction for the Royal Navy, four were cancelled right away. At the same time the General Board of the US Navy was pressing for the construction, in addition to the *Omahas*, of a further thirty new light cruisers for their fleet and Japan was pressing ahead with her own plans which included at least ten new cruisers. Eight of these new Japanese ships were to be armed with 8-inch guns to the new limit, and to counter these the British estimated that they would require no less than seventeen of the same type, eight for fleet work and at least nine to guard the Pacific trade routes of the Empire which the Japanese ships might threaten. This was in 1922 and a year later the above mentioned minimum needs for cruisers was put at seventy vessels of this type. It was suggested therefore that no less than eight 10,000 ton cruisers should be built each year from 1924-26 and four a year thereafter to give a total of 48 light cruisers.* This plan of course, even ignoring the desirability of building so many of the largest type, was quite unrealistic in the economic conditions then prevailing.

Neither was the US Navy backward: they wanted a start on sixteen such vessels and held up the example of the light battle-cruisers *Courageous* and *Glorious* as part of the reason for them, even though they knew full-well that these exceptional vessels were being converted into aircraft carriers, as were their own *Saratoga* and *Lexington* battle-cruiser hulls. Both France and Italy had commenced their own 'Treaty' cruisers of the *Tourville* and *Trento* classes. In the face of these even the reluctant Labour Government of Ramsay MacDonald had to assent to a modest start and lay down five of the eight *County* class 8-inch ships that the Admiralty had been asking for for two years.

Once the go-ahead had been given there was a tendency for the

---

* The 10,000 ton, 8-inch type were still called 'light cruisers' at this time. Not until 1929 were they re-classified as 'heavy' cruisers.

British to try and cram everything possible into the 10,000 tons. Not only was a whole new type of 8-inch gun to be carried by these ships but they insisted, in advance of their time it would seem, that these should be capable of anti-aircraft fire as well and they were required to have an extreme elevation of 70-degrees. This in itself was very commendable but the problems which arose by this additional technical innovation contributed much to the already massive teething problems of this new gun, and they were initially not very satisfactory in service. As Captain Grenfell was to point out, 'The new design of 8-in turrets fitted in *County* class cruisers took five years or more to make reasonably efficient. In their early years, they could seldom get off the eight rounds per gun of a practice shoot without falling to pieces.'*

In 1923 the Admiralty submitted their requirements asking on 21st November of that year for a full eight 10,000 ton cruisers spread over five years. This was followed by the approval of the legend for these ships a month later. The Government reacted sharply to such a massive programme and questioned the need to build such large ships. The Admiralty pointed out that, even should the whole eight be built by 1929, the Royal Navy would still only have 59 modern cruisers of all types, 31 of which would be required for fleet duties leaving only 28 for world-wide trade defence, and that all the other powers were building to the limits. They added this was but stage one of the full replacement programme of seventeen such ships. The Conservative Government of the day was almost immediately replaced by a minority Labour one heavily committed to retrenchment of armaments. With its arrival any hope of the Admiralty's full plan, or even of its first stage, vanished forever.

The plan was cut down in January 1924, only four being asked for in that year with five the following but the Government, swayed far more by the need to mitigate unemployment than by any consideration of Imperial defence, finally agreed to lay down five 10,000 ton cruisers, *Berwick*, *Cornwall*, *Cumberland*, *Kent* and *Suffolk*. The situation was mitigated by the decision of the Australian Government to build two such vessels to the same design, and these became the *Australia* and *Canberra*. Thus seven of the initial eight 10,000 tonners were safely begun. The subsequent programme, however, was to undergo more serious opposition.

Designed by Sir Eustace Tennyson d'Eyncourt, they were unlike

---

* Grenfell, Captain Russell, *The Bismarck Episode*, (Faber, 1953), p 199.

any contemporary vessels anywhere. Indeed their whole appearance seemed to be a throwback to the late Victorian or Edwardian period of warship design and brought visions of the *Powerful* and *Terrible* of that period; high white hulls on the China Station made the similarity even more pronounced. Described by some as classic and handsome, to the common sailor they stuck out of the water like great barns, and references to P & O Liners and the like had more than a hint of justification in them. Their enormous freeboard and three tall funnels made them stand out and presented glorious targets for rangefinders and guns. Nor then did these great blank hulls with their rows of scuttles hide the fact that their armour protection was pathetic for vessels of such size and cost. In truth to gain the maximum armament and speed called for the designer had little left over for defence and they had no main belt protection. A 3-5 inch belt was added later. The 1½-inch armour on their decks and 1-inch on their turrets resulted in spreading what protection there was across their magazines and machinery. Another retrograde step was their anti-torpedo bulges which were external instead of internal as in most modern heavy ships. The five-rounds-a-minute main armament might have redressed the balance somewhat, had it been achieved. As completed they all came out at just under the 10,000 ton limit, but foreign ships like the *Trento* cast a blind eye to such niceties as Treaty Limits and displaced over 12,000 tons, so these first 'Treaty' ships were already outclassed before they took to the water.

By April 1924 it was already manifest that the Admiralty were having second thoughts on the wisdom of constructing such costly vessels of limited value, and it was hoped that a 7,000 ton limit might come about. The United States, however, was firmly against any such reductions in size at all, nor would it agree to scale down the maximum calibre of the guns to 6 inches. In October the Labour Government were overthrown and the Conservatives reinstated but already fears of a new building race, in heavy cruisers rather than battleships, was hardening opposition to the construction of the full Admiralty programme. However much Their Lordships might wish to restrict the upper limits of individual ships, they were still as opposed as ever to restrictions on *total* tonnages, as we have seen, and they remained so, but with decreasing hopes of seeing their views carrying weight at international levels.

Beatty's next battle was with Churchill, who as Chancellor was opposing Navy expenditure with all the passion with which he had campaigned to uphold it six years before! So great was the fight for economy that the 8-inch cruiser programme had to be split; although seven such ships were to be laid down in the years 1925-26, a new type carrying only six main guns instead of eight, was introduced. In addition a further three of the older cruisers had to be scrapped despite the fact that the Admiralty wished to retain even over-age ships to redress the shortage in numbers.

The subsequent conference at Geneva has been mentioned, and it was in the aftermath of this that the Admiralty decided to drop any further 8-inch ships and concentrate on heavily protected 6-inch armed ships, despite what other nations did. By this time the four ships of the *London* Class, *Devonshire*, *London*, *Shropshire* and *Sussex* had been followed by the two surviving ships of the *Norfolk* Class, *Dorsetshire* and *Norfolk*, but two others, *Northumberland* and *Surrey* had been cancelled by the Labour administration newly returned to office.* These six ships followed the general lines of the five earlier *Kent* Class with minor modifications by Sir William Berry to that design, which consisted of fitting internal bulges which marginally increased their speed but little else. The five smaller 8-inch cruisers of the *York* class had been reduced to two, *Exeter* and *York*, and thereafter 8-inch construction lapsed.

Twin funnelled, and with a lower freeboard, they were, with a shallow 3-inch belt, slightly better protected than the *Counties* but of course dropped one twin turret aft. A knot faster, they presented a more modern appearance to the world but were still much of a hasty compromise dictated more by costs than actual fleet requirements. Their legend had been approved in 1927 against the wishes of the First Lord, Bridgeman, who wanted to go for 6-inch gun vessels to show Britain's lead and good faith in reducing armaments.

In 1927 Churchill again blocked any expansion of the cruiser plan, proposing that the six ships of the 1927-28 programme should not be commenced and the Board gave way on this issue, despite the fact that this threatened their whole long-term plan. Captain Roskill concludes that the fact that considerable controversy on exactly what type of cruiser was required had a lot to do with their easy compliance on this occasion. Indeed Admiralty policy of what type of cruiser was needed was in a considerable state of flux

---

* These would only have been far more powerfully armoured ships with a slight loss in speed. See Sturton, J.A. *HMS Surrey and Northumberland*, Warship International, No 3, 1977.

at this period.* Arguments ranged from 7,000 ton ships armed with only four 8-inch guns, 10,000 ton ships with 6-inch calibre weapons as their main armaments, the continued original programme and, in 1928, Chatfield, the Controller, came up with a new type of 'trade defence' cruiser with six 8-inch guns but with speed reduced to only 21 knots to give extra-long endurance. Such a vessel would have been decidedly inferior to any other cruiser in the world and hardly worth wasting valuable tonnage on, but the Board were impressed and a staff requirement was prepared and much discussion took place. The First Sea Lord, Sir Charles Madden, was against such a wasteful concept, taking Bridgeman's line that smaller 6-inch ships in large numbers were much more of an asset.

Churchill remained adamant that fifty cruisers had been originally put up as a total requirement by Beatty at Washington and pressed that seventy were unnecessary. With the arrival of the Labour Government in May 1929 even more stringent measures were to come and, as we have noted, one of their first steps was the cancellation of the *Northumberland* and *Surrey*. Admiralty-modified requirements for a steady programme of three cruisers per year also came under scrutiny at this time. Madden's ideas bore fruit for in September 1929 it was proposed that the first ship of a much smaller type should be built. This was the 7,000 ton *Leander*, armed with eight 6-inch guns, and even smaller ships were contemplated.

The London Naval Conference which followed saw the British stating that they would be happy with only fifteen 8-inch cruisers but required a further forty-five 6-inch ships to protect their trade. If this could be agreed to they would not object to the United States building eighteen of the former type and another ten large cruisers with 6-inch guns. But the Americans wanted the British total reduced to fifty in all by 1936. In January 1930 the Cabinet agreed that fifty were 'amply adequate'. The final terms left Britain with a total cruiser tonnage for the period covered by the Treaty (1930-36) of 339,000 tons and fifty ships. As the existing 8-inch ships totalled 149,000 tons and the old 6-inch ships 100,000 tons, 90,000 tons remained to be utilised in replacement programmes. The Board decided therefore to use this by construction of fourteen new ships, three of these were to be in the 1930 programme and the remainder spread over the following three years. On completion of this

---

* Roskill, Captain Stephen, *British Naval Policy Between the Wars, Vol. 1. The Period of Anglo-American Antagonism, 1919-1929* (Collins, 1968), pp 555.

programme a further 86,000 tons would be ready for replacement as the 'C' class cruisers reached their age limit.

Of the new 6-inch ships were the eight *Leander* class vessels. They mounted four twin 6-inch turrets, with elevations of up to 60-degrees to tackle long-range aircraft but as these weapons were modifications to the already well-tried twin semi-automatic weapons fitted in the *Enterprise* and tested at sea their adoption was far more happy than the 8-inch design of the *Counties*. The first five ships, *Achilles*, *Ajax*, *Leander*, *Neptune* and *Orion*, were strikingly handsome ships, and the innovations of concentrating the boilers in a unit of four and trunking their outlets into a single funnel, although theoretically risky, proved well justified. Their initially weak anti-aircraft armament was later improved by the twinning of the 4-inch mountings in most, just before the war. The later three ships of this class, *Amphion*, *Apollo* and *Phaeton* were built to a modified design which resulted in a no less pleasing two-funnelled appearance, but soon after their completion they were transferred to Australia and renamed *Perth*, *Hobart* and *Sydney*.

Of even more modest dimensions were the little *Arethusa* class cruisers, the first products of the 'numbers through modest dimensions' call. There were to have been two squadrons of these ships making eight in all, and the first, the name ship of the class, was included in the 1931 programme, with one more included in each of the following years' estimates. However the second squadron of four was finally dropped by the Admiralty when it was seen that in response to Britain's lead in reduction of size and tonnages the American answer was the cold slap in the face of the 10,000-ton *Brooklyn* class armed with *fifteen* 6-inch guns. Japan was no less disdainful of such British gestures coming back with the *Mogami* class similarly armed (and with secret built-in provision to convert these in 8-inch gunned ships at a later date), while France started her *Gloire* class and Italy her *Garibaldi* classes, all much greater in tonnages and armaments than the little *Arethusas*.

Displacing some 5,250 tons on average when completed, these four ships, *Arethusa*, *Aurora*, *Galatea* and *Penelope* were armed with six 6-inch guns of the same general type as the *Leanders*, in twin turrets, two with eight 4-inch guns giving a more realistic AA potential. They were virtually unarmoured, their main belt and decks having only 2-inches and their turrets and director control towers 1-inch, but, despite many doubts, they had brilliant war records, as we shall see. Their size and handiness made them ideal ships for employment as Rear-Admiral (D)'s commands, and they were often used in this role, but it was not the one for which they were designed. In contrast the Japanese small cruisers built in the 1920's were built with leadership of destroyer flotillas as one of their main functions, following the lead of the Royal Navy in the pre-1914 era before proper destroyer flotilla leaders, which were merely enlarged destroyers, came into a short-lived vogue between 1916 and 1938.

The reaction of the other major powers caused considerable concern to the Admiralty. It was suggested that the tonnage of the *Leanders* should be increased by 500 tons to give them more balance but to do so would reduce the number that could be built under the terms of the London Treaty from fourteen to thirteen, and even then their foreign opposite numbers would mount almost double their main armament. The old dilemma of numbers or size again raised its insoluble head. It was belatedly realised that the triple 6-inch mountings of foreign designs would have to be adopted if our future ships were to match this and the go-ahead was looked at afresh with a view to arming them with nine 6-inch guns, or ten if the twin mounting was retained for the time being.

As a result of progress made, the 1933 programme saw the dropping of the original *Leander* design and the larger and much more powerful *Minotaur* class were put forward, to displace almost 10,000 tons and carry twelve 6-inch guns in the new triple turret. Only a limited number were at first contemplated, Nine of these large ships were proposed, while the continuation of the *Arethusas* would also allow for extra numbers and another five of these were also contemplated. But these plans were also overtaken by events.

The strait-jacket of the London Treaty was a constant irritant to Their Lordships and Lord Chatfield worked long and hard on the Prime Minister, MacDonald, to have the old yardstick of seventy re-introduced. With only fifty-two cruisers on hand and seven of those due to be scrapped within a year, it was a close thing but finally the Premier gave way on this issue, helped perhaps by the Abyssinian crisis of 1935 and the breakdown of the General Disarmament Conference in October 1933 with Hitler's statement that Germany intended to withdraw from both it and the League of Nations.

This also led to a review of the 1933 programme and as a result three of the new *Minotaurs* and one *Arethusa* were accepted and the *Leander* type terminated. After construction had commenced on the first two, *Minotaur* and *Polyphemus*, these traditional names were regrettably changed and town names substituted; they became

Newcastle and *Southampton*, also former cruiser names. It has been suggested that this was because the name *Minotaur* had unhappy associations with the armoured cruisers which carried those names in the Great War, but this explanation is not convincing to us. It is perhaps possible that the substituting of the fine classical names for those of cities in the United Kingdom was to promote belated interest in Naval affairs in the country as a whole at a time when the funding of the services was far from popular. Another reason put forward was that the modern sailor would not be able to pronounce these traditional and honoured names, a very poor excuse and one that the light cruisers ignored. (It is true however that *Penelope* was known on the lower deck as *Pennyloap*.)

Although it was stated at the time that the *Town* class were built as a reply to the *Brooklyn* and *Mogami* types their design aroused some criticism at home. For a start on the same displacement as these ships they still mounted three less 6-inch guns, but the British design was more sound in the long run. The *Mogamis* were obviously of far greater tonnage than the 10,000 admitted to and, although it was not known at the time that they would be re-armed with 8-inch guns anyway, test firings early in their life showed up their hull weakness with such a large main armament. The extra triple turret in the American cruisers was blind over a considerable proportion of their 'A' arcs, which meant that for much of the actual combat period this extra turret was just so much deadweight. Even though the British *Towns* were far more seaworthy creations, after eight had been completed two further ships had to be modified with enlarged hulls and extra horsepower. These latter two became the *Belfast* and *Edinburgh*, and after very early war damage the *Belfast* was rebuilt even more completely with extra protection and bulges. The first two squadrons comprised the *Birmingham*, *Glasgow*, *Gloucester*, *Liverpool*, *Manchester*, *Newcastle*, *Sheffield* and *Southampton*; all completed pre-war and most were to have distinguished war lives. Their twin sloping funnels and piled up bridge structure gave them a slightly 'alien' appearance at the time away from the traditional clean lines of British cruisers. Other innovations incorporated were the splitting of the four boilers into twin units again and their being placed alternately to the engine rooms to minimise battle damage after criticism of the *Leander* arrangement. They were also the first British cruiser class to be designed with fixed aircraft catapults and hangars, items that were added to most modern cruisers during the 1930's as well as heavy ships. This considerable expenditure of money and space proved a mixed blessing. The considerable extension of the ship's patrolling range by the use of such amphibions was very desirable in the wastes of the deep oceans on patrols against surface raiders, but for fleet work the appearance of more and more carriers during the war rendered them unnecessary and most captains were thankful to discard their Walrus or Seafox aircraft as soon as possible, for they were a considerable fire hazard in action.

Until the expiry of the London Treaty the construction of these big cruisers brought to a head the critical situation as regards numbers. Now that seventy had been established as the desired minimum once and for all, the only way it could be achieved was for the retention on the fighting lists of a large number, of the old 'C' class cruisers which by rights should have gone to the breakers' yards from the mid-1930's onward. In 1934 £2 million was allocated for this and within a short time the paucity of anti-aircraft defence for the fleet made itself manifest and the happy expedient of utilising these small cruisers' old hulls for the task presented itself, giving them a viable role for several years to come. The Abyssinian crisis was the catalyst which first brought this about and the *Coventry* and *Curlew* were the first two so converted. Their original armament of five single 6-inch guns, two 3-inch AA guns and eight 21-inch torpedo tubes, was stripped from them, replaced with ten single 4-inch HA and two quadruple 2-pdr pom-poms substituted. This made them formidable anti-aircraft ships for their time and plans were at once put in hand for further such conversions.

Money however, was still tight and this proceeded more slowly than was desirable. By the time war broke out only the *Calcutta*, *Cairo*, *Carlisle*, *Colombo* and *Curacoa* were taken in hand. Their modifications were somewhat different from the two earlier proto-types and consisted of eight 4-inch in four twin shielded mountings. This gave more protection to their crews and reduced topweight, but was not universally popular in war service as it meant restricting the arcs of fire which could be covered when under dive-bomber attack, the ten single open mountings (later reduced), being far more flexible in this respect.*

The continued search for the ideal smaller cruiser to fill the

---

* See for example, Connell, G.G. *Valiant Quartet* (William Kimber, 1979), for an example of this viewpoint.

numbers gap continued after the adoption of the ten 10,000 ton *Town* class ships. In 1935 no less than five different types were studied all of them armed with 6-inch guns, ranging in tonnage from 3,500 to 5,000 tons, all of which proved impracticable. In the event the threat from the air was seen as becoming an ever increasing factor and with wise foresight the Board decided to adopt a dual-purpose armament for the new generation of small cruisers, utilising the brand-new twin 5·25-inch gun which was to constitute the secondary armaments of the new battleships to be laid down on expiry of the Treaty in 1936-37.

This was to be a happy choice, for although such a calibre appeared small when compared to foreign designs, no less than five mountings could be shipped giving a respectable armament of ten guns on a tonnage of under 5,500. Thus came into being the famous *Dido* class which achieved lasting fame with the 15th Cruiser Squadron in the Mediterranean during the darkest days of World War II. The 5·25-inch gun proved a very valuable weapon in such waters, indeed at one time it was contemplated arming the big destroyers of the 'L' and 'M' classes with this gun, as a more worthwhile reply to the Japanese *Fubukis* than the low-angled 4·7-inch carried by the disappointing *Tribals*.*

Not that there was not some opposition to arming cruisers with a smaller gun than foreign types. There was. The main roles when employed as fleet cruisers were listed in an attempt to define how they fitted into the scheme of things. The priorities in that respect were put as: (1) reconnaissance; (2) screening; (3) shadowing; (4) AA defence of the Fleet and (5) supporting the light forces. Some opinions were expressed that the ships would not be able to press home the first three and the last of these functions against 6-inch armed enemy cruisers. Even the small German ships of the *Köln* class carried nine 5·9-inch guns. Some experts would have preferred the tonnage allocated to some of the *Dido* class to have been spread instead to provide more destroyers of the larger types, as contemporary Japanese ships of the *Fubuki* type far outgunned current British ships. Nonetheless the decision to go ahead with the *Didos* was upheld, and proved more than justified in the war years. Initially three ships were provided for along with two 'Improved' *Southampton* class ships, *Belfast* and *Edinburgh*; but a grave crisis developed in 1935 over the Italian invasion of Abyssinia, a crisis

* Smith, Peter C., *Fighting Flotilla* (William Kimber, 1976), p 38.

that at once threatened war with Italy over 'sanctions' and exposed the grave overstretch of the Royal Navy. Having to plan with such a war, as well as the re-birth of the German Navy and the undiminished threat of Japan, which would take up most of the main forces available in commission, a series of Supplementary Estimates were rushed through, the first in April 1936 and the second in July. Under the second of these, additional funding was coupled with a strong call from Chatfield in February that large numbers of the smaller cruiser type would be needed, and as a result five *Didos* were included. The question of building any more of the 10,000-ton 6-inch type was under examination, and it was indeed suggested that no more should be built.

In the midst of this the calling of the Second London Naval Conference to consider disarmament began to look more and more irrelevant but nonetheless it went ahead and it prompted Chatfield to review the situation again and stress the minimum needs of the Royal Navy in cruiser types as seventy ships, fifteen 8-inch, ten of the big 6-inch types and forty-five smaller cruisers. The total tonnage this represented was 562,000 which was certain to raise American hackles again if put forward. Not surprisingly the Foreign Office hedged at making this public again. Nor was the Premier any less anxious to placate American feelings on this sensitive matter, despite ardent pleas by the First Sea Lord. Chatfield re-iterated the argument that 8-inch cruiser building should be terminated; only a limited number of the 10,000-ton *Minotaur* type should be continued but that small handy types of 7,000 tons and 6-inch guns were required in large numbers and that no limit should be agreed as to how many we could build. This the Government baulked at, lowering their sights to a total of sixty under-age ships with ten over-age vessels to back them up, or even the acceptance of fifty cruisers. This was in 1934. That autumn the Americans came some way to accepting our demands, but were far from happy about total numbers. The final outcome was, in a limited sense, a victory, for the British viewpoint for 8,000 tons was agreed to as the upper limit for new cruiser construction.

The Treaty was signed in March 1936 and the building programme of that year reflected the spur to modernisation that resulted. It was a race against time, however, that the Admiralty had lost, for ships provided for in 1936 would not, in the main, be ready before 1940 and by that date we found ourselves at war. All in all, under the 1936-38 programmes eleven of the new *Didos* were commenced, and aroused enthusiasm from Chatfield, and fury and scorn from Winston Churchill. The first group consisted of the *Argonaut, Bonaventure, Charybdis, Cleopatra, Dido, Euryalus, Hermione, Naiad, Phoebe, Scylla* and *Sirius*. Their displacement came out at 5,450 tons but owing to wartime shortages of the new mountings *Charybdis* and *Scylla* had to embark an inferior armament of eight 4·5-inch guns in twin open shields instead of the five 5·25-inch twin turrets of most of the others. Consequently they were dubbed in the fleet, 'The Toothless Terrors'. In the event these shortages, the test of war, and additional equipment embarked, forced modification of this armament and some dropped one twin turret, while the five ships of the second group, which comprised the later 1939 programme, were designed with only four turrets. They differed in appearance by having shorter and straight funnels against the first group's raked funnels. These five displaced 5,770 tons and became the *Bellona, Black Prince, Diadem, Royalist* and *Spartan* but did not join the fleet until late in the war, and thus did not enjoy the opportunities of the first group to earn their laurels.

Eight thousand tons now being the new upper limit, the plans for the 6-inch cruisers had to be re-examined by the Board in some detail. Although an improved *Dido* with fourteen 5·25-inch guns was considered, it was felt that these ships should be able to stand up to the light cruisers under construction abroad and by careful design the same main armament as that carried by the 10,000 ton *Minotaurs* was fitted into these smaller ships, no mean achievement. In fact too much had been attempted. The names selected seemed to be a further extension of the *Town* class idea although extended to the Empire. They became known as the *Colony* class and the names had even less tradition behind them than the *Towns*. They presented however a similar profile although with upright funnels. Weight saving was produced by the squared-off transom stern (as against the traditional cruiser stern) a feature which was designed to increase speed, but, on the whole this squeezing of the 'quart into the pint pot' worked surprisingly well. Once limitation ceased the three latter ships of the class, *Ceylon, Newfoundland* and *Uganda*, had, in July 1937, their tonnages raised to 8,800 and dropped one triple turret to facilitate additional anti-aircraft weaponry. Their main belt armour was 3¾ inches against the 3 to 4 inches of the *Town* and *Improved Town* types, and the 2-inch of the *Dido*, and they were one or two knots slower. Eventually eleven ships of this type were under construction *Bermuda, Ceylon, Fiji, Gambia, Jamaica, Kenya, Mauritius,*

Newfoundland, *Nigeria*, *Trinidad* and *Uganda*.

By the time the estimates came round to being discussed in 1938 much had taken place throughout the world to dispel most illusions that war could be averted. The Spanish Civil War, the repeated demands and military adventures of Italy, Germany and Japan and the frenzied pace of their armament and so on. In Britain the end of restrictions brought about the New Standard to which the strength of the Royal Navy was to be built up should funds (and time) permit. As far as cruiser strength was concerned this meant raising the upper limit on numbers from seventy to eighty-eight (one hundred being expressed as an ideal but realised as probably unattainable). In August 1938, around the time Hitler marched into Czechoslovakia, the actual numbers of fairly modern ships built or building fell far below this utopian number, with but forty-two such cruisers built and fourteen building. These were given as being the fifteen *County* class, 8-inch ships, ten *Town* class and nine *Colony* class, eight *Leander* class, ten *Dido* class and four *Arethusas* plus the rather more elderly vessels, the three *Hawkins* class and two 'E' class ships. As a result four *Improved Colony* ships were begun along with three *Didos*.

These followed the lines of the *Ceylon* and the other modified *Colony* ships, having three triple turrets and heavy anti-aircraft batteries in their place. The original name of the *Town* class ships were re-adopted, thankfully, for these new ships which became the *Minotaur* class. As *Polyphemus* had been appropriated for a new aircraft carrier however, the four became the *Minotaur*, *Superb*, *Swiftsure* and *Tiger*. Of 8,800 tons other details were the same as the *Colony* class, save that speed was increased by a knot, but these were not finally funded until the 1941 War Programme. Once the war was underway the needs of the situations changed from day to day and the cruiser building programme was modified frequently, being cut right out at one period. Thus the projected sister ships of the above class, *Bellerophon*, *Blake*, *Defence* and *Hawke*, along with larger 8-inch versions, *Centurion*, *Edgar*, *Mars* and *Neptune*, never got very far and most were merely projected or later cancelled. Three of them, after a whole series of re-namings, were completed in the late 1950's to very different designs as the *Blake*, *Lion* and *Tiger*, but as such fall outside the scope of this book.

The fluctuations of British cruiser strength is perhaps best summarised in Table One.

Table One
British Cruiser Strength 1919-1946

Year	Completed	Sunk or Wrecked	Scrapped	Total
1919	6	-	2	133
1920	-	-	44	89
1921	2	-	27	64
1922	3	1	8	58
1923	-	-	6	52
1924	1	-	1	52
1925	1	-	-	53
1926	2	-	6	49
1927	-	-	-	49
1928	7	-	2	54
1929	4	-	4	54
1930	3	-	1	56
1931	1	-	2	55
1932	-	-	-	55
1933	2	-	1	56
1934	2	-	5	53
1935	3	-	2	54
1936	3	-	1	56
1937	6	-	-	62
1938	2	-	-	64
1939	3	-	-	67
1940	7	3	-	71
1941	6	10	-	67
1942	6	13	-	60
1943	7	2	-	65
1944	2	3	1	63
1945	2	-	-	65
1946	-	-	8	57

* * *

Thus it can be clearly seen that, after 1920, the Admiralty's 'Minimum' figure for cruisers was never achieved. The wartime total figures were always far less than shown because of ships damaged in action and undergoing repairs, so the apparent peak figure shown for 1940 of seventy-one was not in fact the total number of cruisers available for service at that time. Perhaps a true wartime figure would be about ten to fifteen below the totals shown.

Although new construction was obviously the most talked-about aspect of the cruiser building policy in the years leading up to the war, it was clear that time would run out before the desired number of ships could be attained. Some considerable time and expense was therefore devoted to bringing a few of the cruisers already built up to reasonable strength for the forthcoming conflict. Although this is never sound policy and the putting of new wine into old bottles rarely justifies the time and effort involved, it was all that could be done with the restrictions of treaties, cash and time allowed.

We have already seen how the increasing awareness of how much the air would come into the scheme of things, and the lamentable state of unpreparedness the Royal Navy found itself in with regard to AA defence as result of wrong policies on armaments and systems to counter aircraft taken in the 1920's, had resulted in the old 'C' class cruisers, due for the scrapyard, being given a new lease of life. But the renewing process on most classes was a continuing policy and we shall examine next how each class was affected prior to the outbreak of war.

The 'D' class in general were slightly more modern than the 'C' class, and little affected by any radical changes pre-war, the only concession to the power and threat of the bomber being the substitution of 4-inch guns for 3-inch and the addition of a single 4-inch HA gun on the after shelter deck, small enough provision. But it was not expected to employ them in the front line and this was considered adequate. The two 'E' class ships, being larger again and already carrying three such guns plus a pair of 2-pdr AA weapons, received no such additions before 1939 but they were included in the programme of fitting cruisers with catapults and seaplanes to improve their scouting abilities. The *Raleigh* was wrecked in the West Indies in 1922 on her first commission but the remaining ships of her class underwent widely varying transformations during their lives. *Frobisher* had been equipped as a training ship for a long time in the 1930's and her sister ship *Vindictive* had just completed a long re-fit to take her place in this capacity in 1939. The latter was too far changed to make her worthwhile re-converting in a fighting role and she spent the war as a mobile repair ship. *Frobisher* was not modernised but re-shipped her original guns, dropping two of the 7·5-inch singles and adding additional HA guns in lieu. *Effingham*, by contrast, was completely rebuilt and brought up to modern standards. She completed carrying nine 6-inch guns, four single 4-inch HA later twinned, and two quadruple 2-pdr pom-poms well equipped to take her place in line. Unhappily she was lost on her first voyage when she ran aground on rocks off Norway and so all this work was wasted. *Hawkins* remained in her original state with a few light AA weapons added.

The bigger the ship the more that could be done to improve her. On this principle, and because satisfaction with the *County* class, the 'Ruddy Haystacks', was always muted, the earliest vessels of this type were scheduled for modernisation early on. In the end only the *Berwick*, *Cornwall*, *Cumberland* and *Suffolk* were fully treated of the first group. All were fitted with a narrow armour belt to enable them to stand up to the Japanese heavy cruisers a little better, their single 4-inch guns were twinned and 2-pdr pom-poms were added. Their aircraft stowage was increased from one to four and a large box-like hangar was constructed to house these abaft the funnels, which did absolutely nothing to enhance their already top-heavy silhouette. *Berwick* and *Cornwall* were otherwise unchanged but *Cumberland* and *Suffolk*, the first pair to undergo this refit, had lost a deck abaft 'Y' turret in an attempt to improve seaworthiness caused by these additional fittings.

A more ambitious re-building was undertaken with *London*, which completely altered her appearance. The *Dorsetshire* was originally to have undergone similar treatment but the accelerating pace of war preparations caused this to be aborted and *London* remained unique. To give her a worthwhile protection against 8-inch shell fire she was re-equipped with a belt of up to 5-inch thickness over her vitals and the extra weight this entailed was compensated for by the fitting of entirely new machinery and boilers and in a complete re-design of her superstructure. Her 4-inch guns were paired, as in all post-1930's ships and sixteen pom-poms shipped. Her new profile was modelled on that of the *Colony* class cruisers with slab-like bridge forward, two upright funnels replacing the old-fashioned triple layout. At a quick glance she might have been taken for a *Colony* save for her distinctive twin 8-inch turrets and her extra high flush decks. She should, in theory, have been a most potent British cruiser when she eventually rejoined the fleet but the time taken (from 1938-41) was as long as to build a brand new ship, and she never had the chance to test her much improved capabilities against the Japanese, serving instead with the Home Fleet for her war career and only going east later on when the fighting was all but over.

Among the more modern ships little could be done but to improve AA gun power by twinning the 4-inch mountings and adding pom-poms and multiple ·5-inch machine guns. The hard experience of war however was soon to lead to radical changes in most of the cruisers employed then in the front line. As a general rule light AA was massively increased with every refit, but this was done as the ships and weapons became available and no set pattern emerged. As well as this the most common extra topweight was embarked in the form of radar equipments. The first cruiser to be so fitted was the *Sheffield*, while the AA conversion *Curlew* followed her in 1939 with a much improved set. But here again, as with the AA armament, sets were fitted as and when the ships came in for refitting and wide variations were found on ships of the same classes. At this top hamper steadily increased it was found necessary to land one turret to compensate. Ships which had this modification were the *Emerald* (one 6-inch gun), *Enterprise* (two 6-inch guns), *Devonshire*, *Norfolk* and *Sussex* ('X' twin turret removed), *Achilles* and *Leander* ('X' twin turret removed), the surviving *Town* class ships ('X' turret), all the *Colony* class save *Gambia* and *Nigeria* ('X' turret) and *Cleopatra* of the *Dido* class ('Q' turret) (The *Phoebe* never shipped her 'Q' mounting at all due to shortages.)

Severe war damage could, conversely, lead to a great degree of modernisation among ships worth saving. The earliest example of this resulted from the mining of the almost new *Belfast* in the Firth of Forth soon after the outbreak of war. Her back was broken and repairs required were so extensive that the decision was made to incorporate extra protection and armour to withstand 8-inch shellfire as well as a host of other technical improvements. When she emerged from Devonport dockyard three years later she was unique among her 6-inch sisters. Additional underwater protection in the form of external bulges transformed her into the portly lady now on view on the Thames; her beam was increased to 69 feet, and her tonnage, all questions of limitations forgotten, went up to 11,500 tons. As such she was probably only second to the re-built *London* in overall power, but like the 8-inch cruiser, never had the opportunity to show her mettle against the Japanese heavy cruisers she was designed to combat.

Perhaps the most extensive transformation which took place as a result of war damage other than *Belfast*, although far less important, took place to the old 'D' class cruiser *Delhi*, improbable as it would appear. Her conversion resulted from the failure of pre-war planners to devise an effective dual-purpose gun to arm British destroyers. Despite the fact that the 16-inch guns of the *Nelsons*, the 8-inch guns of the *County* ships and the 6-inch guns of the smaller cruisers, had all been designed to give good high elevations and facilitate anti-aircraft fire. The problem of giving destroyers the same capability appeared beyond the Admiralty. This was partly due to opposition to the basic need for such a weapon. Between the wars the trend of thought was still that the chief role of the destroyer was to fight off torpedo attacks on our own battle fleet by enemy destroyers, with delivery of their own torpedo attack second and limited anti-submarine capability third. The vulnerability of destroyers to both dive- and torpedo-bomber attack was frequently pointed out but to no avail and all British ships of that type were fitted with the 4·7-inch low angled gun up to and including the over-rated *Tribal* class and the later 'J' and 'K' classes which were just entering service as war broke out.

A belated attempt to solve the problem resulted in the 'L' and 'M' class destroyers being fitted with an improved, but highly complex mounting, but this was still far inferior to the 5-inch turrets that had been fitted in Japanese and American destroyers for a decade or more earlier. In discussions on how to overcome this problem the stumbling block was always tonnage; British ships of the destroyer type were on average always 300-400 tons lighter than their foreign counterparts. This ruled out the adoption of the 5·25-inch gun as we have seen. Free discussion between the American and British navies had gradually developed by July 1941 and at that time the merits of the 5-inch single mountings carried by the current US destroyers were much admired. Among the interchange of information was the fact that details of both the standard British 4-inch and 4·7-inch guns were exchanged with Captain Cochrane of the USN for details of this 5-inch weapon which was being fitted to the big destroyers of the *Fletcher* class. No contemporary British destroyer was of a size sufficient to mount this weapon in any numbers but the larger hull of the *Delhi* was considered a more-than-adequate platform on which to experiment and in that month she sailed to the USA under the terms of Lease-Lend and underwent a year-long refit. When she sailed from New York in August 1942 she was a fully fit fighting unit, she had shipped five of the American guns, two forward, two aft and one awkwardly sited abaft her funnels and before her mainmast which restricted its air arcs. She also had two quadruple pom-poms and no less than ten

Oerlikon 20-mm weapons along with radars of the latest type and other refinements. As such she made a splendid addition to the fleet. Again unfortunately she was extensively damaged by bombing soon after joining the Mediterranean Fleet which put her out of the war for another three months and, by the time she re-joined, the situation vis-à-vis German air power in that theatre had completely changed. Like *London* and *Belfast*, therefore, she had little or no opportunity to show her worth in her new guise.

All these three major conversions show how important it is to have ships ready *before* the outbreak of war rather than attempt to rectify faults *after* it has got underway, but of course funding is always restricted prior to war and more-or-less unlimited after it has commenced. Another cruiser that received extensive modifications as a result of war damage was the 8-inch ship *Sussex*. While refitting on the Clyde in November 1940 she was hit by a large bomb and the resulting fires completely gutted her. Following explosions inside her, and to save the dockyard, she was flooded and as a result she capsized and sank. Not surprisingly her repairs were extensive and she was in dockyard hands for almost two years. Even so her changes were far less sweeping than those of her erstwhile sister *London*. The frail pole masts were replaced by tripods to take the weight of the extra radars and directors with which she was equipped, her single 4-inch guns were 'twinned' and extra light weapons added. However her appearance was not greatly altered by these improvements and little or no extra armour was incorporated.

The dockyard availability in Great Britain was also a cramping restriction on too many of these major refits and time was always lacking. The need was to get ships away to sea again as quickly as possible. It was fortunate indeed that the massive dockyards of the United States were able to step in and help under the Lease-Lend agreement and the list of British cruisers that underwent major repairs on the other side of the Atlantic is a long one: *Caradoc, Delhi, Durban, Ajax, Leander, Orion, Penelope, Glasgow, Newcastle, Liverpool, Manchester, Argonaut, Cleopatra, Dido, Phoebe, Newfoundland, Nigeria* and *Uganda* all spent varying periods in US dockyard hands during the war, the majority after receiving bomb damage. Indeed the menace of the dive bomber accounted for far greater casualties and damage than any other form of enemy attack save submarine, as the following table shows:

Table 2
Analysis of British Wartime Cruiser Losses 1939-45
Principal Cause: Main reason for loss.

Dive Bomber	Submarine	T.B. or G.B.	Mine	Surface Action	Other
Calcutta	Bonaventure	Spartan	Neptune	Canberra	Curacoa
Carlisle	Cairo			Charybdis	Dragon
Cornwall	Calypso			Edinburgh	Effingham
Coventry	Dunedin			Exeter	
Curlew	Galatea			Manchester	
Dorteshire	Hermione			Perth	
Fiji	Naiad			Sydney	
Gloucester	Penelope			York	
Southampton					
Trinidad					

* * *

It was attrition from the air, mainly from the land-based bombers of the Axis powers in the restricted offshore waters of Europe that caused the greatest casualties and it was possibly the form of attack that British warships in general were not equipped to deal with. With surface to surface actions restricted, more by the fact that neither Germany nor Italy sought such battles any more between 1939 and 1945 than they did between 1914 and 1918, it is inevitable that such a disparity would occur.

These figures are further emphasised when one studies the areas in which the greatest losses took place, as in Table 3 on page 40:

No hard and fast conclusions can be reached from figures of course, for there are too many imponderables but certain generalities can be made within wide frameworks. The first is that British cruisers were ill-equipped to defend themselves against dive bombing by skilful opponents, like the German *Stukagruppen* in the Mediterranean and the Japanese Navy carrier-based crews in the Indian Ocean. A massed concentrated attack by such aircraft on individual ships was almost certain to result in either hits and heavy damage or loss and few aircraft were destroyed in return. This was a general failing among warships of all types in the Royal Navy. Adequate carrier-borne fighter cover was the only real answer to this type of attack whereby the vulnerable dive bombers could be decimated before reaching their attack positions. The tendency for British cruisers to catch fire easily was noted early in the war and damage control appeared to lag behind current methods in most ships.

Ship-to-ship actions were so rare, for the reasons already stated,

Table 3
Analysis of British Wartime Cruiser Losses 1939-45
General Area of Losses

Mediter-ranean	Norway & Arctic	Indian Ocean	Far East	N and S Atlantic	Home Waters
Bonaventure	*Curlew*	*Cornwall*	*Canberra*	*Curacoa*	*Charybdis*
Cairo	*Edinburgh*	*Dorset-shire*	*Exeter*	*Dunedin*	*Dragon*
Calcutta	*Effingham*	*Sydney*	*Perth*		
Calypso	*Trinidad*				
Coventry					
Carlisle					
Fiji					
Gloucester					
Galatea					
Hermione					
Manchester					
Naiad					
Neptune					
Penelope					
Southampton					
Spartan					
York					

*   *   *

that little valid comparison could be made. On paper the German, Italian and Japanese heavy cruisers looked more than a match for the *County* class but they hardly ever clashed. The *Berwick* certainly came off second best in her brief duel with the *Hipper*, but she had already been damaged at Spartivento and one turret was not operational. The *Exeter* with her six 8-inch guns was overwhelmed by four Japanese 8-inch ships and stood no chance whatsoever. She certainly caused little damage in return before she sank in her final action, but she too was damaged and her crew fatigued. The *Canberra* was likewise overwhelmed and caught by surprise and put up little resistance at Savo Island. In the light cruiser category the Italian cruisers would have proven easy meat, as shown by *Sydney*'s destruction of *Colleoni*, but they had the advantage of three or four knots extra speed and were difficult to pin down as they invariably avoided action. The *Sydney*'s fate at the hands of the armed merchant raider *Kormoran* would seem to indicate that their slender protection would not have stood up well in a prolonged slugging match with a real light cruiser. Again *Exeter*, *Ajax* and *Achilles* stood up fairly well to the pounding from *Graf Spee*, although had the German ship elected to stand her ground, all three would have been sunk or badly damaged. As it was, *Exeter* took enormous punishment well, although the lighter guns of the British ships were unable to cause serious harm to even a pocket battleship's limited protection.

The virtues of British cruisers would appear to have been, in common with most other types of British warships at this period, their general overall durability and sea-keeping abilities. The little cruisers of the 'C' and 'D' classes were over twenty years old and designed for the North Sea rather than the Arctic Circle and the battering they took on the Northern Patrol Line in the early months of the war made this point obvious. Only shortage of more suitable ships led to their employment in this role and they were soon withdrawn. The modern ships stood most weather conditions well, even the fury of the Arctic storms. The *Sheffield* received the most severe buffeting of all in those waters and was damaged, but it is true to say that British cruisers stayed at sea in conditions which would have made life impossible for most of their foreign rivals and the Italian and Japanese ships would never have been able to operate thus.

Whatever their faults, and these were not altogether obvious pre-war, the truth was that, as predicted in the 1920's, there were never enough of them, especially in the critical period from 1939 to 1943. So critical indeed did the position become that at one stage it was seriously considered that the brand-new battleship *Duke of York* should be exchanged for eight American 8-inch cruisers. This was in February 1941 and was a typical brainchild of Winston Churchill, the man who had fought so hard against the 8-inch cruiser programme in the 1920's! Nothing ever came of it but it reflected the short-sightedness of politicians as a whole and if the Admiralty are accused of not providing the right sort of cruisers in sufficient numbers when the need was acute then they have greater justification than most in pointing out that this was hardly their fault.

Ubiquity was the corner-stone of the cruiser and British cruisers found themselves in situations which could hardly have been envisaged when they were first planned and designed. Nonetheless the Admiralty showed greater foresight than they have been given credit for. It is true that much effort and money was wasted in equipping cruisers with scouting aircraft, but there was every justification for this in their role of trade route protectors and on this duty they were remarkably efficient. Indeed it is fair to say that this role was made redundant for them by their very effectiveness and by 1942 the threat of the armed merchant raider had been almost entirely eliminated.

The provision of the *Dido* class was also a master-stroke and was indeed widely copied by other nations, especially the USA with their *Atlanta* class ships which were almost direct copies. But the design of the cruisers depended on the tactical requirements of the time they were built and to gain a more deeper understanding of why the ships were built as they were, and why they had to alter to meet the changing demands on them we must turn to their role in modern warfare, both as envisaged in the 1920's and 1930's and how it developed in the fluctuations of actual world-wide combat.

CHAPTER TWO

The Role of the Cruiser

The origins of the cruiser type, which was always diffuse, have never been better described than by N.A.M. Rodger. He points out that although the light cruiser as it had evolved by the early twentieth century might have inherited the *functions* of the sailing frigates of Nelson's day it was by no means true to say that this necessarily implied any sort of continuous lineal descent or unbroken succession of steadily improving types. The process was far more complex than this. From the enormous variety of widely differing ships to which the label cruiser was subsequently applied, only slowly did a distinct and readily identifiable warship type appear. It was, in Mr Rodger's apt words; 'the first modern light cruiser evolved by a process which might be called unnatural selection.'*

The development of the armoured cruiser was in comparison, more easy to plot. Either as cheaply built second-class battleships for distant stations, or as direct British replies to foreign types then building which threatened our supply lines, the armoured cruiser followed a more straightforward path.

The first vessel designed and built abroad which came into the definition of armoured cruiser was the Russian vessel *General Admiral* (a singularly Russian name which reflected her attitude towards her fleet for many years including World War II as a kind of subordination to the Army). She was an open central-battery ship equipped with four 8-inch and two 6-inch guns, but her hull along its waterline was protected by the provision of a shallow belt of armour. She was laid down in 1870 and completed in 1873.

The first British vessels to come into a similar classification were the *Shannon* completed in 1877 and the *Nelson* and *Northampton*, completed in 1881 and 1878 respectively. The first ship mounted two 10-inch, seven 9-inch and six 20-pdr guns on a displacement of 5,670 tons. Fully rigged as were most ships at this time she was

* Rodger, N.A.M., *The First Light Cruisers, The Mariner's Mirror,* Vol 65, No 3, August 1979.

single-screwed and her engines could push her along at twelve knots. She had a limited protecting belt of 9-inches' thickness tapering to 6-inch rather than a complete belt of armour. She was classed officially as a broadside armour-belted cruising vessel and was designed specifically to act as a flagship on distant stations. Too weak for a battleship, too slow for a true cruiser, she saw little employment. Her successors were similar hybrids. They displaced around 7,500 tons and were capable of fourteen knots as designed. They mounted four 10-inch and eight 9-inch guns. These guns were carried broadside fashion, the last of the battleships, if they can be described as part of their status, to do so.

In fact their duties were described quite precisely at the time by the Controller of the Navy thus: – ' . . . their object was not to take part in a close engagement but to roam over the seas and drive away unarmoured fast cruisers from harrying our commerce . . . '

The increasing prosperity of the Empire and the increasing dependence of an increased population at home on imported goods and foodstuffs as well as raw materials brought about an ever increasing concern of the vulnerability of the trade routes. Beaten so often before in straight combat with the Royal Navy, and with little hope of matching her ship-for-ship because of Britain's dominance of the new technology France naturally considered the severance of these links as an easy way to bring her old enemy to her knees and the traditional policy of the weaker naval power, the *guerre de course*, was an open secret. To by-pass the unassailable British battle line was an attractive (and cheap) alternative for any potential enemy. Thus the French pronouncements, later repeated when the torpedo seemed to favour such attrition with the *Jeune Ecole* school of thought, led to the advocacy by admirals like Sir Alexander Milne, of large numbers of cruising vessels of our own to patrol the sea lanes as protection against such a threat.

Yet there was no co-ordinated policy and the transition from sail to steam saw an enormous number of vessels carrying the old ratings of frigate, corvette and sloop, as well as gunboats and torpedo-carrying craft, all of which could come under the wide embracing title of cruisers in some of their functions. It will be convenient before discussing the role of the cruiser as it changed and developed, to trace briefly the diffent lines of ancestry that led to the first hard and fast classifications of 'Armoured' and 'Protected' cruiser which finally emerged from this chaos.

If the armoured cruiser as it eventually emerged can be regarded as the natural evolutionary successor to the 2nd rate battleship as represented by the *Research* (1864), *Enterprise* (1864), *Favourite* (1866), *Lord Clyde* and *Lord Warden* (1866-67), which were the earliest light-weight armoured ships, then their origins can be traced through the *Pallas* (1866)* type of experimental battleships to the *Shannon*. As we have seen, she was first of these types to qualify for the title of 'armoured cruiser' though opinion was divided as to what exactly her true role was. The same fuzzing of definitions led to the *Imperieuse* and *Warspite* (1886-88) before reaching fruition with the *Orlando* class of 1886-87, *Aurora, Australia, Galatea, Immortalite, Narcissus, Orlando* and *Undaunted* which sprang from the Northbrook Programme of 1884. These dispaced 5,000 tons and carried two 18-ton guns and ten 6-inch guns, with 10-inch armour. (*Aurora* and *Immortalite* were 5,600 tons when completed later.) The same programme produced the *Archer* class of torpedo cruisers right at the other end of the scale. But after the *Orlandos* the armoured cruiser fell into disfavour, and the protected cruiser came to the forefront.

The difference lay in their chief form of protection. The armoured cruisers, as their name implied, depended on thick belts of armour along their hulls in the traditional way. Protected cruisers had their vitals shielded by decks varying in thickness from ½-inch to 6-inches, with their hulls sub-divided internally and coal bunkerage substituting for side armour. These cruiser types were further sub-divided into rates, 1st, 2nd and 3rd class, all had their place in the Navy of this period. But following a ten-year break the armoured cruiser was re-introduced following a large French programme of such ships and the introduction of the Krupps armour which made it a viable proposition again. The first of the new type were the *Cressy* class, based on the *Diadem* class of protected cruisers, but with the armoured belt and the new 9·2-inch gun as the principal weapon. As the French programme continued to pre-occupy the Admiralty, successive classes were built to match their armoured cruisers. Thus followed the *Drake* class (1902-3), *Monmouth* class (1903-4) and *Devonshire* class (1903-04). Twenty-five of these ships were built in that short period before Sir William White gave way to Sir Philip Watt as Director of Naval Construction. His arrival heralded a new batch of giants, and in rapid succession the *Duke of Edinburgh* class (1906), *Warrior* Class (1907) and *Minotaur*

* For details of these experimental types see Parkes, Oscar, *British Battleships* (Seeley Service, 1966).

Table 4
Final Development of the Armoured Cruiser 1902-08.

Ship	Nominal Displacement	Armament (as fitted)	Max Belt.	Speed Knots
Aboukir				
Bacchante				
Cressy	12,000	Two 9·2-inch guns	6-inch	21
Euryalus		Twelve 6-inch guns		
Hogue				
Sutlej				
Drake				
Good Hope	14,100	Two 9·2-inch guns	6-inch	24
King Alfred		Sixteen 6-inch guns		
Leviathan				
Bedford				
Berwick				
Cornwall				
Cumberland				
Donegal	9,800	Fourteen 6-inch	4-inch	23
Essex				
Kent				
Lancaster				
Monmouth				
Suffolk				
Antrim	10,850	Four 7·5-inch	6-inch	22
Argyll		Six 6-inch		
Carnarvon				
Devonshire				
Hampshire				
Roxburgh				
Duke of Edinburgh	13,550	Six 9·2-inch	6-inch	23
Black Prince		Ten 6-inch		
Achilles		Six 9·2-inch	6-inch	23
Cochrane	13,550	Four 7·5-inch		
Natal				
Warrior				
Defence	14,600	Four 9·2-inch	6-inch	23
Minotaur		Ten 7·5-inch		
Shannon				

Class (1908) arrived. But their day was done and the armoured cruiser as a type was finally terminated with the arrival of the *Invincible,* battle-cruiser, a ship with the speed of the big cruisers but the guns of a battleship.

The details of these final products of the Armoured Cruiser end of the cruiser story are contained in Table 4 and show just how large the type had become by the eve of the Great War.

If the tracing of the armoured cruiser lineage raises problems then the protected cruiser raises even more. As the traditional 'Three-deckers' of the wooden-walls of Britain with their ranks of broadside guns carried as in Napoleonic days gave way to the new capital ships, the armoured frigate initiated by the *Warrior* (1860), so the old classifications fell into disuse but the transition was gradual. Thus the forerunners of the smaller cruisers show a wide variety of origin types. If the term 'cruiser' is to be accepted as any ship other than a ship-of-the-line which was detached for independent duties, and these could include convoy protection, training, raiding enemy trade and the suppression of piracy, then the most common types utilised were the original frigates, corvettes and sloops. These types continued to be built as the armoured frigate became the battleship in the 1860's. From the *Inconstant* (1868), through the armoured *Shah* (1873) until the last frigate to be so rated – the *Raleigh* (1873) – can be traced one line of descent: *Raleigh* herself was re-classified as a cruiser as late as 1889. Similarly the *Active* and *Volage* (1869) were followed by the *Diamond* and *Sapphire* (1874) which were the last wooden corvettes in the Royal Navy: The *Bacchante, Boadicea* and *Euryalus* (1875-77) were rated corvettes and were diminutive versions of the *Raleigh*, while the *Opal* class* corvettes (1875) were followed by the nine ships of the *Comus* class† which incorporated armoured decks at the instigation of Sir Nathaniel Barnaby. The *Calliope* and *Calypso* followed (1883-84), but already this type had become much criticised with the launching of the Chilean *Esmeralda* designed by Rendel and built at Low Walker yard of Armstrongs in Britain. She was five knots faster than the *Comus* class ships and far outgunned them; she had an armoured deck and carried breech-loading guns against their muzzle loaders. Just as revolutionary in their way were the *Iris* and *Mercury* (1879) described as the first high speed steel cruisers, but they lacked the armour

* *Emerald, Garnet, Opal, Ruby, Tourmaline* and *Turquoise.*
† *Canada, Carysfort, Champion, Cleopatra, Comus, Conquest, Constance, Cordelia, Curacoa.*

deck of *Esmeralda*. This was added to a new design based on their specification and the call for fast cruisers to protect trade and the result was the four ships of the *Leander* class (1882-83).[1] They displaced 3,800 tons and carried ten 6-inch breech-loading guns at 17 knots.

Meanwhile separate development was going ahead with regard to the torpedo-cruiser concept. Great difficulty was encountered in deciding just what armament they should carry. Eventually these four ships[2] carried on a 3,500 ton displacement an armament of two 8-inch and ten 6-inch guns and as such were more heavily armed than most of their contemporaries, though not with torpedoes other than a few experimental types! Sir William White, having discarded the armoured type at this time, was pressing ahead with new ideas for improving on the protected cruiser type, including the *Medusa* class,[3] which he described as 'a protector of commerce . . . '. These carried six 6-inch guns on a displacement of 2,800 tons at a speed of 20 knots. He followed this class up with the *Pearl's*,[4] of 2,575 tons displacement designed for service with the Australian Government and these can be truly said to have been the first of what was to become the modern concept of a light cruiser.

Meanwhile in an attempt to solve the torpedo-cruiser problem two experimental ships, *Fearless* and *Scout,* appeared on the scene in 1887. Displacing 1,596 tons they carried four 5-inch guns and three torpedo tubes. These were followed by the *Archer* class, but this road proved to be a dead end with the development of the torpedo-gunboat and ultimately the torpedo-boat destroyer.

Following the Naval Defence Act of 1889 a great expansion of the fleet took place. The smaller cruisers based on the *Pandora* class followed through the *Pallas* class[5] of 2,575 tons (1889-90) to the *Pelorus* Class (1897-1900), which carried eight 4-inch guns, two 14-inch torpedo tubes at 20 knots. The 1st rate cruisers *Blake* and *Blenheim* were expanded versions of this basic design intended as colonial flagships. They displaced 9,000 tons while the *Bellona* class 3rd class cruisers[6] took the design the other way, displacing 1,830

[1]   *Amphion, Arethusa, Leander, Phaeton.*
[2]   *Forth, Mersey, Severn, Thames.*
[3]   *Magicienne, Marathon, Medea, Medusa, Melpomene.*
[4]   *Katoomba, Mildura, Ringarooma, Touranga, Wallaroo.*
[5]   *Pallas, Pearl, Philomel, Phoebe.*
[6]   *Barham, Barrosa, Barracouta, Bellona, Blanche, Blonde.*

tons. But the *Powerful* and *Terrible* displaced 14,100 tons when they joined the fleet in 1896, and were at the other end of the scale.

Charles Rathbone Low, writing in 1892, defined the work of cruisers at this time as: ' . . . scouting, protecting convoys and harassing an enemy's communications . . '* To this, in peacetime, could be added the roles of training of seamen, showing the flag and controlling the more remote and restless races of the Empire.

The development of protected cruisers continued from this in successive classes, which are described in Table 5.

* Low, Lieutenant Charles Rathbone, *Her Majesty's Navy, Vol 3* (Virtue, 1892) pps 326.

* * *

Table 5
Final Development of the Protected Cruiser 1893-1905

Ship	Nominal Displacement	Armament (as fitted)	Max Deck	Speed Knots
Crescent	7,700	One 9·2-inch gun	5-inch	19½
Royal Arthur		Twelve 6-inch guns		
		Four 18-inch TT		
Edgar				
Endymion				
Gibraltar		Two 9·2-inch guns		
Grafton	7,700	Ten 6-inch guns	5-inch	19½
Hawke		Four 18-inch TT		
St. George				
Theseus				
Astraea				
Charybdis				
Cambrian				
Bonaventure	4,360	Two 6-inch	6-inch	19½
Flora		Eight 4·7-inch		
Forte		Four 18-inch TT		
Fox				
Hermione				
Andromache				
Aeolus				
Andromache				
Apollo				
Brilliant				

Ship	Nominal Displacement	Armament (as fitted)	Max Deck	Speed Knots
Iphigenia				
Intrepid				
Latona				
Melampus		Two 6-inch guns		
Melpomene	3,440-3,600	Six 4·7-inch guns	6-inch	20
Naiad		Four 14-inch TT		
Pique				
Rainbow				
Retribution				
Scylla				
Sappho				
Sirius				
Spartan				
Sybille				
Terpsichore				
Thetis				
Tribune				
Pactolus				
Pandora				
Pegasus				
Perseus				
Pelorus	2,135-2,250	Eight 4-inch guns	2-inch	20½
Pioneer		Two 14-inch TT.		
Pomone				
Proserpine				
Prometheus				
Psyche				
Pyramus				
Diana				
Dido				
Doris				
Eclipse		Five 6-inch guns		
Isis	5,600	Six 4·7-inch guns	2½ inch	19½
Juno		Three 18-inch TT		
Minerva				
Talbot				
Venus				
Arrogant				
Furious	5,750	Four 6-inch guns	3-inch	19
Gladiator		Six 4·7 inch guns		
Vindictive		Three 18-inch TT		
Hermes				
Highflyer	5,600	Eleven 6-inch guns	3-inch	20
Hyacinth		Two 18-inch TT		

Ship	Nominal Displacement	Armament (as fitted)	Max Deck	Speed Knots
Challenger *Encounter*	5,915	Eleven 6-inch guns Two 18-inch TT	3-inch	21
Andromeda *Amphitrite* *Argonaut* *Ariadne* *Diadem* *Europa* *Niobe* *Spartiate*	11,000	Sixteen 6-inch Two 18-inch TT	4-inch	23
Amethyst *Diamond* *Sapphire* *Topaz*	3,000	Twelve 4-inch Two 18-inch TT	2-inch	22

* * *

The end to this long progression of widely different form and capabilities came around the same time as the armoured cruiser was terminated. The final class (*Gem* class) marked the next logical progression for it was the first to carry the new steam turbine engine. But with the termination of this period of relative stability the cruiser type crystallised into two extremes. At one end of the scale the introduction of the battle-cruiser type saw enormous ships armed with the guns of the battleship; at the other a new type completely was introduced to work in harmony with the new enlarged destroyers of the *River* and *Tribal* classes. These were termed Scouts and in size and dimensions bore some of the lineage of the old torpedo cruisers which had been such failures.

The basic requirements were a sea speed equal to that of the latest destroyers and a handy armament compatible with that of their charges. The first classes were built to this limited function as conflict with Germany began to replace the traditional bogey of France. They were only required in limited numbers and the first eight were built in pairs, each builder responding to the Admiralty requirement in his own fashion, as was general policy at the time. *Adventure* and *Attentive* by Armstrongs displaced 2,670 tons. *Patrol* and *Pathfinder* from Cammell Laird's yards displaced 2,940 tons, *Forward Foresight* from Fairfields and *Sentinel* and *Skirmisher* from Vickers, 2,900 tons, but all were later armed with nine 4-inch guns, one 3-inch HA gun and two 14-inch TT. Their deck armour was only 1½-inches and their best speed was 25 knots. All were completed in 1905.

Such ships were fine for the *River* class destroyers; their function was to act as leaders for such ships and co-ordinate their attacks, but with destroyer speeds and sizes increasing an improvement on this type was an obvious requirement and two more classes were built to fill this need. They featured turbines instead of triple expansion which increased their speed by a knot although their displacement went up to 3,300-3,440 tons to carry ten 4-inch guns and two 21-inch torpedo tubes. All were constructed by Pembroke Dockyard; the first four *Bellona*, *Blanche*, *Blonde* and *Boadicea* joined the fleet in 1909-11, the second three *Active*, *Amphion* and *Fearless* in 1912-13. But already their type was superseded and after fifteen Scouts they passed into history.

Since the completion of the medium sized *Challenger* and *Encounter* in 1905 moderate dimension type protected cruisers had not been built. This was largely due to the theories of Jackie Fisher who saw no use at all for such ships. He preferred to rely on large destroyer types, like the experimental *Swift* to carry out scouting functions ahead of the fleet and report back by R/T. But across the North Sea Germany was steadily building a whole succession of medium size cruisers and an improvement on the Scouts was considered necessary. As these ships were expected to act in addition as a screen for the battle fleet some armour had to be re-introduced and a heavy fire power. The result was the first of the *Town* group of cruisers which featured an armoured deck of up to 2-inch thickness, and two 6-inch guns to tackle enemy ships of that type. On a displacement of 4,800 tons they also carried ten 4-inch guns and had a best speed of 26 knots. These five ships, the *Bristol* class,[1] were followed by a somewhat larger class, the *Weymouths*,[2] in which displacement rose to 5,250 tons to enable the main battery to be a more realistic one of eight 6-inch guns, although there was a slight loss of speed as a result. The nine ships of these two classes were completed in 1910-1912, and were still officially known as 2nd Class cruisers. But in the latter year these old terms, no longer having much meaning any more, were replaced and all the small protected cruisers still with the fleet were known for the first time officially as light cruisers.

[1] *Bristol, Glasgow, Gloucester, Liverpool, Newcastle.*
[2] *Dartmouth, Falmouth, Weymouth, Yarmouth.*

In the next group, the *Chatham*[1] and *Birmingham*[2] classes, the protected deck concept went by the board and they were given a 3-inch armoured belt. Tonnage was increased to 5,440, speed remained the same and one extra 6-inch gun was carried by the ships of the latter class. Two cruisers building for Greece in British yards were taken over in 1915 that bore a rough resemblance to this type. These were the *Birkenhead* and *Chester*, which, on a 5,200 ton displacement mounted ten 5·5-inch guns.

All these *Towns* were still considered too slow for the duties for which they were built and so a completely fresh design was instigated for the new light cruisers, a design which, with various modifications, spanned nine classes and the whole period of the Great War. They were highly successful and formed the bulk of the Grand Fleet and Harwich Force cruisers throughout most of that conflict. They continued to be built after the end of the war and thus bring our story up to date. The easiest way to list their various differences is to consult Table 6.

[1] *Chatham, Dublin, Southampton,* plus *Brisbane, Melbourne, Sydney* (RAN)
[2] *Birmingham, Lowestoft, Nottingham.*

* * *

Table 6: Early Development of the Light Cruiser 1914-1919

Ship	Nominal Displacement	Armament (as fitted)	Protec-tion	Speed
Arethusa *Aurora* *Galatea* *Inconstant* *Penelope* *Phaeton* *Royalist* *Undaunted*	3,512	Two 6-inch guns Six 4-inch guns Four 21-inch TT	3-inch	28.5
Caroline *Carysfort* *Cleopatra* *Comus* *Conquest* *Cordelia*	3,750	Two 6-inch Eight 4-inch Four 21-inch TT	3-inch	29
Calliope *Champion*	3,750	Two 6-inch Eight 4-inch Two (Subm.) 21" TT	4-inch	29
Cambrian	3,750	Three 6 inch Six 4-inch Two (subm.) 21" TT	3-inch	29

Canterbury		Two 6-inch		
Castor	3,750	Eight 4-inch	3-inch	29
Constance		Two (subm.) 21" TT		
Centaur	3,750	Five 6-inch guns	3-inch	29
Concord		Two 3-inch guns		
		Two 21-inch TT		
Caledon				
Calypso	4,120	Five 6-inch guns	3-inch	30
Caradoc		Two 3-inch guns		
Cassandra		Eight 21-inch TT		
Cardiff				
Ceres		Five 6-inch guns		
Coventry	4,190	Two 3-inch guns	3-inch	30
Curacoa		Eight 21-inch TT		
Curlew				
Calcutta				
Cairo		Five 6-inch guns		
Carlisle	4,290	Two 3-inch guns	3-inch	30
Colombo		Eight 21-inch TT		
Capetown				
Danae		Six 6-inch guns		
Dauntless	4,650	Two 3-inch guns	3-inch	29
Dragon		Twelve 21-inch TT		
Delhi		Six 6-inch guns		
Dunedin	4,650	Two 3-inch guns	3-inch	29
Durban		Twelve 21-inch TT		

Daedalus, Daring, Desperate and *Dryad* of the above class cancelled. Also the *Despatch* and *Diomede* completed in 1922.

*   *   *

The development of the *E* Class and the *Improved Birmingham* classes threatened to set off the spiral yet again until the Washington Treaty finally settled two distinct types, the heavy cruiser and the light cruiser. It did not stabilise for long; already the minelaying cruiser was in existence with the construction of the *Adventure* (1927). Her type was perpetuated with the *Manxman, Welshman, Latona, Abdiel* and *Ariadne* of the war years but these fall outside the scope of our book. Then came the advent of the anti-aircraft cruisers and the type sub-divided yet again.

Having examined in some detail the ships built under the general heading cruisers between 1870 and 1919, let us now look at the role of the cruiser as it was applied at various times over that period and how this led to its role as envisaged for World War II.

To recap, the larger cruisers came about partly as cheap 2nd-rate battleships, a policy which never worked but was always attractive to politicians. Partly it was continued as a response to foreign ships building at the time, Russian designs, French types designed to swoop on our far-flung commerce, matching class-for-class cruisers built in France, Japan and Germany. This was not satisfactory either, for rarely if ever did the ships designed to match each other come up against each other. The Admiralty had decided after the Great War that a more sensible policy was to build the type we needed for ourselves and let others go their own way, but the various treaties, as we have seen, brought up pressures to build to the limits to have ships equal to other nations again. Again it did not work.

Smaller cruisers came about partly by inheriting the duties of the older types frigates, corvettes and this was more justified. The range of types stemmed as much from the whole experimental transition from sail to steam, from muzzle-loaders to breech loaders and arguments about armour as anything else. The stability achieved in the early twentieth century was thrown into disorder with new technical advances, the turbine, radio telegraphy and so on and specialised types again began to emerge: the Scouts to aid destroyer flotillas, the need for ships with anti-aircraft capabilities in the 1930's. It would almost seem as if the rule of thumb on this process was that if there was a new duty to be performed the cruiser would do it! Always the most adaptable of warship types and the most prolific in the Royal Navy, it can be readily understood why the Admiralty kicked so hard against having such a versatile unit of seapower restricted in numbers, something which the Americans with only limited objectives, could never understand.

The First World War was of course the measure on which inter-war plans and most tactical discussion were based. The expected role of the cruiser therefore was most influenced by the lessons of that conflict and we can examine it under the main headings and compare and evaluate accordingly.

The Battle Fleet Concept

This was the main corner-stone of Admiralty policy between the wars, despite much criticism since that such a concept was already outdated by the 1930's. Most major exercises came down to the locating of an enemy battle fleet and placing our own in the correct position to engage it on the lines of the Battle of Jutland. In the 1930's only Japan (our most likely enemy) and the United States possessed enough battleships to form such a likely opponent. Nonetheless the long-range duel between heavy ships was the climax of fleet action as envisaged at the time and everything else was sub-ordinated to that. This continued right up to the Combined Fleet exercises of March 1939 and Captain Roskill concludes that: 'Plainly the principle that sea warfare would be decided by such means was far from dead on the eve of World War II.'*

The cruiser's place in this was the old established one of scouting ahead of the main fleets in extended line abreast until contact was made with the opposing fleet. Once contact was made the cruisers would brush aside any enemy light forces they encountered and press in as close as possible in order to ascertain the strength, course and speed of the enemy battle line. This information was to be signalled back to the C-in-C in order that he might make his own dispositions accordingly to bring them to action. Contact was to be maintained, even at the extent of self-sacrifice, in order that continual updates of this information could be transmitted until the C-in-C himself had the enemy in sight. Once this had happened the cruisers were to place themselves ahead of the battle line in order to counter-attack any attempts by enemy destroyers to intervene against our own battleships and also in order to maintain further contact should the enemy try to escape from his position. Cruisers were also to take any opportunity to support our own flotilla craft in their attacks and prevent interference from the enemy's cruisers on such an attack.

The scouting line ahead of the fleet was termed the 'A – K' line. This in itself dated back to First World War days when the ideal spread of such scouting cruisers consisted of two squadrons of light cruisers: six ships in each for a total of twelve, would be thus deployed; each cruiser was allocated a code letter from A to K on the battle chart. That the days had long gone when we could hope to muster as many as twelve cruisers to form such a line was obvious but the term was retained.

Great emphasis was placed on the early and accurate sending of sighting reports and on their regular updates so that the C-in-C was always fully aware of the enemy's intentions. Lack of such precise and continued reporting was held by many to have brought about

* Roskill, Stephen, *Naval Policy between the Wars*, Vol 2 (Collins, 1976), pp 431.

the indecisiveness at Jutland and every cruiser was left in no doubts that its first duty was to see that no such lamentable omission was to mar the second chance in any future war! That our own small fast cruisers might run into the *Mogami* 8-inch ships when trying such tactics called for the inclusion of at least one 8-inch cruiser squadron with the main fleet to match them, and the same applied to the Italians.

When Max Horton was in command of the 1st Cruiser Squadron in the Mediterranean during the period of the Abyssinian Crisis in 1935-36, it consisted mainly of 8-inch ships, *London* (Flag), *Australia*, *Berwick*, *Devonshire*, *Exeter*, *Shropshire* and *Sussex*. His principal task he decided was the destruction of the Italian 8-inch ships and it is interesting to note that this ex-submariner applied the Battle Fleet concept to this task:

> A number of different situations *may* arise, but the most urgent for our consideration are those involving battle between the two forces of eight-in cruisers. The general principles governing the tactics of our battle fleet now apply equally well to our eight-inch cruisers.*

The fate of the armoured cruisers *Black Prince*, *Defence* and *Warrior* at Jutland, all three of which were destroyed by battleship fire after pressing in too close, behove some caution for these bulky high-sided *Countys* in similar circumstances. Against 8-inch cruisers their high standard of training and skill and their undoubted leadership would have stood them in good stead, but in a main fleet action big lightly-armed cruisers, no matter how bravely led and fought, had been shown to be nothing more than death traps for their large crews.

Against the smaller 6-inch cruisers of likely opponents, the Japanese *Sendai*, Italian *Condottieri* and German *Köln*, British ships like the *Leanders* or *Towns* had every chance as they were both more powerfully armed and protected; only in question of speed were they at a disadvantage, and in persuading a reluctant enemy to stand and fight which was to prove a grave handicap in the years ahead.

The fact that the 'A – K' line would probably be composed of six cruisers rather than twelve was less important thanks to the fact that

---

* Chalmers, Rear-Admiral W.S., *Max Horton and the Western Approaches* (Hodder & Stoughton, 1954), pp 42.

the cruisers all carried amphibian aircraft to carry out searches for them and this would extend their range many times. Conversely of course the enemy would be similarly served and on balance, remembering that the British would be seeking combat whereas the enemy on the basis on World War I would be avoiding it, these additions tipped the advantage away from the hoped for set-piece battle. It was not forgotten how, in August 1916, a sortie by the High Seas Fleet had been misled by reports from Zeppelins scouting ahead of them and had turned back in time to avoid being trapped by the Grand Fleet who were seeking vengeance after Jutland a few months earlier.*

There was also the mitigating fact or that the speeds of modern battleships were almost as good as the battle-cruisers of the First World War, but cruiser speeds had not improved. This meant even less chance of their being able to maintain a safe distance from the enemy heavy guns and still being able to give clear, concise reports. In heavy weather any slight speed advantage would be lost, for the big ships would be able to maintain their speeds whereas the cruisers would have to slow down or risk weather damage in close proximity to the enemy. The 'A – K' line however was still justified in a fleet action because poor weather conditions and the unreliability of aircraft could negate their positive qualities, and the flotillas still required support.

Another result of the Jutland battle was that British ships were intensively trained in night fighting which would give the cruisers some chance of fulfilling their job of maintaining contact and which ruled out aircraft playing any part. The Japanese were similarly skilled in this but the Italians shunned any attempts to master it and paid heavily as a result during the war. The development of radar which came later added to this dimension and tipped the night fight scales heavily in favour of British, and later, American ships, although it was far from infallible as the latter found out at the Battle of Savo Island in 1942.

Striking Forces

Also associated with surface-to-surface action as envisaged was the setting up of special striking forces to probe and harry the enemy in coastal waters. The restricted number of battleships available

* See for example Marder, Arthur J., *From Dreadnought to Scapa Flow, Vol 3* (O.U.P., 1978), pps 285-300 for how this came about.

would ensure that they would, in the main, be husbanded, and anyway they would not be risked in such areas. The cruiser on the other hand would provide the nucleus for such forces based on the ideal of the Harwich Force of World War I.

Such forces would be mainly offensive in character and consist of fast cruisers supported by modern destroyers. Such a combination would be able to descend rapidly and without warning on exposed enemy convoys or units and cause considerable damage with the advantage of surprise. Again night fighting gave British formations of this type the edge, as was demonstrated in the Mediterranean in 1941. In 1939 the Humber Force was the earliest example of such a force to be set up in Home Waters. But they could also be defensive in character; witness the setting up of special anti-invasion squadrons in 1940, based on a kernel of light cruisers. The effectiveness of such striking forces depended much on their expendability to achieve a desired result. Examples abounded in the war to follow, which illustrated both the need for strong nerves when employing such forces and the consequences of over-extending them beyond their capabilities. Above all team-work and training held the key to their success. Ships which trained and fought together for long periods would generally have good records of success. Haphazard use of such forces, with ships merely brought together for one-off operations, rarely enjoyed such success.

Protection of Trade Routes

For as long as the cruiser type existed this was regarded as one of its prime functions, if not *the* prime. Whether in convoy or sailing independently the merchant ship presented a huge and vulnerable target to even comparatively small men-of-war on the loose and such was the vast extent of our world-embracing trade that seeking out such raiders was very much a needle-in-the-haystack operation. This was why large numbers were always needed, but the fact remains that in 1939 on outbreak of war only fifty-eight cruisers were on hand, and of these many were required for fleet work. This reduced to a paltry of 23 the number available to guard the sea lanes, a number clearly totally inadequate. On any one day in 1939 some 2,500 British merchant ships would be at sea; to protect them with less than one cruiser per 100 ships was the task that faced the Admiralty.

The only alternatives, apart from the introduction of the convoy system in limited form, which means one cruiser could guard ten to fifty ships more effectively, was the introduction and deployment of armed merchant cruisers, liners fitted with old guns that served to act as proper cruisers. They were almost as vulnerable as their charges, stood little or no chance if they encounted a proper warship for they were completely unarmoured, but they had to suffice, thanks to the treaties that had so bound us in the inter-war period. The heroic sacrifice of the *Jervis Bay* and *Rawalpindi* are well-known and are accorded the honour that is their due. But this does not mitigate by one jot the fact that real cruisers would have done the job better, and indeed would probably have been sufficient deterrent to prevent such slaughter taking place. This was the price paid for misplaced idealism in the 1920's and 1930's, but it was paid by seaman not statesmen.

As long ago as 1870 the 'Liberal' school of thought had maintained that armed merchant cruisers would suffice for policing the trade routes without the need to embark on costly cruiser programmes. This trend of thought surfaced again in the 1920's, led by Admiral Sir Herbert Richmond. He argued that no ship of war need exceed 7,000 tons, the size he considered sufficient to defeat an armed merchant raider.* His theory was used to attack any renewal of battleship building and greatly influenced MacDonald at Washington. This of course disregarded the fact that any nation that ignored this ruling and built bigger ships would rule the seas. To emphasise this, the appearance of the 14,000-ton 'pocket battleships' in Germany's new navy, as fast as heavy cruisers and armed with six-11-inch guns posed a new threat to merchant shipping on distant sea routes.†

Such a ship made a formidable adversary and clearly outclassed even the *County* class, let alone the smaller cruisers. Against such a foe only *numbers* would avail, but with only twenty-three cruisers available where were the ships to form the necessary squadrons and could we afford to concentrate them, thus reducing their area of search? In the event we had to do just this, as well as divert much-needed battleships, battle-cruisers and aircraft carriers to this end. Although the Battle of the River Plate ended in a victory it is just as well that Germany had few such vessels.

---

* Richmond, Sir Herbert, *Sea Power in the Modern World*, (Bell, 1934) pp 6.
† To achieve so much on this displacement armour protection was poor, nonetheless it proved sufficient to be effective against the 8-inch shells of *Exeter* when put to the test. Its striking power was vast and the range of ships enormous, they were, in fact, the prophets of *Guerre de Course* strategy's ideal.

Obviously then although the convoy system was to be introduced immediately on the outbreak of hostilities, there could be no question of providing even a single cruiser to guard each one of them. Priority had to be given to the most important. The Canadian Troop Convoys, for example, had battleships as escorts as well as cruisers, while the same principle was applied, although usually with cruisers as the main escorts, for the Australian troop convoys across the Indian Ocean to the Middle East. Special convoys with troops and vital war equipment were given the protection of two or even three cruisers across the Bay of Biscay to Gibraltar but for the average convoy no such luxury was available. If an AMC could be allocated it was, but most ordinary convoys rarely saw a cruiser for more than part of its journey.

This applied to the first years of the war, when threat of attack from pocket battleship or armed merchant raider was almost as likely as submarine attack. However the cruiser patrols proved themselves so efficient at rounding up and despatching these raiders that this role gradually became redundant later on. In the North Atlantic it was mainly the big HX convoys that benefited from at least one cruiser as flagship of the escort. As the old 'C' class conversions became available it was policy for at least one or two of these to be based in the Western Approaches to provide anti-aircraft cover for convoys approaching our western ports, especially so after the fall of France when long-range German bombers could, and often did, seek out these convoys that had survived the U-boat packs further out. In the Mediterranean these little cruisers were of course invaluable for such purposes, as Admiral Cunningham was quick to point out: 'We now had the three small anti-aircraft cruisers *Coventry*, *Calcutta* and *Carlisle*, and no convoy was complete without one or the other of them.'*

Desirable, and indeed, necessary though it was considered to have at least one cruiser available to protect the more valuable convoys from enemy surface attack, it should not be forgotten just how vulnerable this made the cruiser itself to attack from below the water. The cruiser was never designed to fight the submarine and lacked the battleship's underwater protection to protect it from torpedoes. Whereas battleships, even old ones like *Malaya*, might absorb a submarine's torpedo hit and still reach port, cruisers had little or no protection in this manner. So a cruiser would normally

---

* Cunningham of Hyndhope, *A Sailor's Odyssey*, (Hutchinsons, 1951), pp 309.

zig-zag at speed across the face of the convoy to give it its immunity.

In the same way cruisers on distant patrols against enemy raiders were almost always without the protection of destroyers. There were no destroyers to spare for such purposes, and even if there had been their restricted range would have ruled this out and merely tied the long-ranging cruiser down and restricted it in one of its chief assets. Just how vulnerable cruisers were to submarine attack had been amply demonstrated within the first weeks of World War One when one small U-boat had despatched three large cruisers *Cressy*, *Hogue* and *Aboukir*,* within a short while causing enormous casualties. As well as taking independent evasive action while with a convoy, often indeed lurking hull-down over the horizon to be on hand if needed but not in the submarine target area, those cruisers in distant waters relied a great deal on the remoteness of their war zone from the normal submarine hunting areas. However the German submarines of the Second World War had far greater range than their First War ancestors, and this, plus the use of the refuelling 'Milch-Cow' system, meant that even the 'safest' areas became dangerous in time. The odds of such a needle-in-the-haystack encounter might be considered huge, but it must be remembered that such cruisers would be patrolling natural trade routes for independently-routed shipping which could become known to enemy submarines. This lessened the remoteness of such an encounter, as witness the tragic loss of the *Dunedin*.

The use of cruisers to guard convoys in this way was on the whole successful, though it is perhaps again fortunate that the ultra-caution of such enemy raiders as did approach such convoys meant that they were not often put to the test. When *Hipper* attacked one such convoy in the Bay it was because she did not realise that the cruisers *Berwick* and *Bonaventure* were present, and, after getting a shock, she soon retreated. The deterrent value of just one cruiser was therefore worth its weight in gold. But the possibility of someday running into something that they could not handle was ever-present. In such an instance not even a squadron of cruisers could have prevailed, as against the *Bismarck* or the *Scharnhorst* and

* Much of the blame for this was the stupid location of these old slow ships close in to the Dutch coast in the old 'Close blockade' manner, and also in the natural gallantry of surviving ships to go to the rescue of their comrades, thus offering large, stationary targets. It was against all natural instinct to leave comrades struggling in the sea, but the potential of the submarine was not fully realised at that time.

Gneisenau for example, but it was then that they would be expected to sacrifice themselves by engaging such an enemy, and thus enabling a scattering convoy to escape, as in the classic case of the *Jervis Bay* AMC, that even one old, or weak cruiser, would still play a vital part. It was in just such an expectation of throwing themselves upon the *Tirpitz*, which was believed to be just over the horizon, that Admiral Hamilton's cruisers deployed during the ill-fated PQ17 in 1942. The fact that she was not anywhere near the convoy, and that, left to its fate, alternative methods of destruction, the submarine and the bomber, were then able to decimate it, in no way lessens the validity of the cruiser escort; but the intelligence was interpreted incorrectly in Whitehall.

Use as a Destroyer Flagship

We have seen how, with the development of the destroyer as a full-scale seagoing vessel, the desirability of having the control of so many ships concentrated in a larger vessel able to accompany them into battle, led to the development of the Scouts, and from them the long line of light cruisers in the period 1905-1918. The subsequent development of specially built flotilla-leaders for a time did away with this need, but in the co-ordination of several flotillas it was still felt desirable for Rear-Admiral (D) to exercise his command from a ship of light cruiser size overall. In the 'tween-wars period this duty was normally performed by the newer 'C' class cruisers, and then later, by the little *Arethusas*, which proved ideal.

However this was based on the 'Large Fleet' concept, which, in practice, soon proved impractical. Only the Home and Mediterranean Fleets ever justified such a special cruiser, and most commands were reduced to one, or at best, two flotillas for much of the war. Also the needs of the fleet for cruisers in more normal roles were always more pressing. Thus although the *Aurora* performed this function for the Home Fleet flotillas and the *Galatea* for the Mediterranean Fleet flotillas, this set-up did not long survive actual combat requirements.

Nonetheless the function was revived from time to time for special circumstances. These were flexible and encroached on the Striking Force concept, as with the use of one light cruiser with the Plymouth Command flotilla to sweep the Channel in 1943; the convoy escort role, as in PQ18 when the *Scylla* embarked Rear Admiral (D) to command the four half-flotillas of Home Fleet destroyers which formed the main escort; and in the Battle Fleet concept in miniature, as with the final stages of Malta convoys, when the Sicilian Channel was barred to larger ships, and cruisers like the *Cairo* acted as flagship to the destroyers fighting their way through to Malta. One of the earliest successes in the Mediterranean came from such a combination with the *Sydney* co-operating with a destroyer flotilla to bring about the destruction of the Italian light cruiser *Bartolomeo Colleoni*.

It is of interest to note that the Japanese, modelling their fleet on the Royal Navy, continued to use their specially-built small cruisers in the traditional manner long after other navies had discontinued the idea, and that they proved most successful in this role.

Anti-Aircraft Defence
It has already been seen how the glaring deficiencies in protection of the fleet from air attack had been made patently obvious during the Abyssinian Crisis of 1935-36 and how this had led to the conversion of the *Coventry* and *Curlew* as AA ships. The American Admiral Leahy described their function as that of 'base defence' but this was never the main *raison d'être* of their conversion. They were intended to provide convoys with an umbrella of flak against enemy bombers, and, as Captain Roskill states: 'This pouring of new wine into very old bottles proved useful for convoy protection work, especially after short-wave radar sets had greatly increased the efficiency of their armaments.'*

Thus this conversion programme was extended.

But in the case of the *Dido* class cruisers, built with the new 5·25-inch HA/LA gun as their principal weapon, it was air defence of the Main Fleet which was listed as one of their *primary* functions, with their orthodox light cruiser potential a close second. The Admiralty's reliance on the anti-aircraft gun as the main defence against aircraft can be seen as highly optimistic. The carrier-borne fighter aircraft of good performance proved itself, in the long-run, to be the ideal form of defence against this form of attack. But that is not to say that the policy of building ships like the *Didos* was wrong. The remarkable war record of these ships more than justified their construction, but even without the benefit of hindsight the Admiralty were surely more correct on their estimation of their value than was the ill-informed criticism of Winston Churchill.

Remember that at the time these ships were designed and built,

---

* Roskill, *Naval Policy, op cit*, pps 422.

the aircraft supplied to the Royal Navy came from the Air Ministry, a body that showed itself completely uninterested in the special needs and requirements of the Fleet. Obsessed to the point of fanaticism with the theory that long-range bombing of Germany would win the war on its own, little enough effort was put into the construction of high-performance fighters of their own, the Spitfire and Hurricane owing as much to their dedicated designers as the RAF, and with regard to carrier-borne aircraft these were so far down the list of priorities as to be almost invisible. The Navy was also at fault here, the need to cram as many roles as possible into each new aircraft type meant that modern fighters, like the Fulmar, also had to double as reconnaissance aircraft and carry an observer. Not surprisingly their performance *vis-à-vis* modern land-based aircraft was lamentable. The thought seems to have been that they would never have to operate against land-based aircraft, a fallacy which the Norwegian Campaign of 1940 quickly exposed.

Whatever the reasons, the Admiralty knew that the fighter aircraft on its limited numbers of aircraft carriers would not only be inferior in performance but also outnumbered and therefore provision of special anti-aircraft cruisers was a good investment for a modern fleet. The provision in the larger modern cruisers of batteries of eight to ten 4-inch HA guns, pom-poms and multiple ·5-inch mg's, was also well thought out; indeed for the scale of air attack envisaged these defences would seem perfectly adequate. Unfortunately attrition from the air became *the* major enemy policy in European waters and on occasions proved overwhelming. The *quantities* of shells used to beat off prolonged air attacks was quite beyond that envisaged, and both the pom-pom and the multiple machine-gun proved to lack range or hitting power against modern bomber types. Only after the adoption of the 20-mm Oerlikon and the 40-mm Bofors cannon in large numbers was anything like the scale of defence required gained. Radar helped further, as did proximity fuses, but even with all these improvements over 1939 the Aegean Campaign of 1943 showed that determined and well-led bombers, in particular dive-bombers, would often get through and ships designed to withstand 8-inch shells were unable to stand up to 1,000-lb bombs.

Against determined attacks, well pressed home by dive or torpedo bombers the answer was always *volume* of fire, whether long or short range. The same defence, saturation fire, was part answer to the ultimate in manned bombers in the Pacific theatre, the

Kamikaze. An example of this was to be found during operations off Okinawa when the two British battleships accompanying the carrier fleet were withdrawn, leaving their air defence to their own fighters and the cruisers. With the huge batteries of the capital ships not available, the Kamikazes pierced both screens and hit several carriers badly.

However there was *no* defence against the radio-controlled stand-off weapons developed by the Germans later in the war, as the *Uganda* found to her cost off Salerno, and the loss of the brand-new *Spartan* off Anzio to such weapons a few months later, in January 1944, only drove this unpalatable fact further home.

Shore Bombardment
Probably the least-expected role for the cruisers of the Royal Navy pre-war, it was in the role of army support during amphibious landings that the multi-gunned light cruisers achieved a new and highly successful reputation in the second half of the conflict. Being often the only large ships on far-off station since Victorian days, cruisers had frequently been called upon to assist in combined operations of the most limited types. These usually involved landing parties of Royal Marines and sailors equipped with naval Gatlings and small guns to assist the soldiers ashore. The guns of the cruisers *Powerful* and *Terrible* featured thus in the Boer War, and light weapons landed from cruisers in the Red Sea also helped in the Sudan Campaign at Tamai and El Teb in 1884*, and in many lesser fights.

Direct support from the guns of the anchored warships themselves was even more infrequent. At the bombardment of Alexandria in 1882 no cruisers were present, unless one can somehow stretch the term to include the ancient *Penelope* with her 8-inch muzzle-loading guns in that category. In the First World War there were more chances for cruisers to adapt to this form of warfare. During the final stages of the German advance to the Belgium coast and before the Western Front congealed into one vast dugout and trench system to the Swiss frontier all manner of warships bombarded the seaward flank of the enemy.

It was here that the lesson was learnt early that saturation fire from large numbers of smaller guns was more effective against targets like troop concentrations and field pieces than the heavy

* See Smith, Peter C. *Per Mare Per Terram* (Balfour, 1974), pps 79-82.

guns of the battleships. The latter had a more spectacular effect, and were the most likely to knock-out fixed shore batteries, although it took a lot of luck to score direct hits and extreme ranges on such small targets, but the more rapid fire of the cruisers could smother a target more efficiently. This same lesson was to be re-learnt in World War II. The other lesson was as old as the hills: no matter how powerful or skilful a warship, the fixed and protected guns, well dug-in and firing on pre-determined fixed bearings, would always have the edge.

Although warships' guncrews were among the most expert and highly-trained in the world and capable of engaging small moving targets at long ranges, counter-battery work was never very satisfactory without spotters to plot the fall of the shells and make corrections. And even in ideal conditions such targets were hard to locate and pin down. A mobile battery of howitzers behind a line of dunes for example did not present a clear silhouetted target like an enemy warship on which to make ranging estimates. The lesson was re-learnt at the Dardanelles where, as at Alexandria, it was found that only direct hits on the guns themselves would do, a very difficult feat to achieve.

Mining Operations

The Royal Navy had never been at the forefront in mine warfare before 1914, regarding the weapon as that of the weaker power and only limited experiments had been made. By contrast certain European navies of this era gave the mine a high place in their armouries, and also gave much thought to methods of delivery into enemy waters. Minelayers were generally old and slow vessels in the Royal Navy, converted to lay fixed fields in defensive areas. Little thought had been given to the requirements for high speed dashes into enemy coastal waters to lay minefields from surface ships.

By contrast Germany had given this much thought. During the war they developed this concept by converting two light cruisers, *Graudenz* and *Regensburg*, into fast minelayers. These were 5,000-ton vessels with a speed of 27 knots and armed with seven 5·9-inch guns and could carry 120 mines apiece. All subsequent classes of light cruiser built in Germany had this minelaying capacity built-in to their original specifications; the ten ships of the *Frankfurt*, *Elbing*, and later *Königsberg* and *Dresden* classes all had a capacity for 120 mines. A logical extension of this policy was the building of the special cruiser-minelayers *Bremse* and *Brummer* in 1916. Of 4,000-

tons displacement and armed with four 5·9-inch guns they had the great virtues of speed of 34 knots and enlarged capacity for 360 mines each.

The use of light cruisers for minelaying was a common factor in other nations' fleets at this time. The Italian lights cruisers *Marsala*, *Nino Bixio* and *Quarto* were so equipped, and in addition Italy built several specialised ships. Many Russian cruisers were similarly fitted out. The Admiralty turned first to Mercantile conversions for fast minelayers with the *Princess Irene* and *Princess Margaret*, but the earliest cruiser conversions for conventional defence minelaying were seven ships of the *Apollo* class during 1905-10. Their guns were stripped from them and they only carried six 6-pdrs, but they could stow 150 mines. These conversions were the *Andromache*, *Apollo*, *Iphigenia*, *Intrepid*, *Latona*, *Naiad* and *Thetis*. In their designed role they were quite successful, acting as a squadron in 1914. *Iphigenia* and *Intrepid* went to North Russia in 1915-16 for this work, and *Andromache* and *Latona* to the Mediterranean where mines laid by the latter scored the biggest success of any British minefield when the battle-cruiser *Goeben* was badly damaged and the cruiser *Breslau* was damaged by mines in 1918.

For offensive operations however something better was obviously required. Many destroyer conversions proved a good answer; their only problem was that their capacity was small. So various small cruisers with good speeds were adapted as the war went on and acted as a squadron with great success during 1917-18 in the North Sea. Among those which operated in this role from time to time, utilising bolted-on mine rails which could be rapidly landed when the ships were required for more conventional duties, were the *Aurora*, *Penelope*, *Blanche* and *Boadicea*.*

Post-war however the answer seemed to lie in a cruiser size ship built specially for the task and the first experiment in this idea was the *Adventure* of 1927. She was described as a cruiser-minelayer, displaced 6,740 tons, was armed with four 4·7-inch guns and could carry either 280 large or 340 small mines. Her chief drawback was her lack of speed: 27 knots. After being worked as a test-bed she herself was damaged by mines and was converted to a repair ship and it was in this capacity, rather than as a cruiser or a minelayer, that she spent most of the war. The requirements of speed and a

* A detailed study of such minelaying *Into the Minefields*, by Peter C. Smith is under preparation.

good defensive armament took priority over capacity in the next class of this type, the famous *Abdiel* class which were completed between 1941 and 1943. On a displacement of only 2,650 tons they carried a mine load of 160, but had good dual-purpose guns and were credited with phenomenal speeds of around 40 knots. These six ships, *Abdiel*, *Apollo*, *Ariadne*, *Latona*, *Manxman* and *Welshman* were splendid vessels but proved to be too valuable for many other tasks in actual combat conditions and saw as little actual minelaying as *Adventure*. The running through of badly-needed supplies to Malta was one of their main duties in 1941-42, and while engaged in such duties they sometimes doubled up as small cruisers. *Ariadne* went out to the Pacific Fleet and did some good work there, but they really fall outside the scope of this book and were the Royal Navy's final attempts at combining minelaying and cruisers in one design.

Although the Germans, Italians and Russians continued to give their light cruisers this function as high priority no British cruiser carried out such missions in World War II.

When war came in September 1939 therefore British cruisers were fully stretched to meet their expected roles. New roles emerged and old ones gained new prominence, but, as before, the cruiser was capable of meeting the new demands made on it. Numbers were inadequate, but a good programme of new construction was underway. Before turning to examine in detail just how the British cruiser responded to the circumstances both old and new, the effective strength and its allocation are listed in Table 7 on page 70.

Thus was the stage set.

Table 7
Disposition and Cruiser Squadrons September 1939.

Fleet/Area	Unit	Ships
Home Fleet	18th Cruiser Sqdn	*Belfast, Edinburgh, Sheffield, Newcastle*
(Scapa Flow)	12th Cruiser Sqdn	*Cardiff, Dunedin, Effingham, Emerald Enterprise, Delhi*
	7th Cruiser Sqdn	*Caledon, Calypso, Diomede, Dragon*
	Destroyer Command	*Aurora*
(Humber)	2nd Cruiser Sqdn	*Glasgow, Southampton*
(Portland)	Attached	*Caradoc, Cairo, Ceres*
Mediterranean	1st Cruiser Sqdn	*Devonshire, Shropshire, Sussex*
Fleet	3rd Cruiser Sqdn	*Arethusa, Penelope*
(Alexandria)	R/Ad (D)	*Galatea*
	Attached	*Coventry*
North Atlantic Station (Gibraltar)	Attached	*Capetown, Colombo*
South Atlantic	9th Cruiser Sqdn	*Danae, Dauntless, Despatch, Durban*
Station	South American Div	*Ajax, Cumberland, Exeter*
(Freetown)	Attached	*Neptune*
America and West Indies Station (Bermuda)	8th Cruiser Sqdn	*Berwick, Orion, Perth, York*
China Station (Hong Kong)	5th Cruiser Sqdn	*Cornwall, Dorsetshire, Birmingham, Kent.*
East Indies Station	4th Cruiser Sqdn	*Gloucester, Liverpool, Manchester*
R.A.N. (Australian Waters)		*Adelaide, Australia, Canberra, Hobart, Sydney*
R.N.Z.N. (Pacific)		*Achilles, Leander*

*   *   *

CHAPTER THREE

Cruisers Against Warships

It has been noted how the policy of cruiser building had been constantly influenced over the years by two main themes. The first, of constructing ships specifically designed to oppose and counter cruisers building for other nations, re-occurs again and again in our story. It is not difficult to understand the motivation behind this, but it has rarely, if ever, proved to be a satisfactory course to follow. The second, of building the type of ships which the Admiralty considered the best for the job in hand, is obviously more sound and was long recognised as being so. Despite this the first, often because of outside influences, politicians, treaty restrictions etc, has frequently intruded upon the second, no matter what the Admiralty's wishes.

When the failings of building ship to match ship are examined, it is not hard to make out a case against it. Foreign ships were built and designed for strictly limited roles, mainly, as in the case of Russia and France in the nineteenth-century, and Germany in the twentieth, as commerce raiders able to exploit the weakest link in the power of a world-wide Empire such as Britain's. With such strictly limited functions in mind they could concentrate on essential features and sacrifice all-round capability, whereas the reverse would always be true for the Royal Navy. Other powers, the examples of Italy, Japan and the United States, would build their cruisers with a main fleet type action as the predominant rationale and place trade protection in a much lower category. Again the Royal Navy would have to place equal emphasis on both these facets, or construct cruisers in such numbers as to provide superiority in both types. This latter policy was, in fact, the one adhered to in the golden years of British seapower from 1888 to 1914. The wealth of the country and the national will was such that for every outstanding cruiser type produced abroad the Royal Navy was able to construct whole classes of cruisers that outmatched their particular characteristics. This meant costly programmes and high manning levels but the Navy was at that time able to carry this burden.

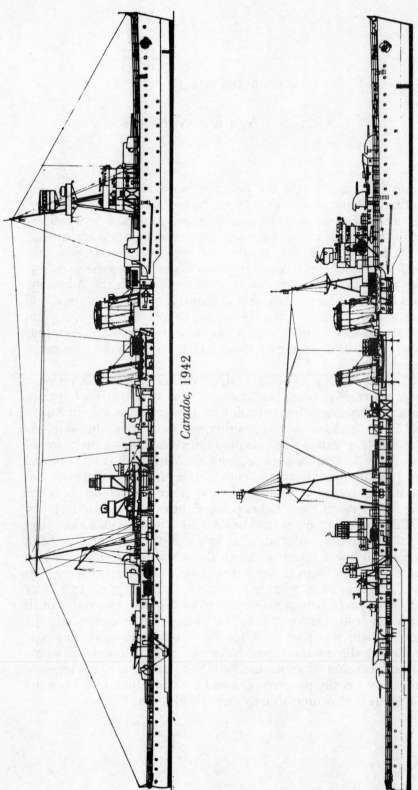

Caradoc, 1942

Caledon, 1944

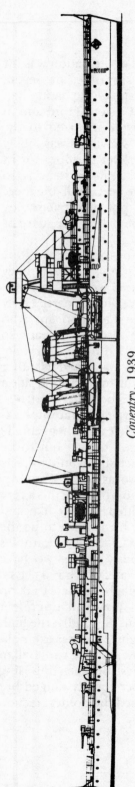

Coventry, 1939

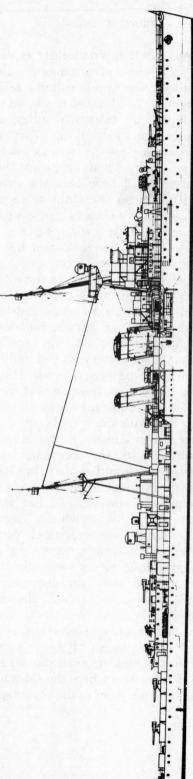

Coventry, 1940

After 1922 this no longer applied. The will of the nation was for the abolition of armaments altogether if possible, or severe restriction on numbers if that failed. The wealth of the nation had been expended in the mud and wire of the Western Front and in propping up exhausted allies, and debts were incurred to the United States for fighting a Continental-type war which was totally unnecessary for the world's premier naval power to adopt for its own security. Then there came the additional treaty limitations, so that even had the will and the money still have been available there was no longer the scope to outbuild every potential enemy, by laying down a class of cruisers for every two or three Japanese or American ships that appeared.

It might be thought that such severe limitations on what had gone before would have forced upon the Navy the adoption of the policy which they themselves favoured anyway, but, as we have seen, for various reasons this was in the main not so. We did not particularly want 10,000-ton cruisers with 8-inch guns, but the Americans, who were in the chair, and the Japanese, not to be outdone, did, and so we had to follow suit. Not until the late 1920's did the Admiralty revert to the better policy of building the ships that suited us rather than following foreign trends. This of course is an over-simplification of the problem, but one that could be said to be generally true.

The biggest drawback in the ship-for-ship type programmes was that the actual chances of ships designed to fight each other actually meeting in combat in the event of hostilities, turned out to be almost nil. In a set-piece major naval battle each ship would have its designed role and its place, but World War Two, as World War One, saw the introduction of too many random factors to make this a very frequent occurrence. So like was rarely pitted against like and comparisons about which design ultimately turned out to be the best compromise were rarely put to the test. Of the few examples where such comparisons might be cautiously made, we have selected four. Firstly the Battle of the River Plate, which is a classic example of how a combination of heavy and light cruisers took on and, by superior tactics, defeated a more powerful opponent designed specially to defeat such combinations. Secondly, the high speed dash and cut-and-thrust of opposing light cruisers is exemplified in the action off Crete between the *Sydney* and two Italian cruisers. Our third example is that of a rare clash between opposing 8-inch cruisers where the sides were on paper equally ranged but the decision went to the commander who used the boldest tactics:

the Battle of Savo Island. And finally the only daylight encounter between the heavy cruisers of Japan and a British ship carrying the same armament, the Battle of the Java Sea. Into all these clashes other elements imposed to a greater of smaller extent but they are the closest comparisons available for study of ship-for-ship combat.

The Battle of the River Plate (13th December 1939)

The results of the Great War as they affected German Naval thinking were apparent throughout the Second World War. They had built a fleet which they had hoped would match both in size and efficiency Britain's Grand Fleet, and it had not worked. Although their ships were in many cases the equals, and in some respects the superiors, of individual British ships, they could never compete in two vital areas. One was in the building, which, put simply, lay in the fact that once Britain had accepted the challenge to her long-established superiority she always had the vital building expertise and capacity to out-build any such challenge from Germany. In other words the 'Two keels for one' type response meant that by the end of the war the Grand Fleet was in fact far superior in numbers to the High Seas Fleet than it had been at the beginning, despite losses. There was no way Germany could match such an expansion.

Secondly, there was the elusive factor of *morale* which three centuries of uninterrupted victories had given British seamen over any opponent. Again in basic terms it could be said that whereas the British were always confident that should a stand-up fight take place they would win, and win decisively, the Germans never expected any more than limited success and tried to avoid such a confrontation. As would be expected, the results of the sea fighting only reinforced these respective viewpoints and no such challenge was made in the second conflict.* On the other hand in such *matériel* subjects as shells, fuses, mines, torpedoes, searchlights and gunnery equipment, the Germans were, at the outset anyway if not in 1918, superior.

Where Germany achieved spectacular victories at sea was in the adoption, not always by choice, of the *guerre de course* type strategy advocated by France during the years she had been cast in the same role as Germany as an inferior fleet challenging a dominant one.

---

* Although it should be stressed that such a challenge *would* have been presented had time allowed for it with the proposed 'Z-plan' which called for the building of an enormous fleet of modern ships by 1945.

The major success was the U-boat campaign and, not surprisingly, this policy was adopted without question as the basis for the second struggle, and again came close to success. But with regard to surface fighting the Germans had achieved some isolated, if short-lived, victories by the exploits of her detached cruiser squadrons in the early days of the First War. Thus for example Coronel, when a German squadron wiped out a British one, and also the effect that raiding cruisers like the *Emden* had on British merchant shipping and the vast amount of effort that had to be taken to bring such elusive raiders to book. The escape of the *Goeben* and *Breslau* was also widely acclaimed; it had the effect of drawing Turkey into the war on the German side and was another short-lived victory as were raids later in the war by German cruisers against the weakly escorted Scandanavian convoys.

Although these made a deep impression on German thinking, the Allies appeared to have somewhat overlooked their effects when drafting the limitations of the Versailles Treaty and German naval architects were quick to seize their opportunities. By limiting the tonnage of German capital ships to a mere 10,000 tons the Allies in effect gave a spur to revolutionary new thinking and can almost be said to have forced the 'pocket-battleship' concept onto their opponents by this.

Whether forced or eagerly adopted, however, there is no doubt that the resulting new type of armoured ship, as the Germans termed their new raiders, presented the Royal Navy with a grave threat and one to which they could reply with no immediate answer. The *Deutschland* and her sisters were the nearest thing yet to the ideal surface raider and when they appeared on the scene in the early 1930's many felt that the traditional British cruiser would stand little or no chance against them. It was often said that the only ships afloat which could both catch *and* destroy the three German vessels were Britain's own rapidly ageing battle-cruisers, *Hood, Renown* and *Repulse*. Even two *Counties* were held to be no match for a *Deutschland*, while the smaller *Leanders* and the like were given no chance of survival at all.

The pocket battleships were of about 13,700 tons displacement (Germany having no scruples, even in the pre-Nazi era, of cheating on international agreements in this manner). Even so on such a modest displacement and within dimensions just as small, they packed a great deal of offensive power. Each was armed with six 11-inch guns, in two triple turrets fore and aft. These guns heavily outranged any British cruiser weapon of course, and fired a shell which could penetrate any envisaged cruiser armour with ease. Their secondary armament was also considerable, each ship carrying eight 5·9-inch guns, the equivalent of the most powerful British light cruiser types. Supplementing these were six 4·1-inch guns and heavy (for their time) AA armaments of semi-automatic cannon constituting a far superior system to any British warship. They were also equipped with eight 21-inch torpedoes, carried in two quadruple mounts on the quarter-deck, and obviously placed there to ward off any heavy ship coming up astern of her. They carried a scouting aircraft on a catapult.

Coupled with such a powerful *offensive* array of weaponry were other features which marked them as unique vessels. Their main propulsion units were MAN diesel motors, four to each shaft, which gave her almost 60,000 shp and a top speed of 26 knots. These new engines saved considerable weight, as did the extensive use of electric welding in her actual construction itself. These features all helped to give her an extensive range of operations (10,000 miles at her economical speed of nineteen knots) giving immediate lie to the story put out that these ships were built solely for the purposes of escorting troop convoys in the Baltic! Indeed, when war actually came two of these ships had actually sailed from Germany days earlier, vanishing into the wastes of the Atlantic awaiting their chance to show their worth. Evading all British air patrols they were on station ready to pounce before the Royal Navy could take their measure.

It had long been recognised that single cruisers would be unable to stand up against the pocket battleships. The only hope of bringing such ships to book was for special groups of cruisers, backed up when possible by battle-cruisers and aircraft carriers (the former for the guns large enough to beat the enemy, the latter to scour the wide waters and locate them) to operate together. This meant reducing considerably the area of search and thereby increasing the enemy's chances of evading detection. But to be effective they had to strike, and when they did it was hoped that slowly but surely they would draw a net around themselves.

As Captain Roskill states, 'The effectiveness of surface raiders depends not only on* the actual sinkings and captures which they accomplish but on the disorganisation to the flow of shipping

* Roskill, Captain S.W., *War at Sea, Vol. 1* (HMSO, 1954), pp 111.

which their presence, or even the suspicion of their presence, generates.'

Admiral Raeder had despatched his two ships with instructions that they were to cause the maximum disruption and destruction possible on the Allied shipping lanes, but they were warned to avoid at all costs getting involved with equal or superior naval forces, and even inferior warships were to be left alone unless it was absolutely certain that an easy success could be achieved without damage to the pocket battleships themselves. This order the German captains carried out rigorously throughout the war and thus the *deterrent* of even small and isolated British cruisers had a major effect out of all proportion. The raiders were further restricted by Hitler himself initially. While the Polish campaign was underway he held them back hoping that once Poland was brought to heel Britain and France would not be willing to go on with the war. When that became apparently just so much wishful thinking, he instructed that French ships should be left alone, hoping to divide the Allies. He was also concerned to keep the powerful US Fleet out of the way and kept his ships well away from the so-called 'Neutrality Zone' to start with. Therefore it was not for some weeks after the war had started that the two raiders, still undetected, began operations in earnest.

The first to sail had been the *Admiral Graf Spee* which left her home port on the 21st August. On the 24th the *Deutschland* also sailed, and by the end of the month the former was on her waiting position in the South Atlantic and the latter in the North Atlantic, each with an attendant supply ship in company.

The Admiralty had no firm knowledge that these ships had escaped their patrols, and although they suspected one might have got loose had no confirmation. The general policy adopted from pre-war thought was to rely mainly on the evasive routeing of all merchant shipping to escape detection by such raiders. Behind this tactic the limited number of available cruisers were to patrol the main concentrations off well-used ports and in the most threatened areas or the most vulnerable, convoys were immediately formed, which, if although but poorly protected (other than troop convoys which had old battleships allocated to their defence) at least reduced the profile of the thousands of merchantmen at sea on any day of the year and made them less easy prey to locate. Of course such measures could never be totally effective and many scores of independently routed ships continued to ply the oceans totally undefended. With the resources available it could not be otherwise.

At the end of September Hitler finally threw off the fetters and the two pocket battleships began to operate in earnest. The *Deutschland* sank her first victim, the *Stonegate*, on the Bermuda-Azores route on 5th October. *Admiral Graf Spee* beat her by destroying the *Clement* on 30th September and thereafter both ships began to operate in earnest with increasing success. These initial sinkings gave the Admiralty their first confirmation of their fears, although the survivors' reports were often inaccurate and confusing. Nonetheless it was established beyond doubt that the pocket battleships were out and immediate steps were taken by the Admiralty to try and find and defeat them. On 5th October eight powerful Hunting Groups were formed to patrol both the North and South Atlantic. These groups are shown on Table 8, and are as modified by Admiralty Postgram 1210/31st October 1939 and put into effect.*

* The original intended, but *not used*, plan is in Roskill, *War at Sea*, Vol. 1, pps 114.

* * *

Table 8
Hunting Groups formed 5 October 1939.

Force Code	Ships (Types, Nationality etc)	Area
F	*Berwick, York* (British 8-inch cruisers.	Employed as North Atlantic convoy escorts.
G	Two Ships from *Cumberland, Exeter* (British 8-inch cruisers) and *Ajax, Achilles* (British 6-inch cruisers added later)	Eastern Seaboard of South America.
H	*Shropshire, Sussex* (British 8-inch cruisers)	Cape of Good Hope
I	*Eagle* (British aircraft-carrier) *Cornwall, Dorsetshire* (British 8-inch cruisers)	Indian Ocean
J	*Malaya*, (British battleship) *Glorious* (British aircraft-carrier)	North Atlantic
K	*Renown* (British battle-cruiser) *Ark Royal* (British aircraft-carrier)	Covering all the Central Atlantic

Neptune (British 6-inch cruiser)
Hardy, Hero, Hereward, Hostile (British
destroyers)

L   *Repulse* (British battle-cruiser)   North Atlantic
Furious (British aircraft-carrier)

X   *Dupleix, Foch* (French 8-inch cruisers) Western Atlantic

Y   *Strasbourg* (French battle-cruiser)   West Indies.
Hermes (British aircraft carrier)
Neptune (British 6-inch cruiser, initially,
later to Force K)

*   *   *

Such a heavy drain on the Allies' main fleets, one battleship, three
battle-cruisers, five aircraft-carriers, ten heavy and six light cruisers
and four destroyers, showed just how much disruption even *two*
pocket battleships were able to cause, and this must be counted as
part of their success even as much as the limited sinkings they
achieved. Indeed the *Deutschland* only sank two merchant ships in
the North Atlantic before being recalled to home waters. She again
evaded all detection and anchored at Gdynia on 17th October,
while the Allies were still vainly hunting her in the North Atlantic.

Admiral *Graf Spee* continued to score easy victories in the southern
oceans, roaming from the west coast of South America to the east
coast of Africa and back again before switching her hunting area
into the southern part of the Indian Ocean in November, laying a
false trail there and doubling back into the South Atlantic again.
Throughout these months she remained elusive and her tally of
kills steadily mounted, reaching nine ships by 7th December when
she sank the *Streonshalh* almost mid-way between the two continents.
But her spectacular career was now drawing to a close.

From the steady build-up of reports from her victims the
Admiralty was gradually able to narrow their search. All of forces G,
H and K had been placed under the overall command of Admiral
G.H. d'Oyly Lyon, the C-in-C, South Atlantic and after a long
period of unrewarded toil his measures began to bear fruit. The
German raiders, lacking any bases in these distant waters, relied
totally on their supply ships to keep them going in oil, foodstuffs
and other essentials and if the head of this hydra remained
unaccounted for, the concentration of Allied ships patrolling in

search of her gradually whittled down the tail. Three German merchant ships, blockade-runners, fell victim to their net in November, the *Uhenfels*, *Adolph Woermann* and *Emmy Friederich*, which somewhat offset British losses. *Graf Spee*'s supply ship, *Altmark*, had some narrow escapes herself during this period. Later sweeps picked up the German vessels *Watussi* and *Adolf Leonhardt* and on the 5th yet another, the *Ussukuma*: the cruisers *Neptune*, *Caradoc*, *Shropshire*, *Ajax* and *Cumberland* all had a share in these successes. But still the principal enemy remained free.

Meanwhile Commodore H. Harwood, commander of Force H, the South American Division, with his broad pennant flying in *Exeter*, had re-distributed his forces. At the same time as *Graf Spee* was disposing of the *Streonshalh* and heading for the traffic-congested area around the River Plate estuary, Harwood, playing a hunch that that was *indeed* her next area of operations, was directing his ships to the same area. His flagship, *Exeter*, had been undergoing repairs in Port Stanley while Harwood tranferred to the *Ajax* to continue the hunt. Meanwhile the *Achilles* had taken the former's place. His most powerful ship, *Cumberland*, was in the Falkland Islands at the beginning of December in case the German captain, Langsdorff, should attack on the anniversary of the First World War battle in those waters. Basing his guesswork on the probable lure of the waters off Rio de Janeiro and the Plate he calculated that *Graf Spee* could reach that region by 12th December. He was prepared to meet her there. *Exeter* was sailed on 9th and *Achilles* joined forces the next day. By dawn on 12th December all three British cruisers were patrolling some 150 miles to seaward in anticipation. Just twenty-four hours later, at 0608 on 13th December, the pocket battleship steamed into their arms when *Ajax* reported smoke to the north-west.

At once Harwood sent *Exeter* to investigate this tell-tale trail and at 0616 she sent back to him the stirring signal: 'I think it is a pocket-battleship'. At last they had cornered the enemy. But they had cornered him with the most weakest of all the hunting groups. One 8-inch cruiser, and she mounting but six guns, and two of the smaller 6-inch *Leanders*, now had to find some way to bring the *Graf Spee* to bay before being knocked out by her much more powerful armament. It was a problem that, naturally, Harwood had contemplated in some depth on many occasions. He had long ago decided to attack and if possible get in under those lethal 11-inch salvos to a range where his smaller weapons could inflict some damage. He

Calcutta, 1940

Cairo, 1942

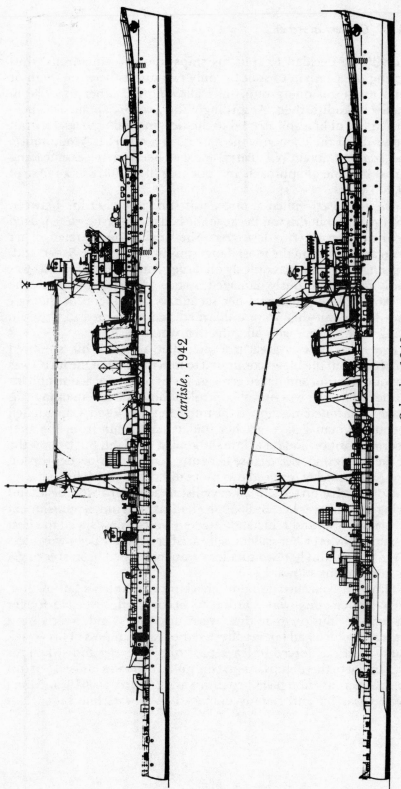

Carlisle, 1942

Colombo, 1943

accordingly decided to split his ships into two squadrons, thus forcing the German to split his only two turrets between them or concentrate on one group, thus allowing the other to close in relatively undisturbed. Accordingly the *Exeter* (Captain F.S. Bell) turned out of line and steered to the west intending to attack from the south of the enemy, while *Ajax* (Captain C.H.L. Woodhouse) and *Achilles* (Captain W.E. Parry) engaged her from the east heading across her line of approach and opening fire at 0618 at a range of 19,000 yards.

The *Graf Spee* replied at once, at first dividing her fire between both groups, but this was because she had thought she was engaged by one cruiser and two destroyers. She quickly concentrated all her main armament on the most dangerous opponent, the *Exeter*, and, utilising her radar, was quickly on target. Almost at once *Exeter* was badly hit and seriously damaged by two 11-inch projectiles. The pocket battleship reserved her secondary armament for the *Ajax* and *Achilles* but they were unharmed and continued to close in, firing as they went with all guns that would bear.

Exeter was now in great trouble. After a further hit, she fired torpedoes but the blows continued to rain in on her. One turret was put out of action and her steering gear was put out of action and for a brief while she was out of control, although her remaining two turrets continued in action as the range rapidly closed. Captain Bell eventually managed to get her under helm again from the after steering position and for a time she kept in the fight. But by now the pocket battleship was so close her guns were firing a low depression and *Exeter* quickly received two more direct hits which left her with but one active turret and a heavy list to starboard with dead and dying men all over her. By 0650 she had taken as much punishment as she was able and reluctantly steered west at slow speed to effect repairs. However her gallant self sacrifice had not been worthless for in the interim her two smaller companions had been able to get in some telling blows.

Firing in concentration and checking each other's fall of shot, their lighter guns were starting to become effective. No longer under the illusion that they were destroyers and, receiving a battering which had not yet affected the seaworthiness of his vessel, Langsdorff was forced to leave the crippled *Exeter* and switch his armament to these ships. At first only one turret was utilised but this was dangerous enough, as first *Ajax* was straddled, at 0640, and then *Achilles* was hit and slightly damaged by a waterline burst. Not surprisingly their own accuracy fell away for a while under such a deluge, and conditions were made doubly difficult by the laying of a smokescreen by the *Graf Spee* and the failure of *Achilles'* gunnery wireless set. Indeed the enemy appeared to think he had silenced them and made a turn to the south with the apparent intention of going after the damaged *Exeter*, which was steering south-east under a pall of smoke.

Fortunately the 6-inch cruisers recovered themselves and, with the range down to 16,000 yards, resumed their battering of the enemy at 0708. This forced the German ship to change course back to the north-east and once again Langsdorff gave the *Ajax* the benefit of his 11-inch guns to some effect: a direct hit at 0725 put both her after turrets out of action. Still the two little ships continued to close in; the range rapidly came down from 11,000 to 8,000 yards and at 0738 *Ajax* took another heavy shell which sheered off her topmast. *Achilles* still remained scot-free, but this clearly could not last for the enemy was shrugging off their puny blows with apparent immunity while still maintaining his own accurate replies. Harwood was forced to turn away under cover of smoke to assess the situation further at 0740.

It was expected that the undamaged *Graf Spee* would take this opportunity to close and deliver the *coup de grâce* to both British squadrons, but, to their surprise she declined the invitation, seemingly content with merely driving off her little tormentors. Far from pursuing them the pocket battleship instead continued to the west and, after a short interval, at 0748, Harwood took his two ships back in pursuit.

And so the strange conflict continued, with the larger German vessel steadily steering away from her two British adversaries and making a beeline for the neutral haven of Montevideo in Uraguay. From time to time the *Graf Spee* swung round and fired still accurate salvos from her main armament but she never seriously threatened *Ajax* or *Achilles* and it was plain that these were merely warning shots to make them keep their distance. All through that strange winter afternoon the chase continued, and on through the dusk. As Maldonado Bay came into view on their starboard bow the *Ajax* turned south to cover the southern exit from the Plate, while *Achilles* kept steadfastly astern of the enemy. By 2317 that night it was clear beyond doubt that *Graf Spee* was entering Montevideo and *Achilles* was recalled. The German ship actually reached that port at midnight. The battle was over as far as the cruisers were concerned.

They had achieved much, *Graf Spee* had been hit by two 8-inch shells, one of which penetrated the armour belt and armoured deck. She was also hit by eighteen 6-inch shells and suffered one officer and thirty-five men killed and sixty wounded.

The curious diplomatic war that went on afterwards and resulted in the scuttling of the *Graf Spee* and the suicide of Langsdorff form no part of our story. The battle was the first victory at sea, or indeed, victory of any sort for the Allies in the war and has been much analysed and fought over again since. A recent television documentary further covered this well-worn ground without revealing more facts on the battle itself.

What conclusions can be reached from the point of view of cruiser tactics in such circumstances? On paper the three British ships hadn't a chance and in fact they inflicted very little serious material damage on *Graf Spee* despite their gallant behaviour. In contrast the light protection of the three British ships was in no way meant to stand up to 11-inch shells and the battering that *Exeter* took is, in its way, a testimony to the skill of her builders. Quite why Langsdorff denied himself the satisfaction of finishing off at least two of his crippled opponents will always be something of a mystery, although his crew have paid frequent tributes to his own overriding concern for his young crew and his distaste at the waste of lives unnecessarily. It was probably this humanity in the German captain that saved the *Exeter* and *Ajax* as much as anything else, another example of an inponderable influencing events in war.

Mediocre British propoganda reduced this to basic terms, 'a good British little 'un will always defeat a bad German big 'un' and the like which was a dangerous attitude to adopt at the beginning of a long and uncertain war. But certainly the instinctive British attitude of attacking first, and not giving the enemy time to utilise his superiority cannot be faulted in this instance. It was certainly a welcome change to the caution and half-heartedness that had marked events in the Great War and showed that the Royal Navy had lost none of its old aggression since that conflict. In handling an inferior force Harwood's tactics cannot really be faulted and they made a deep impression on Churchill, always one to back attack no matter what the consequences. Unfortunately in war it is usually attrition that decides the issue, not individual battles, no matter how well conducted or how successful the outcome, and this was to become apparent later. The euphoria that accompanied this cruiser action in the South Atlantic was reinforced by similar actions against the Italian Navy in the Mediterranean a few months later, and it is to one of these that we must now turn.

The Destruction of the 'Colleoni' (19th July 1940)

There had long been a tradition in the Italian Navy of building ships which carried heavy armaments on light, comparatively unarmoured hulls. Speed rather than strength had often been associated with their warships. This was probably due to their late blossoming as a naval power of any note and by the fact that their horizons were bounded by the almost land-locked Mediterranean. In particular, having no world-wide commitments they could concentrate on their immediate needs, which was eminently sensible, and produce vessels which related to the requirements of their own home waters. In the First World War their attention was almost entirely concentrated on the Adriatic which was so restricted both naturally and by minefields and net barrages that speed was indeed a very desirable attribute.

This was certainly the case with their light cruiser and destroyer designs laid down between the wars as part of Mussolini's grand expansion schemes for his armed forces. While the heavy cruisers might cheat on tonnages to incorporate heavy armour protection the light cruisers of this era, designed as they often were with high-speed dashes into enemy waters to lay mines, speed was the essence. Typical of these fast thinly hulled ships were the cruisers of the *Condottieri* class, of which there were several sub-groups.

The first ships of this class were designed in the mid-1920's and laid down in 1928, all being completed three years later. They featured a straight-stemmed bow, a raised fo'c'sle with a flush deck from abaft the bridge, much like contemporary destroyer designs in fact, which was no co-incidence. They were powered with 2-shaft geared turbines, their forward uptakes being trunked in the case of the fore-funnel giving them a distinctive profile. Shp was 106,000-126,200 giving them speeds of up to 38 knots plus. Compare the comparative figures for a contemporary British light cruiser, the *Leander*, with a shp of 72,000 for 32 knots while the armour protection allocated each ship further emphasises the different concepts under which they were constructed. Both ships carried similar armaments on these different hulls: the Italian ships mounted eight 6-inch in four turrets, as the *Leanders*, with six 3·9-inch and eight 37-mm and twelve 20-mm AA guns with four 21-inch torpedo tubes. The *Condottieri* also had a built-in minelaying capacity for 96 mines and carried two aircraft.

In all the Italians built twelve ships to this same general design of which the *Bartolomeo Colleoni* and the *Giovanni Delle Bande Nere* were of the first group. When war was declared in June 1940 the former was with the 2nd Division at Naples and the latter was with the 6th Division at Messina in Sicily. Both were serving with the 2nd Division at the Battle of Calabria in July when they first had a taste of British shells and the Italian fleet was driven into harbour by Admiral Cunningham's Mediterranean Fleet.* Despite this set-back the Duce's orders that his naval and air forces take the offensive throughout the Mediterranean were still, at this stage of the war, being carried out to a limited extent and with this in view the Italian Naval High Command, *Supermarina*, decided soon after Calabria that an attempt must be made to interrupt the free-flow of British convoys to and from the Greek ports from the Suez Canal and the Levant by reinforcing their small naval forces based on the island of Leros with the 2nd Division.

The *Bande Nere* and *Colleoni* accordingly sailed from Tripoli to comply with this order on the evening of 17th July and steered north-eastward. Aerial reconnaissance had been conducted by the *Regia Aeronautica* over the approaches to the Aegean and they had reported that the area they had covered was free of any British movements. Perhaps the two cruisers should have been dubious of such reports following events at Calabria where they had been badly let down by the air force, but, whatever their feelings, they pressed on towards Leros through the Eastern Mediterranean under the command of Admiral Casardi. As they sped through the waters south of Greece during the daylight hours of the 18th however their initial escort of the destroyers of the 10th Squadron left them and returned to harbour at Mersa Matruh leaving the two Italian cruisers on their own for the last leg of their hazardous journey.

Unknown to the Italians, light forces were also at sea in the Aegean that day. Sailing from Alexandria on the 18th were two groups: the first consisted of the Australian light cruiser *Sydney* (Captain J.A. Collins, RAN), the second of the five ships of the 2nd Destroyer Flotilla (Commander H. St. L. Nicolson), with the *Hyperion*, *Havock*, *Hero*, *Hasty* and *Ilex*. Their mission was almost identical to that of the Italian cruisers, for they were to enter the

---

* See Smith, Peter C., *Action Imminent*, (William Kimber, 1980), for a full account.

Aegean and intercept any Italian shipping they encountered moving in or out of the Dodecanese islands. Following this at dawn on the 19th the *Sydney* was to take one destroyer and enter the Gulf of Athens in search of such targets, while the rest of the destroyers were to divert along the north coast of Crete in an anti-submarine hunt from east to west to see if they could flush out any of the Leros-based submarines.

Thus it came to pass that first light on the 19th found both groups on a collision course, neither aware of the other's purpose. The resulting engagement later took the name of the Battle of Cape Spada, which is the westernmost tip of the island of Crete.

The *Bande Nere* (Captain Franco Maugeri) and the *Colleoni* (Captain Umberto Novaro) had just entered the channel between Crete and the island of Cerigotto at 0717 on the morning of the 19th steering almost due north while the four destroyers under Commander Nicolson, *Hyperion*, *Ilex*, *Hero* and *Hasty*, had reached the end of their beat and were steering on directly opposite course across the Bay of Kisamo when they sighted each other at a distance of about 19,000 yards. The two Italian cruisers were making 30 knots by 0727 and opened fire on the destroyer flotilla. Commander Nicolson immediately turned his ships about and signalled to the *Sydney*, then some forty-five miles north of him, that he was leading the two Italian ships towards her. *Sydney*, on receipt of this signal, immediately turned south to rendezvous and worked up to full speed.

Although the morning was misty neither side had any difficulty in identifying the other as cruiser and destroyer, although whether he was up against 8-inch or 6-inch ships was not immediately clear to Nicolson. On their side Admiral Casardi and his staff clearly identified their opponents as destroyers and, to avoid the expected counter-attack by torpedoes he ordered his two cruisers to steer a diverging course towards the eastern tip of Cerigotte. This had the effect of opening up a gap of more than 20,000 yards between the two forces, which meant that the Italian gunners could still continue their fire on the rear of the British destroyer line while remaining well out of range from any reply their opponents' 4·7-inch guns could make. Thus for a long time it was hot work for the British ships but in the main no destroyer was seriously threatened at this range. To keep them at a respectful distance the rear destroyer launched two torpedoes at 0743 and the 2nd Flotilla then laid smoke while on a parallel course to the enemy. Ten minutes later they resumed their original heading and the Italian ships complied. As the British destroyers increased speed up to 32 knots the range steadily opened up to 22,000 yards. This headlong chase continued for the best part of an hour with the Italians making no progress in closing the gap but being drawn nicely into *Sydney*'s path in the classic manner.

By 0830 the destroyers were still far ahead under intermittent fire, no more accurate than before, at 36°N with a thick bank of low-lying mist on their starboard quarter which the two Italian cruisers were fast approaching. Meanwhile *Sydney* and *Havock* were drawing closer to the north of this mist and, at 0826, the Australian cruiser had the enemy in sight through it, and, three minutes later she opened fire on the leading Italian cruiser at 19,000 yards range. Almost immediately the *Sydney* straddled the *Bande Nere* and then scored a hit on her, which, although causing no serious damage, caused the Italian squadron to veer sharply away and lay smoke to cover their withdrawal.

According to one source Casardi could only dimly make out their opponents and mistook the *Havock* for a second cruiser. However debatable this and other conjecture is, the result was abundantly clear for, after running south-east under cover of smoke for ten minutes, at 0840 the helms of both Italian cruisers were put over further and further and they were soon in full flight back through the Cape Spada-Cerigotto channel at their best speed.

There was little doubt that the Italian cruisers could out-run the *Sydney*. The question was could her very accurate gunnery score sufficient damage to the enemy to slow them down before they drew safely out of range? Commander Nicolson had of course turned his flotilla into line abreast to assist in the hunt but they were so far astern now that they were unable to close the gap to become effective participants, while their speed was no greater than the Italian cruisers. So the battle's second phase now developed into a high speed chase south with the *Sydney* trying to catch her two flying opponents and the British destroyers trailing along astern hoping for good pickings for their torpedoes if one of the enemy was forced to drop out.

Thus it continued for another hour with *Sydney* slowly but surely . being left behind but with her 6-inch salvos falling accurately around her sternmost opponent, the *Colleoni*. Her patience was finally rewarded when the enemy were crossing the Bay of Kisamo for, at 0923, she scored a vital hit on *Colleoni* which penetrated into her engine room and brought her quickly to a stop. Leaving the cripple to the good intentions of Commander Nicolson's destroyers, *Sydney* continued the chase after the *Bande Nere* which continued at her full speed to the south. But the gap continued to widen and after an hour-and-a-half of long-range shooting the ammunition supply for *Sydney*'s two forward turrets was beginning to run low. The Italian flagship, after clearing the channel, set a straight course for the haven of Tobruk, and, at 1030, Captain Collins called off the pursuit. By that time just four 6-inch shells remained for 'A' turret and one for 'B' turret. *Banda Nere* had been hit twice, at 0835 and at 0950, with eight dead and sixteen wounded.

The *Colleoni* offered no resistance when Nicolson's destroyers came storming up. They quickly lowered their boats to take off the survivors and between them the *Havock*, *Ilex* and *Hyperion* rescued 525 members of her crew. Much of the time they were carrying out this mercy mission they were under air attack from Italian bombers who continued attacking them, fortunately without scoring any hits, while their own countrymen were being picked up from the sea. On conclusion of this work the *Ilex*, and *Havock* put *Colleoni* on the bottom with torpedoes and then rendezvoused with the returning *Sydney*, *Hasty* and *Hero*. The whole force then returned to Alexandria.

It had been a neat and efficient little action, marred perhaps by the escape of damaged *Bande Nere* but nonetheless satisfactory for that. Captain Collins was awarded the CB for his part in the action. Admiral Casardi claimed that his ships had been up against the *Sydney* and *Gloucester* during the action, but the *Havock* resembled the much larger *Gloucester* even less than she did the *Sydney*.

Little that was new was learned from the Cape Spada encounter, but much was confirmed about the differences between the two nations' light cruisers. As at the River Plate the British had not hesitated to close with a superior opponent and tackle them head-on. The long patient training between the wars had been reflected in the accuracy of *Sydney*'s long-range gunnery against a fast flying target and was most commendable.

That the Italian cruisers were built for speed and would always out-pace our own cruisers, and even our destroyers, was expected, as was the heavy expenditure of ammunition naturally entailed in such a chase. It was unfortunate that the stocks of 6-inch shell at Alexandria were very low at this stage of the war, a defect that cannot be laid at the cruiser designer's door. It was to be accentuated by frequent further actions of this type in the months ahead; *Ajax* in particular was involved in similar high speed chases during which three Italian destroyers were sunk.

All-in-all then, the Royal Navy could feel after Calabria and Cape Spada that it had more than the measure of the Italians as surface ship fighters, as it had over the Germans from the experience of the River Plate and *Renown's* action off Norway against *Scharnhorst* and *Gneisenau* in April. This pattern once established, never changed. Unfortunately the hope that every Axis power would react in the same way to even inferior Allied cruiser forces did not hold up when the third partner entered the fray. The cruisers of the Imperial Japanese Navy were to prove far tougher nuts to crack as our next two examples are to show.

The Sinking of the 'Exeter' (1st March 1942)

The Japanese attack on Pearl Harbor on 7th December 1941 eliminated the US Navy as a major hazard to their conquest of South-East Asia. Although the aircraft-carriers and cruisers survived almost intact they were utilised as fast striking forces in the Pacific proper and not risked at any time during the hard-fought surface battles that marked this period of conquest between January and March 1942. Nor, with the sinking of the battleship *Prince of Wales* and the battle-cruiser *Repulse* off Malaya a few weeks later, did the Allies have any warship larger than a heavy cruiser to contest the Japanese surface ship dominance of these waters. The rapid conquest of Malaya, Borneo, the Philippines and the Dutch East Indies by seaborne troops was therefore a matter of cruiser/destroyer task groups locked in unequal struggle and the results of these battles were almost complete victory for the Japanese. Japan had battleships in these waters which could have been called upon to decide the issue had it have been necessary, but, in the event, it never was. The cruisers and destroyers, the latter armed with the deadly long-range torpedo, the 'Long Lance', were able to decimate with ease the hotch-potch of British, Australian, Dutch and American ships ranged against them.

The largest battle of this bitter period of defeat for the Allies was the Battle of the Java Sea which took place in a series of confused encounters off the north coast of the island of Java between the Japanese cruiser and destroyers guarding their troop convoys and a mixed squadron of about the same size and composition of the Allies trying to get at them. In this battle the Japanese were absolute victors. The Allied ships got nowhere near the transports and suffered almost 90 per cent casualties in the process. Two British cruisers took part in this heroic failure, the 8-inch cruiser *Exeter*, refitted and re-armed after her damage at the River Plate, and the Australian cruiser *Perth*, sister of the *Sydney*. The battle has been described in some detail* and will not concern us here other than to say that as a result of it the *Exeter* had been damaged by 8-inch shell fire from the *Nachi* and set on fire. Reduced to fifteen knots speed and with her communications centre destroyed she had put back to the port of Surabaja for emergency repairs. The *Perth* survived the battle relatively unscathed but was sunk along with the American 8-inch cruiser *Houston* in the Battle of Sundra Strait on 1st March 1942 by Japanese destroyers.

As the Japanese covering forces had only suffered one destroyer slightly damaged it was largely intact and *Exeter*'s chances of survival were decidedly thin right from the outset. To give some idea of what this single damaged 8-inch cruiser was up against, with her attendant destroyers *Encounter* (British) and *Pope* (US), the force that she had to evade was the same one that had wiped out most of the combined Allied squadron on the 27th, and contained four 8-inch cruisers, *Nachi*, *Haguro*, *Ashigara* and *Myoko* of the Eastern Covering Force under Rear Admiral Takagi and Vice-Admiral Takahashi's 3rd Fleet.

These four vessels were sister ships, the first of the heavy cruisers that Japan had laid down and which forced the Royal Navy to follow suit. Their actual tonnage was 13,380 tons against *Exeter*'s cut-down 8,250 tons and, not surprisingly they individually outmatched her in every way. A comparison is given below in Table 9.

It is to be wondered whether the advocates of the *Exeter*'s design ever considered that she would have to face up to not one, but *four* of the Japanese heavy cruisers when they contemplated her design.

The *Exeter* (Captain O.L. Gordon) sailed from Surabaja at 1900

---

* For the Allied side see Thomas, David, *Battle of the Java Sea*, (André Deutsch, 1968). For the Japanese side see Dull, Paul S. *The Imperial Japanese Navy* (1941-45), (USNI, 1978), pps 71-93. *Exeter*'s story is told in detail in Gordon, Oliver, L, *Fight it Out* (William Kimber, 1957). The forthcoming Volume Two of Arthur J. Marder's study of the Royal Navy and the Imperial Japanese Navy will probably become the definitive account. *Perth*'s last flight is in Mckie, Ronald, *Proud Echo* (Robert Hale, 1957)

Table 9
HMS *Exeter* and I.J.N. *Ashigara, Haguro, Myoko* and *Nachi*.

	Exeter	Japanese Cruisers
Displacement (tons):	8,250	13,380
Dimensions (ft): pp:	540	631
oa:	575	662
breadth:	58	68
draught:	17	21
S.H.P.	80,000	130,250
Max speed: (knots)	32	33.75
Armour. Side: (inches)	3	4
Turrets:	2	3
Deck:	5	2
Armament: (Guns):	Six 8-inch.	Ten 8-inch.
	Eight 4-inch.	Eight 4·7-inch
	Eight 2-pdr.	or 5.1-inch
	Two 20-mm.	Eight 25-mm.
		Four 13-mm.
Torpedo Tubes:	Six 21-inch.	Twelve 24-inch.
Complement:	650.	775.

*   *   *

on the last day of February 1942 with her two destroyers. The plan was for her to strike boldly out west of Madura, then steer northward to the east of Bawean Island towards the south coast of Borneo in the vicinity of Banjarmasin and then turn west, hugging that coast until nightfall when the squadron would make a final run under cover of darkness for the Sundra Strait to Colombo. She might have got through but the fate of *Houston* and *Perth*, and the Dutch destroyer *Evertsen*, all of whom tried that route, would have probably overtaken her. There seem to have been no efforts to co-ordinate all six ships into one concerted breakthrough together. But in the event she was fated never even to cross the mouth of the Karimata Strait, and she was still restricted to a best speed of sixteen knots.

They were sighted by the ever-present Japanese reconnaissance aircraft almost as soon as they left harbour and Admiral Takagi was able to make his dispositions to trap her at his leisure. Thus it was that early on 1st March, at 0400 by the light of the setting moon, *Exeter* sighted unknown ships ten miles off. Hoping to evade detection himself Gordon turned his squadron well clear. But at 0750 the masts of warships were sighted from *Exeter*'s masthead. These were two of the Japanese cruisers and they immediately catapulted their spotting aircraft. Still thinking they could evade their enemies the *Exeter*'s group changed course yet again but the Japanese were now steadily closing the trap.

It was at 0850 that the southernmost group, the cruisers *Nachi* and *Haguro*, with their destroyers *Yamakaze* and *Kawakaze* sighted the three Allied ships at a range of some 33,000 yards to the north-east. For an hour they tracked them steering north-west and turning north-east towards them at 0950 to cut off their line of retreat to Surabaja. Meanwhile, at 0935 *Exeter* again spotted them approaching her and almost simultaneously a further warship appeared dead ahead. There were in fact two Japanese destroyers here, the *Ikazuchi* and the *Akebono*, and behind them out of sight of the doomed squadron the heavy cruisers *Ashigara* and *Myoko* steamed to close the ring from the north. They were caught with no option but to make a fight of it.

At 0940 the first salvos crashed out from the Allied squadron. All ships engaged the *Ikazuchi* at ranges varying from 14,000 to 20,000 yards and held on the north-east; *Exeter* worked up to 25 knots to break through what was thought to be the weakest point in the ring of steel, the solitary destroyer. *Ikazuchi* immediately turned back towards her heavy compatriots. Soon the 8-inch cruisers appeared above the horizon and began to return the fire and *Exeter* could see that the odds had lengthened in his direction.

While her two destroyers laid smoke to protect her course was altered to starboard until by 1000 the Allied squadron was steering due east, *away* from the Sunda Strait. The *Ashigara* and *Myoko* kept in position to the north of them and, as *Exeter* had reached her best speed by now, gradually overhauled her, bombarding her with 8-inch salvos as the range came down to 16,000 yards. Meanwhile the Japanese destroyers slipped to the south of the Allied ships and, at 12,000 yards range opened fire with their lighter weapons. While this was taking place the southern group of Japanese ships cut the corner and began to close, until, at 27,000 yards range, their own 8-

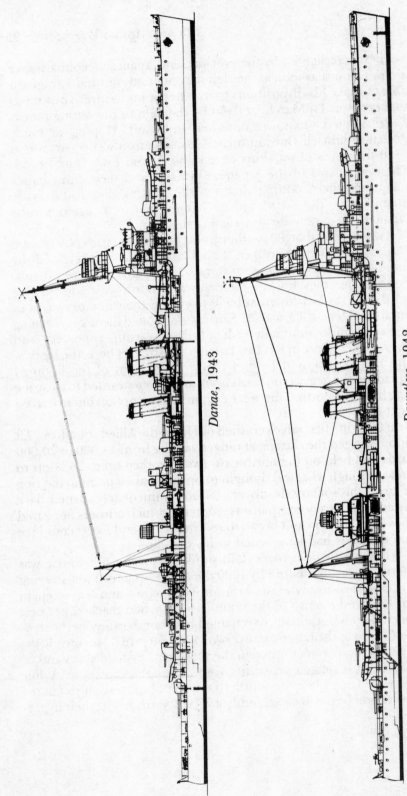

Danae, 1943

Dauntless, 1942

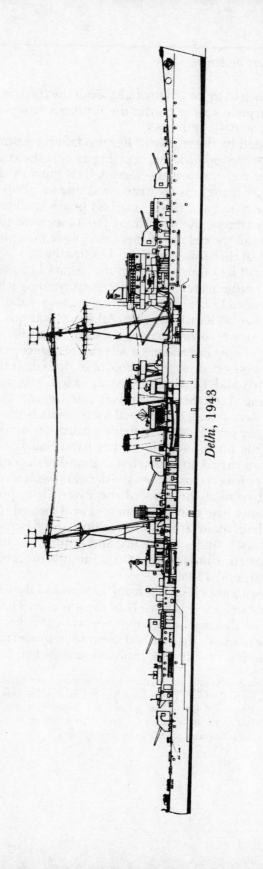

Delhi, 1943

inch salvos began to join in the fight. Both the *Ikazuchi* and *Akebono* launched torpedo strikes, as did the southern group as the range came down at 1040 and 1053.

Still shielded by the smoke of her two faithful destroyers, *Exeter* continued on easterly course, replying as best she could with her three twin turrets against the forty 8-inch guns of the Japanese ships. But her firing was far from good due to failures in her fire control system and she made very bad practice; all her salvos fell wide of their targets. By contrast the Japanese made good practice, although for all the deluge of shells they were pumping out it was not until 1120 that *Exeter* received her first hit.

A rainsquall had loomed up on the distant horizon and it was towards this dubious safety that *Exeter* was running when the blow fell. Unfortunately the first hit was a fatal one; the 8-inch shell penetrated her boiler room again. All power was quickly lost, and she slowed down to four knots, crawling painfully through the water while her big adversaries made careful target practice against her. She was now completely unable to reply to their fire, all power for the 8-inch and 4-inch guns having failed. She was little more than a sitting duck. Seeing she was lost beyond their help the destroyers were released and sped away towards the squall.

The *Ashigara* and *Myoko* now made steady play on the wallowing *Exeter* and the hits poured in on her riven hull fast and furious. Captain Gordon had no option but to abandon ship and at 1130 the Japanese destroyers closed in to finish her off with torpedoes. Thus in unequal combat the hero of the River Plate, put up against hopeless odds just once too often. The Japanese cruisers then switched their main armaments against the destroyers, quickly getting *Encounter* under heavy fire and putting her down at 1135. The *Pope* lasted a little longer then she too succumbed to their gunfire at around 1205.*

It had been a hopeless fight from the start and the best that can be said is that *Exeter* died as bravely as she was able. That she inflicted absolutely no damage on her opponents in either her last fight or at Java Sea is notable, for she had been fully modernised since the River Plate. But the odds were always against her, and even when

---

* Most British and US accounts have it that she was attacked by Japanese dive bombs and crippled before being sunk by the cruisers, but one British historian does not mention these: Kirby, Major General S. Woodburn, *The War Against Japan*, (HMSO, 1957). We are inclined to disagree with Kirby on this issue, and favour Morison's version that the planes came from *Ryujo*.

she was built the hope that a six-gun ship with light armour could stand up to the ten-gun Japanese heavy cruisers was always a bad gamble. Nor did her more powerfully armed sisters stand much more of a chance in the only other cruiser versus cruiser combat that British ships took part in against the Japanese, which we shall now describe.

Battle of Savo Island (9th August 1942)
The onrush of the Japanese during the first year of the war was not checked until the Battle of the Coral Sea in May and the first major defeat did not take place until the next carrier-dominated battle off Midway Island in June. Despite these setbacks the initiative still apparently remained with them until 7th August 1942, when the first US Marines landed on the islands of Guadalcanal and Tulagi in the Solomons Group. Up to that point Japan had been consolidating her stranglehold on the Southern Pacific by preparing to invade New Guinea and developing air bases down the chain of islands towards Fiji in the hope of thereby completing her isolation of the Australian sub-continent. As part of this ambitious programme her construction units had been building a major airstrip on Guadalcanal island and had almost completed it. To forestall such a dangerous intrusion the Americans sent in their Marines to seize it, which they did without too much difficulty. The problem was then, whether they could hold onto it.

Covering the landings of the Marines had been a powerful Task Force under Admiral F.J. Fletcher, with three aircraft carriers, a battleship, six cruisers and many destroyers. The Amphibious Force consisted of twenty-two fully laden transports and they had a close escort of four cruisers and eleven destroyers under Rear-Admiral V.A.C. Crutchley, VC. The cruisers of this force were mainly Australian: the 8-inch ships *Australia* and *Canberra* and the 6-inch cruiser *Hobart*.

The Japanese reaction was immediate, but initially not too effective. Based at Rabaul was the 8th Fleet under Vice-Admiral Mikawa, with five heavy and two light cruisers and a destroyer. The rest of his destroyers were on escort duties. But he had some land-based aircraft at his disposal, mainly twin-engined Betty torpedo bombers and Val single-engined dive bombers, and he also had a combat ready group of troops embarked for the occupation of Rabi Island. The main Japanese Fleet was based well back at Truk in the Caroline Islands but Yamamoto, the C-in-C, ordered Mikawa to take energetic steps to throw out the Americans before they could become established. This he now did.

The laden transports were despatched at once to land their troops, but when later reports came in of the strength of the US invasion force (16,000 men), these were hastily recalled, one of their number was lost to submarine attack. Meanwhile the Navy aircraft were thrown into the attack; forty-three of them attacked the main US covering fleet and damaged one destroyer. A second wave of twenty-six torpedo bombers lost heavily but sank one transport and another destroyer. Although these losses were comparatively light they so worried the US commander that he withdrew his main fleet prematurely at 1807 on 28th August, leaving the transports and their escorts without air cover.

While these preliminary blows were being exchanged a much more powerful threat was developing. Mikawa had sailed from Rabaul aboard his flagship *Chokai* with his full strength, rendez-vousing with the four heavy cruisers already at sea and heading determinedly down through the island chain, along the route which came to be known as 'The Slot'. His full strength is shown in Table 10. Although his ships were in fact detected by aircraft of the RAAF their composition was wrongly reported and, further, what reports there were were delayed so that the commanders ashore at Tulagi had no idea this powerful squadron was rapidly closing their vulnerable transport anchorage. The withdrawal of the Main Fleet created a crisis there as it was felt that the transports would be wiped out in air attacks the following day and a hurried conference was called during the night which Vice-Admiral Crutchley was ordered to attend. He did so, but unfortunately he took his flagship, the *Australia*, with him.

Not expecting a major surface attack, the ships of the Screening Force had taken up their night patrol positions covering the approaches to the Tulagi anchorage both north and south of Savo Island which straddled the 'Slot' to the west. The dispositions of these forces are shown in Table 10 below.

Both the picket destroyers were fitted with radar but despite this further advantage it was the Japanese who achieved complete surprise and who fought with more grasp of what was happening. In all night actions confusion is inevitable and this was never more apparent than in this battle. Mikawa had no idea that the covering aircraft carriers had been withdrawn but was determined to

Table 10
Battle of Savo Island-List of Forces.

Japanese		Allied.	
Striking Force		**Picket Destroyers**	
Chokai		Ralph Talbot	Destroyers.
Aoba		Blue	
Kako	8-inch cruisers		
Kinugasa		**Northern Force**	
Furutaka			
		Vincennes	
Tenryu	Light cruisers	Quincy	8-inch cruisers
Yubari		Astoria	
Yunagi	Destroyers.	Wilson	Destroyers
		Helm	
		Southern Force	
		Canberra	8-inch cruisers
		Chicago	
		Bagley	Destroyers
		Patterson	
		Eastern Force	
		San Juan	Light cruisers
		Hobart	
		Buchanan	Destroyers
		Monssen	

*   *   *

continue. He only had the vaguest ideas of the disposition of his opponents around Savo but his spotter planes were able to give him a rough estimate that he was outnumbered.

It was in a single extended two-mile column that Mikawa's Striking Force bore down on the Allied forces patrolling in the darkness. At 0054 on the 9th they sighted the radar picket destroyer *Blue* patrolling the southern channel but she was steering away from the Japanese line of advance and did not sight them in return. At

0100 Mikawa ordered a slight diversion of three degrees to pass safely astern of *Blue* and then swung his column back on course entering the southern channel. The *Chokai*, *Kako* and *Furutaka* had all earlier, around 2300, launched their spotter planes to provide them with illumination during the battle. At 0125 the Japanese Admiral gave the order 'Independent Command', giving his captains freedom of action once the battle commenced and he followed this up at 0103 with the stirring command 'Every ship attack'. Blissfully unaware of the wrath that was about to descend upon their heads the Allied Southern Force was steaming up the southern channel to meet Mikawa, with the two destroyers ahead on either bow and the *Canberra* leading the *Chicago* in line ahead. Although *Canberra* (Captain Getting) had taken *Australia*'s position in the lead, the senior officer designated by Admiral Crutchley during his absence was in fact the captain of the *Chicago* (Captain H.D. Bode); he had gone to bed, however, expecting Crutchley back on station by midnight.

It was at 26 knots that the Japanese Striking Force sailed in combat-readiness to meet their sleepy opponent and, at 0138 they sighted the second destroyer picket, *Ralph Talbot*, some eight miles off their port bow. She too was on her outward leg, that is steering away from the Japanese column, and she too failed to sight them. The Japanese pressed on without altering formation. Almost at once the dim silhouettes of the *Canberra* and *Chicago* loomed up ahead and, at 0138 *Chokai* launched a full salvo of torpedoes at both these targets from a range of only 5,000 yards, ordering her companions to open fire as she did so. It was not until after they had fired their torpedoes that, at 0143, the destroyer *Patterson* belatedly spotted the Japanese and raised the alarm. Too late!

The float planes from the Japanese cruisers now dropped flares to illuminate their targets and all their ships opened fire. At the same time as *Patterson* sighted the enemy the first torpedoes reached the end of their runs and two of them slammed into the *Canberra*'s starboard side. These two explosions were followed by a deluge of shells which ripped the *County* class ship apart, killing many of her crew before they had time to know what was happening, including her captain. She barely had time to reply with a few torpedoes and shells before she was turned into a blazing inferno. Her fires rapidly got out of control and she drifted northward until sunk at 0800 by orders of Admiral Turner after her survivors were taken off.

The *Chicago*, astern of her, fared no better, being hit by a torpedo as 0147 which wrecked her bows. Then shells brought her mainmast crashing down as her captain struggled to the bridge. He turned his ship away, not catching sight of his opponents. A rain squall passed between the opposing groups and after six minutes one Allied force was eliminated. The Northern Force meanwhile had assumed that the bedlam on their flank was anti-aircraft fire against night attackers and continued on their way. But not for long. Mikawa swung his ships north at 0147, some ships losing touch for a few moments. When they resumed contact the Japanese force was in two columns about 1,000 yards apart which opened up to 7,500 yards after a while. Further reports of Allied destroyers had been received, so Mikawa turned north straight for the Northern Force which his two wings enclosed at and soon the three American cruisers were in sight from the Japanese flagship.

Firing re-commenced at once at about 4,000 yards. All guns, main batteries, anti-aircraft guns and light weapons joined in, and again the Japanese launched their deadly torpedoes. The engagement started at 0149. *Aoba* illuminated the *Quincy* with her searchlights and blanketed her with 8-inch salvos at close range. Then they switched their lights off and left her crippled and blind, under fire from both columns with all her forward guns out of action. She turned to starboard and sank at 0235. *Vincennes*, leading the line, was also smothered without chance for effective reply and after taking numerous torpedo and shell hits sank at 0250. The last ship of the line, *Astoria*, managed to fire eleven salvos against her almost invisible enemies, one of which scored a hit in *Chokai*'s operations room, but did not harm her fighting efficiency. In return *Astoria* was soon reduced to same blazing shambles as the others and she sank at 1215 close by Savo Island after the fires reached her magazines.

With the most powerful ships of the Allied Force eliminated at trifling cost it appeared that the transports were at Mikawa's mercy. However instead of steering towards Tulagi he continued his sweep round Savo and headed off back the way he had come, leaving the carnage of sinking and burning ships behind him in the rain and the night. On their way out the Japanese ran into the *Ralph Talbot* and crippled her with several salvos after she had switched on navigation lights in the assumption, strange as it may seem, that they were 'friendly'. Such chaos is familiar in night fighting. The two light cruisers of the Eastern Force probably owe their survival to Mikawa's decision to break off the battle and to the fact that their commanding officer was so uncertain about what was happening that his ships never got into the fight at all.

Why did Mikawa draw off when absolute overwhelming victory was in his hands? It is thought that two things influenced him. One his ships were losing contact in the wild mêlée and the frequent sightings of destroyers worried him that more Allied heavy ships were about. Secondly that he did not know the carriers were now far away and out of range and feared to be caught with damaged ships by heavy air strikes at dawn. Still, even with these things in mind it seems strange that, having risked everything, all these hazards, and come out an easy winner he should not have risked one final gamble and thus destroyed for many months America's ability to strike back. His decision was to have fateful consequences in the months ahead.

Few lessons on cruiser fighting can be gained from this battle, other than the old one that fortune favours the brave. Ship-for-ship the two sides' cruisers were evenly matched, but with the advantage of surprise, determination and a highly-trained force Mikawa had few problems in overcoming his half-asleep and highly-complaisant Allied opponents, despite their radar. *Australia* never got in the fight, which may be just as well, while *Canberra* had no chance to show what she could do. The only thing certain was that *County* class cruisers could not stand up to the amount of punishment she took in a few ghastly minutes, and survive. But it is doubtful whether any heavy cruiser could have done, and she stayed afloat longer than the American ships.

Other Cruiser to Cruiser Engagements
There were remarkably few cruiser-to-cruiser engagements during the war in which British ships were involved that were anything other than inconclusive. The principal ones are as follows:

25 December 1940: The German 8-inch cruiser *Admiral Hipper* tried to attack troop convoy WS5A off Cape Finisterre. Included in the escort were the light cruisers *Bonaventure* and *Dunedin* and the damaged 8-inch cruiser *Berwick*. *Berwick* received two hits but *Bonaventure* engaged and *Hipper* withdrew without getting closely involved.

28 March 1941:   During the opening stages of the Battle of Cape Matapan the light cruisers *Orion*, *Ajax*, *Perth* and *Gloucester* were heavily engaged by the Italian 8-inch cruisers *Bolzano*, *Trento* and *Trieste* without hits on either side.

7 September 1941:   The 6-inch cruisers *Aurora* and *Nigeria* attacked a German convoy off North Cape and sank the training cruiser *Bremse*.

22 March 1942:   During 2nd Battle of Sirte the light cruisers *Cleopatra*, *Dido*, *Euryalus* and *Penelope* successfully engaged and held off the Italian 8-inch cruisers *Gorizia* and *Trento* and the light cruiser *Bande Nere* with the battleship *Littorio* in support.

CHAPTER FOUR

Cruisers on Trade Protection – Operations Against Merchant Raiders

Whilst inevitably it can be argued that the duties of trade protection are those of the Royal Navy as a whole and not just its cruiser force, the fact remains that of the commerce raiders destroyed, cruisers were primarily involved and responsible.

Strategic thinking between the wars, when not confined to the theory of main fleet action, had envisaged that in the event of war with Germany, the merchant fleet on which we as an island would depend for our existence, would be the subject of attack not only from submarines but surface warships such as the pocket battleships, backed up as in the earlier war by merchant vessels suitably equipped for this purpose.

Similarly, in Germany, Admiral Raeder when reviewing the results of similar operations in 1914 to 1918, had concluded that:

(a) Warships designed for fleet work, were unsuitable for operations in waters where they had no or inadequate base facilities.
(b) Large merchantmen such as liners, were too conspicuous and expensive to operate.
(c) Independence and deception were of greater value than speed and gun power.

Thus, by a combination of circumstances not the least of which were the limitations of the Versailles Treaty, Germany decided to concentrate on the construction of that special type of warship such as the pocket battleship with its long range endurance but in addition, to back them up with auxiliary cruisers. The 1934 Naval Estimates provided for four such vessels (*Hilfskreuzer*) but building priorities being what they were, they were never built. Nonetheless, it is fair to assume that a naval eye was keeping a careful watch for merchant vessels which, should the need arise, could be converted to commerce raiders.

Following the outbreak of war in 1939, steps were taken to

convert the first six ships and to prepare them for early operational service. That this was not done prior to the outbreak of war was fortunate for Britain, because in retrospect it must be obvious that if suitably equipped ships had been on station when hostilities commenced, they would have caused widespread damage and dislocation on the shipping routes at a time when the convoy system was not fully organised and when many of our merchant ships must be sailing independently.

However, conversion was pressed forward and the first six ships known as the 'First Wave' proved to be ships of moderate tonnage and speed, fairly modern in appearance but above all, capable of long endurance. Conversion followed conventional lines. Fuel bunkerage and provision storage facilities were enlarged to give self-sufficiency for long periods and each ship although unprotected, was equipped to a level which compared favourably with that of a light cruiser. Thus, each raider carried:

Six 15 cm guns
One 6 cm or one 7·5 cm guns
Two 3·7 cm guns in twin mountings
Four 2 cm guns
Four to six above water, torpedo tubes in single, twin or triple mountings
One or two aircraft (Arado 196 or He 114)
60 – 300 EMC mines

The first six ships to complete their conversion programme (See Table 11) sailed from Germany between 31st March and 3rd July 1940 and in the knowledge that they were to operate in waters where they had no adequate shore base facilities where action damage which was other than superficial, could be repaired, it is not surprising that as a general rule, they were ordered to avoid attacking ships in convoy, warships or auxiliaries and were to confine their operations to merchantmen sailing independently.

The six ships received logistical support from a fleet of supply ships sailed from German or neutral ports and those supplies were supplemented as occasion arose from stores and provisions taken from their victims. Refuelling was usually undertaken in a so-called 'waiting area' which was remote from the normal sea lanes. Three such areas were:

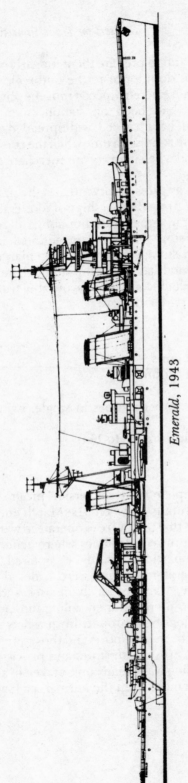

Emerald, 1943

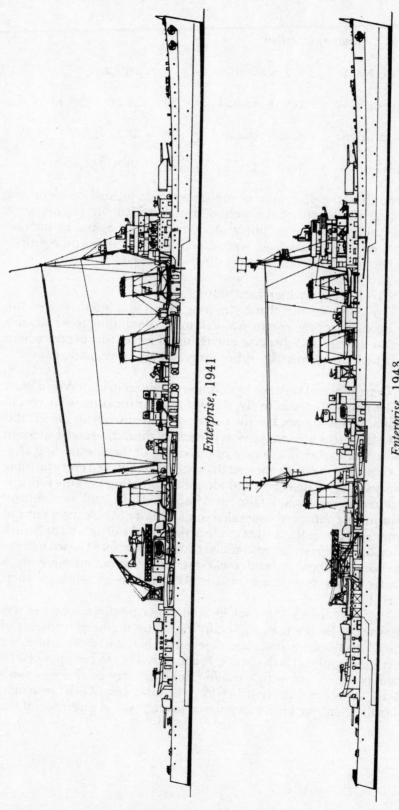

Enterprise, 1941

Enterprise, 1943

Code Name	Location	Position
Bayern	North Atlantic	19° – 26°N.,40° – 47°W
Andalusien	South Atlantic	20° – 28°S.,15°45' – 24°W
Sibirien	Indian Ocean	22° – 30°S.,75° – 85°E

Records show that none of these areas was located or identified during the whole of the period during which the raiders were operating. Of course, other places remote from traffic such as isolated islands and atolls were used for both resting and refitting.

The object of commerce raiding was threefold:

1. To sink enemy merchant ships;
2. To dislocate merchant shipping lines to a point where the economy of the enemy was in danger of grinding to a halt; and
3. To distract and disperse enemy naval forces to a degree where attack on convoys by submarine and air, were made easier.

In fact, the actual sinkings by commerce raiders in both World Wars (4·1% and 6·3% respectively) showed that the measure of success in that area was limited but the presence of the merchant raiders did have far-reaching consequences in terms of distraction and dispersion as we saw earlier in the case of the cruise of the *Admiral Graf Spee*.

Generally speaking, the merchant raiders employed every possible means to delay detection and identification using dummy funnels, telescopic masts and false deckhouses. Guns and fire control equipment remained concealed until the last possible moment and whenever possible, use was made of the identity of neutral or British merchant ships which resembled the raider or were known to be in the locality where the raider was operating and not infrequently, a raider under surveillance, made RRR signals to reinforce their credibility.

Once an enemy ship was located either by the smoke she was making or by the use of aircraft, the raider made adjustments of speed and course designed to ensure that she approached her victim from ahead at daybreak. Frequently, the aircraft operated by raiders were fitted with a trailing hook to carry away the victim's radio aerials and prevent her from sending her 'Raider' warning signal. Then, the customary signal to stop would given and if the merchantman failed to comply, she was attacked by gunfire. Once the ship was stopped and had surrendered, her crew were made prisoner and time permitting, selected items were removed from her cargo and stores before she was sunk. Occasionally of course, some valuable prizes were sent back in the hope that they would run the blockade, others were sent to rendezvous areas for future stripping of stores and equipment and others were used to accommodate prisoners.

As a general rule, the captains of the merchant raiders displayed a measure of humanity to captured crews but one exception, Captain von Ruckteschell of the *Widder* and later of the *Michel*, so violated the provisions of the Hague Convention that he was tried and convicted as a war criminal in 1947.

* * *

Table 11
Operational German Merchant Raiders – First Wave

Name	Number	Admiralty Letter	GRT	Departed Germany	Commanding Officer
Atlantis (Goldenfels)	16	C	7,862	31.3.40	Bernhard Rogge
Orion (Kurmark)	36	A	7,021	6.4.40	Kurt Weyher
Widder (Neumark)	21	D	7,851	6.5.40	H von Ruckteschell
Thor (Santa Cruz)	10	E	3,862	6.6.40	Otto Kähler
Pinguin (Kandelfels)	33	F	7,766	15.6.40	Ernest Felix Krüder
Komet (Ems)	45	B	3,287	3.7.40	Robert Eyssen

* * *

Invariably, the first knowledge that a raider was at large in any given area was that a number of independently routed merchantmen became overdue. It could be argued that, unless of high speed, there should be no independently routed ships and that if there were insufficient ships at any one time to form the nucleus of an adequately escorted convoy, the ships should be held back until a convoy could be formed. Not only would this provide the benefits of convoy protection for its own sake but it would also ensure the best and most economic use of cruisers performing escort duty where in other circumstances they were roaming the trade routes with consequent loss of time and efficiency. These factors were considered but practical considerations dictated that:

1 Unacceptable delays would occur whilst ships were assembling.
2 Frequently the cargoes of such ships were required urgently in Britain.
3 Some ships were so slow that they would unnecessarily impede a convoy.
4 On balance, the risk of independent sailing was justified within the overall picture.

Nevertheless, in the early days of the war, it did mean that once the activities of a raider had become an established fact, warships were hunting for a needle in a haystack because even if they were within reach of the scene of a raider attack, it was almost inevitable that by the time they arrived, the raider had left the area and disappeared into the wide ocean wastes.

Furthermore, as will be seen later, the question of identification led to constant problems and the need to completely identify a suspected vessel as a raider led to warships being tempted far too close to the suspect and it was not until 1942 when the Admiralty developed and put into operation the 'checkmate' system of vessel identification that the problem was resolved to any great extent.

If the hunting warships experienced difficulty in finding the raiders, those same difficulties beset the raiders themselves when it came to locating their victims. Admittedly, those victims followed established routes, frequently aided location by the injudicious emission of smoke and not infrequently, when captured, allowed raiders access to confidential information, books and papers which to the astute reader gave vital information as to ship movements, recognition signals and the like. Nevertheless, despite these advantages and the use by raiders of aircraft, sightings and interceptions were often achieved only at long intervals and the evidence from the logs of raiders showed that sometimes many months elapsed without any ships being sighted, much less intercepted. Nonetheless,

Between the wars the light cruiser squadrons of the Home and Mediterranean Fleets practised evolutions based on the Jutland battle. The *Caledon* is firing a practice torpedo in 1927.

6-inch gun practice aboard the *Caledon* during the 1927 exercises.

The 10,000-ton 'Treaty' cruisers of the various 'County' classes formed the bulk of the new construction in the late 1920's. This photo shows *Suffolk* as first completed in 1927 with short funnels. Unfortunately these soon had to be raised several feet as smoke problems proved as bad as in many pre-1914 designs of Fisher's.

The bulk of the light cruisers which survived into the 1930's had been built mainly for North Sea operations and their endurance was low. Early experiments were conducted with re-fuelling at sea but in this respect the Royal Navy fell behind the navies of Germany and the U.S.A. Here *Cardiff* is shown in 1931 conducting such experiments.

in 1940, the ships of the 'First Wave' sank or captured a total of fifty-four independently sailed merchant ships of 366,644 GRT in addition to which another four ships of 32,200 GRT were lost as a result of mines sown by the *Orion* and *Pinguin*.

From intelligence sources during the second half of July 1940, it was clear that a raider or raiders was operating in the South Atlantic. In fact the *Thor* had already sunk six ships in that month and the cruiser *Hawkins* flyng the flag of Rear Admiral Harwood of River Plate fame, proceeded to patrol the shipping routes between Rio de Janeiro and the River Plate. It was not to be a cruiser but an armed merchant cruiser however, which had the misfortune to come up against the *Thor* and on each occasion that interception occurred, the German ship not only accepted action but left the scene the conqueror.

Although the British AMC's generally had a superiority in speed over the German ships, they were at a considerable disadvantage from their larger silhouette but primarily from the woefully inadequate armament. Although both British and German ships were fitted with old guns, the 6-inch guns in the British ships had a maximum range of 14,000 yards at 20° elevation and had what can only be described as very primitive fire control equipment whereas the German ships had modern fire control systems and guns which had a range of 17,000 yards.

The first AMC to encounter the *Thor* was the former Royal Mail liner *Alcantara* (Captain. J.G.P. Ingham) which was patrolling to the south of Trinidad Island which had been used by German raiders in the First World War. The raider was sighted in the forenoon of 28th July and course was altered to intercept. At 1400 by which time the *Alcantara* had worked up to 21½ knots, the *Thor* turned to starboard, hoisted the German flag and opened fire at a range of 16,000 yards which was well beyond the extreme range of the *Alcantara*'s own guns.

The first salvos carried away the main aerials and put the fire control system out of action and subsequent salvos of well directed fire caused further damage including a hit on the waterline abreast the main engine room. This caused an inrush of water which progressively reduced the speed of the *Alcantara* to 10 knots. Although during the course of the action, the British ship did hit her opponent, little damage was caused and as the primary object of the raider was to escape, she made full use of the British AMC's lack of speed and under cover of smoke she drew away from the scene and at 1530 when last seen, she was at a range of 29,000 yards and steering south at 15 knots.

In what was a relatively short action, the *Alcantara* fired 152 rounds and the *Thor* fired 284 rounds. In the British ship two were killed, four seriously wounded and another thirty suffered slight wounds. In the German ship, three were killed and three were wounded.

It was some hours before Rear-Admiral Harwood knew anything about this action because the *Hawkins* which was about 1,000 miles away, did not pick up the action reports which the *Alcantara* transmitted on her auxiliary W/T set after losing her main aerials.

The *Alcantara* entered Rio de Janeiro on 1st August to carry out hull repairs, but thereafter she was able to continue in service for another three months before she was refitted in England at which time the elevation of two of her 6-inch guns was increased to 30° to give a maximum range of 18,500 yards and she was given a catapult and two Fairey Seafox sea planes.

For a short time following this action, there was a cessation of sailings from Bahia and all Brazilian ports to the southward, because it was reckoned that after breaking off the action, the *Thor* would leave the locality and this is exactly what she did. She steamed as far south as 370°S and then turned eastwards during which time she boiler-cleaned. She then steered north again and after refuelling from the supply ship *Rekum* towards the end of August, her captain felt that it was safe to resume operations. In the area west of St Paul Rocks, she intercepted and sank two more ships after which at the beginning of November she met with the supply ship *Rio Grande* to which she transferred 350 prisoners. Towards the end of that month, Captain Kahler was informed by Naval Staff that there were ten British cruisers or AMC's in the area and in the evening of 4th December when in the area south of the River Plate where the *Thor* was hoping to intercept the whaling fleet on its way to the Antarctic, news was received of the presence in the area of the River Plate, of the British armed merchant cruiser *Carnarvon Castle*, a former Union Castle liner of 20,122 GRT.

The two ships sighed each other at about 0642 on the morning of 5th December at which time the *Carnarvon Castle* (Captain H.N.M. Hardy) was steering towards Montevideo at a speed of 18·3 knots. The British ship increased speed and signalled the other ship to stop, but the *Thor*, anxious to avoid another action which might result in damage which would put a premature end to her raiding, turned away on a south-westerly course. The AMC opened fire at 0757 at a range of 14,300 yards but her shot fell short of the target. Almost immediately, the *Thor* which up to that time had been flying the Jugoslav flag, hoisted the German flag and opened fire.

The two ships then engaged in a series of tactical manoeuvres during which time the *Thor* made smoke to confuse the enemy. At 0830, two torpedoes were fired at the *Carnarvon Castle* but she spotted the tracks in time to take avoiding action. At 0844, the range had come down to 8,000 yards and the well directed fire from the raider was hitting the AMC repeatedly. She was on fire in several places and with fire control and other communications cut, her 6-inch guns were firing in local control and were at one stage, reported to be down to 40 rounds per forward guns remaining.

The end result of the manoeuvring was to end in advantage to the *Thor* which by then had her opponent showing up well against the hazy background, and at 0900 Captain Hardy was compelled to open the range under cover of a smoke screen, in the hope that some of the fires could be brought under control. The *Thor* herself was obviously anxious to clear the area before British reinforcements arrived from the north and she made off at first in a north-westerly direction; when out of range and visibility, she turned south-east and continued along that course until she reached 40°S.

Again, this action showing up the deficiencies of the British AMC's and again, whatever may have been the fears of the *Thor*'s captain, reinforcements for the hard-pressed British ship were too far away to have any hope of giving practical assistance. In fact, the nearest cruiser was the *Enterprise* (Captain J.C. Annesley) which was flying the Broad Pennant of Commodore F.H. Pegram who had relieved Rear-Admiral Harwood on 4th September. She was 450 miles to the south-westward and the AMC *Queen of Bermuda* was 200 miles to the northward.

From any rational assessment of the evidence from these two actions, it is clear that:

(a) Contacts with raiders were fortuitous and not the result of anything other than the sort of astute planning which had brought the River Plate action.

(b) Action was broken off by mutual consent when in terms of guns, ammunition and speed, both ships were capable of maintaining the action; and

(c) The armament and fire control of the German ships was

remarkably superior to that of the British ships, but so far as the latter were concerned there was little that could be done to improve their capability until they could return to British ports for refitting and modification on the lines already described for the *Alcantara*.

So far then, the raiders had had things very much their own way and by the end of 1940 there were still six of them at large because although the *Widder* had returned to Germany on 31st October, she had been replaced by the *Kormoran* of the 'Second Wave' (See Table 12) which had sailed from Germany on 3rd December, under the command of Captain Theodor Detmers.

*   *   *

Table 12
Operational German Raiders – Second Wave

Name	Number	Admiralty Letter	GRT	Departed Germany	Commanding Officer
Kormoran (Stiermark	41	G	8,700	3.12.40	Theodor Detmers
Stier (Cairo)	23	J	4,800	12.05.41	Commander Gerlach
Michel	28	H	4,740	9.03.41	H von Rucketschell

*   *   *

Note: Two other ships in this wave the *Togo* and *Hansa* were damaged when trying to break out and their operations were cancelled.

*   *   *

If 1940 had failed to produce contact and action between the raiders and British cruisers as distinct from armed merchant cruisers, the following year was destined to be one in which the raiders were finally brought under control. Although the six ships at sea managed to sink a total of 44 ships of 226,527, no merchant ship was sunk after 29th July and in the year, three of the raiders were sunk, albeit at great cost, and the other three returned to Germany; although later the two remaining ships of the 'second wave' and one ship from the 'first wave' went on a second cruise, any success they achieved was of a very limited nature.

Before turning to the three actions involving cruisers, mention must be made again of the *Thor* which seemed to have a fatal charm for the armed merchant cruisers. At the beginning of 1941, she was still operating in the South Atlantic but victims were few and far between and it was not until March that she managed to intercept two merchantmen. On 4th April she encountered the *Voltaire* (Captain J.A.P. Blackburn) a ship of 13,301 GRT, armed with eight old 6-inch guns and capable of the relatively slow speed of 14½ knots. She had sailed from Trinidad on passage for Freetown with orders to search the areas to the west of the Cape Verde Islands. The action between the two ships was even more one-sided than on the previous occasions and with her first shots the raider blew away the AMC's main radio aerials and after outranging and outfighting the British ship the end was inevitable. Terrible fires raged aboard the *Voltaire* and she eventually foundered in position 14°25'N., 40°40'W. Only 197 survived and they were taken prisoner by the *Thor* which speedily left the scene, shaped course for home and, after passing up the English Channel, she arrived at Hamburg on 30th April to a well deserved welcome. In the year she had sunk but three ships, excluding the *Voltaire*, of 21,585 GRT.

The first action with cruisers took place in May and involved the *Pinguin*. This raider, as befits her name, had operated with success in the waters of the Antarctic where she had decimated three Norwegian whale-oil factory ships and eleven whale catchers. In search of more fruitful grounds she then moved northwards into the Indian Ocean where she intercepted four further victims, bringing her haul for the year to 17 ships of 57,604 GRT. It was to be the last of these which led to her demise because the tanker *British Emperor* managed to get away her RRR report.

Some 500 miles away the heavy cruiser *Cornwall* (Captain P.C.W. Manwaring) was on passage from Mombasa to the area of the Seychelles and on picking up the raider report from the tanker, she turned northwards, increased speed and commenced to widen the area of her search by using her aircraft. At 0700 on 8th May, one of the Walrus aircraft sighted a suspicious vessel about 100 miles away. On investigation the ship first identified herself as the Norwegian ship *Tamerlane* and as luck would have it, there was sufficient similarity to justify caution. The cruiser continued to close the stranger and the normal game of deception was played out – signals misunderstood, misleading responses given and spurious raider reports transmitted. Finally, the *Cornwall* fired two warning shots and the other vessel realising that she had gone as far as she could to deceive the warship dropped all pretence and at 1715 opened a rapid and accurate fire on the *Cornwall* which had her steering disabled. However, she very soon brought her main armament into action and after repeatedly hitting the raider, she blew up at 1726 in position 3°27'N.,56°38'E. Sixty German survivors and twenty-two prisoners were saved.

In some ways her sighting by the *Cornwall*'s aircraft was a cruel turn of fate, for the *Pinguin* had managed to elude the cruiser in the darkness of the previous night and with a little more luck she might have escaped. This action was the first to raise some criticism from the Admiralty about the practice of warships allowing themselves to come within close range of vessels being investigated. Certainly, with the advantages of torpedoes and excellent gunnery, the raiders were well-placed to disable even a heavy cruiser were she to be caught unawares, but on the other hand what was the warship captain to do? The system of secret call signs was not yet in force nor was the 'checkmate' system. Clever disguise and every ruse open to them were employed by the raiders and the last thing that anyone wanted was for a British warship to open fire prematurely on a ship which indeed turned out to be what she purported. Identification at long range posed many problems and were not wholly resolved even by the use by warships of their aircraft, and the situation was one which put many cautious captains of warships in a dilemma, as the late Captain Agar admitted to us. Certainly, the problem was one which, in the two later actions, was successfully surmounted in one instance and led to tragedy in the other as we shall see.

The *Kormoran* narrowly escaped destruction in January 1941 when sinking the tanker *British Union* on the 18th in position 26°29'N.,31°07'W for the flash of gunfire was seen by the AMC *Arawa*. However although she and the cruisers *Devonshire* and *Norfolk* were rushed to the scene of the sinking, the raider had changed course to the southward and disappeared. During the course of her subsequent operations in the Atlantic and Indian Oceans, she intercepted a total of eleven ships of 68,274 GRT. By November following operations in the Bay of Bengal and the waters around Java and Sumatra, the raider was in the waters to the north-west of Australia and masquerading as the Dutch ship *Straat Malakka*. On the 19th she was scouring the area near to Sharks Bay and at about 1555 she observed what appeared to be two sailing vessels ahead followed by the smoke from what seemed to be a warship escort. At

1600 the warship was identified as one of the three Australian light cruisers and indeed turned out to be the *Sydney* (Captain J.A. Burnett RAN) which had sailed on the 11th, from Fremantle as escort to the trooper *Zealandia*. She had handed over her charge to the light cruiser *Durban* on the 17th and indicated to the authorities ashore that she expected to reach Fremantle in either the afternoon of the 19th or the forenoon of the following day.

There is no evidence that either ship had prior knowledge of the other's presence in the locality and the cruiser's aircraft was not airborne. The captain of the raider has described how on finding himself faced with action with a light cruiser. His one aim was ' . . to gain time; time in which the enemy cruiser would come closer, if possible to within six or eight thousand yards or so, so that when the shooting started he would not be able to outrange (him) . . . ' because he realised that at that sort of range his guns ' . . would not be so very inferior . . . ' to those of the cruiser.

For reasons which will never be explained, the *Sydney*, when faced with a ship whose identity she may have suspected, did not make any identity check with the shore authorities but continued to close the suspect despite the fact that she was not receiving satisfactory answers to signals flashed to her. Captain Detmers has recorded how during the exchange of identification signals the *Sydney* ' . . came gradually closer . . ' until she was ' . . . about three points to starboard . . . at a distance of about 15,000 yards . . . '*

The raider finally hoisted the recognition signal for the *Straat Malakka* and still the cruiser continued to close maintaining radio silence, apparently having no suspicion that she had intercepted anything other than a genuine merchant vessel. She next asked the raider to signal her destination and when that information was given she seemed to be satisfied because she never gave what would have been the customary signal to heave to, which would have been an indication of distrust.

The range continued to come down and the cruiser ' . . . came up steadily with an unchanging bow wave . . ' and was obviously still uncertain; she had brought her 6-inch turrets to bear on the raider but that was the only indication of readiness and as the two ships got closer and closer it was possible to see ' . . pantrymen in white coats lining the rails to have a look at the supposed Dutchman . . '

---

* *The Raider Kormoran* by Captain T. Detmers (Kimber, 1959)

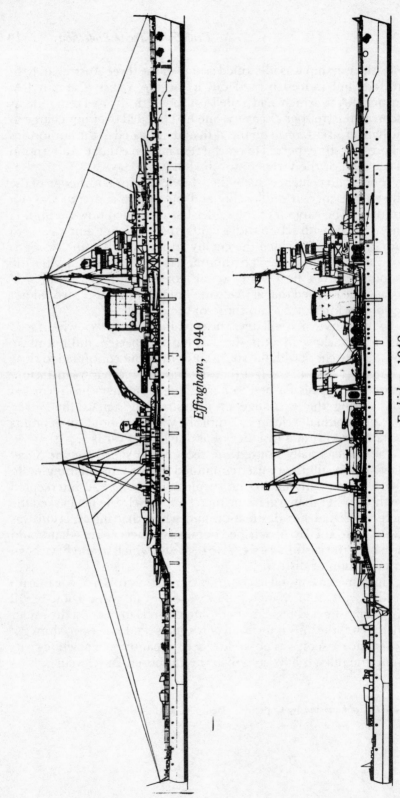

Effingham, 1940

Frobisher, 1942

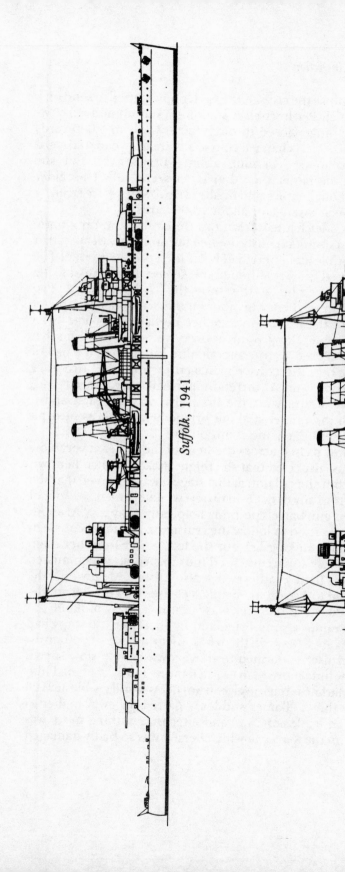

Suffolk, 1941

Cumberland, 1942

To further confuse the cruiser, the raider now started to send off a QQQ signal which Perth wireless station picked up and acknowledged. Still the range closed through 8,000 yards to 3,000 yards and the *Sydney* now ' . . . changed course a point or two to starboard so that (her) silhouette became a little broader . . ' and she demanded that the raider should give her secret call. The raider continued to act out her part and finally the two ships were steering a parallel course at a range of about 1,000 yards.

At 1730 the raider hauled down the Dutch flag and ran up the German flag and simultaneously opened fire and every weapon that would bear scoring hits immediately on the cruiser's bridge. The *Sydney* also opened fire but although the *Kormoran* continued firing the cruiser did not and at this time the raider fired off two torpedoes. One missed but the other hit the *Sydney* below B turret and the force of the explosion together perhaps with that of an exploding magazine, flung B turret over the side. The fifth salvo from the raider set the Walrus aircraft afire but despite the hail of fire directed at her, the cruiser managed to bring her two after turrets into action and Y turret in particular, was fired with ' . . considerable accuracy . . . the first salvo was too high and it ripped through the funnel at about bridge height but its next hit amidships and set the engine room on fire . . . '

The *Sydney* now passed across the stern of the raider at very slow speed and it was suspected that she might try and launch her own torpedo attack but she did not; at that stage it was observed that she was not firing from any of her 6-in turrets which seemed ' . . . out of action with their gun barrels pointing helplessly away . . . ' At about 1800 the *Kormoran* tried to follow the cruiser on a parallel course in the hope of finally sinking her but she lost power from her main engines. The *Sydney* apparently fired four torpedoes which missed and the *Kormoran* fired another which also missed. Meanwhile, the raider continued to fire on the helpless cruiser which ' . . from the forebridge to the stern mast . . ' was ' . . now a mass of flame . . '

At 1825 the raider ceased firing and by that time the ships had opened up the range between them to something like 10,000 yards. The stricken cruiser continued to move away at very slow speed. The *Sydney* now little more than ' . . . a flaming hulk . . . ' faded into the gathering darkness but the glow from her was still visible at 2100 at which time the ' . . flames suddenly darted up even higher as though from an explosion . . . ' and after that nothing more was seen of her from the *Kormoran* which herself was so badly damaged that with no hope of escape she was finally scuttled at midnight, though she did not finally sink until 0035.

In circumstances where there were no survivors from the Australian cruiser and any evidence cannot be verified, any criticism of Captain Burnett should be tempered with caution but if the facts are as related by Captain Detmers, then the close approach of the cruiser to an unidentified ship was fraught with risk and this particularly when the cruiser could have outranged and out-manoeuvred her suspect. The loss of this fine ship and her company was a tragedy but it once again highlighted those identification problems to which we have referred earlier.

The final or almost the final episode was enacted within days of the action just described.

The *Atlantis* continued to hunt in the area of the South Atlantic and the Cape during the first months of the year and despite a narrow escape when she almost ran into the battleship *Nelson* and the carrier *Eagle*, she managed to intercept another eight independently routed merchantmen before heading into the Indian Ocean. In search of further prey, she moved progressively to the sea lanes off Australia and the Pacific and it was not until 10th September after a fruitless eighty day period that she met up with the Norwegian ship *Silvaplana* which she captured and sent back to France as a prize. This was to be her last victim and after replenishing from the *Komet*, she rounded Cape Horn and returned once more to her old hunting grounds. She was ordered home but en route, she was to act as a supply ship to the U-boats operating in the area.

Atlantis re-fuelled *U-68* at a rendezvous not far distant from the Cape-UK route against the better judgment of her captain, and to his chagrin she was ordered to refuel *U-126* in a position to the north-west of Ascension Island. In the vicinity at the time was the heavy cruiser *Devonshire* (Captain R.D. Oliver) which, not being employed on convoy protection duty, was ordered to search the area of St Helena and Ascension Islands because experience had shown in the First World War that this locality had a reputation for known periods of calm weather which was ideal for raider refuelling operations. On passage, it had been the practice for the cruiser to fly off her Walrus aircraft on dawn reconnaissance patrols and on 22nd November the aircraft returned to the ship at 0710, ahead of schedule and reported verbally that a suspicious vessel had been sighted in position 4°20'S,18°50'W. The cruiser increased speed to 25 knots and altered course to intercept. At 0809 masts were sighted on the horizon and the Walrus was flown off again; its observer was reasonably certain that the other vessel was a raider.*

The *Atlantis*, for such it later proved to be, was stopped and refuelling *U-126* whose captain was actually aboard the raider. It has been stated that at this time, the raider's Arado aircraft had been lost and that consequently, she had to rely on visual lookouts but nevertheless, it was not until about the time that the cruiser flew off her aircraft for the second time, that the lookouts in the *Atlantis* sighted the approaching cruiser.

Immediately, the U-boat was cast off and she submerged leaving her captain aboard the raider. The Walrus aircraft continued to circle the *Atlantis* whilst the cruiser maintained a zig-zag course at ranges of between 12,000 yards and 18,000 yards and conducted the formalities of identification. There was an unsatisfactory exchange of signals between the ships, but ultimately Captain Oliver, satisfied that he had intercepted a raider or at the worst a supply ship, fired warning shots. The *Atlantis* worked up to full speed, hoisted the German ensign and under cover of a white smoke screen, turned away under full helm.

At 0837 the *Devonshire* opened fire with full broadsides from her main armament and the second struck the *Atlantis* in No 2 hold where a fire was started. In dire trouble the raider tried to tempt the cruiser into passing across the line taken by *U-126* but Captain Oliver was not to be drawn and with the aid of spotting reports from his aircraft, the *Devonshire* continued to pound the enemy until at 1002 the magazine of the *Atlantis* blew up. At 1012, there was a further explosion and four minutes later, the *Atlantis* sank in position 4°15'S, 18°43'W.

In view of the danger from submarine attack the *Devonshire*, after recovering her aircraft, left the scene, but *U-126* later surfaced and took aboard the survivors from the German ship, which she then transferred to the supply ship *Python*. *Python* was herself intercepted and sunk by the heavy cruiser *Dorsetshire* shortly after.

Of the three actions described, that of the *Devonshire* was the one which showed how unidentified ships suspected of being raiders, should be dealt with. Obviously, the actions of Captain Oliver

---

* For further information see: *The Supermarine Walrus* by G.W.R. Nicholl (Foulis-1966)

could not have been the result of lessons learned from the tragedy of the loss of the *Sydney* but there can be no doubt that the Admiralty had issued warnings to commanding officers, against the dangers of close approach tactics. By any standards however, this was a successful action and that success was marred only by the fact that one of the submarines sent to assist, came by chance across the light cruiser *Dunedin* and sank her with very heavy loss of life.

So, of the seven ships which had left Germany in 1940-41 only one remained at sea by the end of the year, because the *Orion* after little success – one ship of 5,792 GRT – had returned to the Gironde on 23rd August. On 18th May, she had had a lucky escape when sailing off Mauritius, for her aircraft had spotted a British cruiser approaching at a range of about 45 miles. The German ship altered course and departed at full speed but they passed sufficiently close enough for the raider to observe funnel smoke from the cruiser. There is no record that she was spotted by either the heavy cruiser *Cornwall* or the light cruiser *Enterprise* which were the only two British warships operating in that area at that time.

The last ship, the *Komet*, returned to Germany after steaming across the Pacific and rounding Cape Horn, on 30th November. She had enjoyed but modest success in 1941 sinking three ships of 21,378 GRT. She used the Channel route, and escorted by several small vessels she anchored off Cherbourg on the 26th. She sailed up the French coast and her escort became involved in a number of brushes with British light forces but she escaped damage and her luck held again when on the morning of the 29th she was hit on the starboard side of the bridge by a 250lb bomb dropped by a Blenheim aircraft, which failed to explode. She finally arrived in Hamburg at 1800 the following day.

So far, our narrative has been confined to the operations by British cruising vessels against German commerce raiders, but this is an appropriate moment to mention one further encounter which followed the pattern of the actions hitherto mentioned.

When Italy entered the war, there were in the port of Massawa, Eritrea, two merchant vessels and the tropical sloop *Eritrea*. As British and Dominion land forces closed in on the port it became imperative to move these three ships to safety and it was decided to sail the two merchantmen, which had been fitted out as auxiliary ships with four 4·7-inch guns, with the sloop, to Japan where the former would be properly equipped as raiders for operations in the

Pacific. It is with one of the two merchant ships, the *Ramb I* that we are now concerned.

The *Ramb I* was of about 4,000 GRT and had a speed of about 20 knots. She sailed from Massawa on 20th February 1941 and leaving the Red Sea in thick fog she entered the Indian Ocean by way of the Bab el Mendab Strait. It has been suggested* that the Italian vessel intended to act as a raider should the opportunity present itself but there is no evidence that she did and after slipping past Perim, she made her eastward course towards her ultimate destination in Japan.

On the day that the *Ramb I* sailed from Massawa, the New Zealand light cruiser *Leander* took over the escort of the Australian/New Zealand troop convoy US9 from the heavy cruiser *Canberra* and escorted it into Bombay where according to one of her wireless operators† she ' . . . oiled and quickly left that afternoon . . . ' This hurried departure was apparently due to intelligence from the Admiralty that the Italian ship had sailed. Whatever the reason, the *Leander* ran southwards and by the 25th was ' . . slightly north of the Equator . . ' and on the following day, ' . . all obstructions were taken down, provisions were placed in remote action stations and the radio staff busied itself placing spare aerials handy to deck insulators . . ' By that time the cruiser was traversing the Equator and then, at 0510 the following day, she sighted a vessel on the horizon to port. The cruiser went to action stations and increased speed to close the unidentified ship and as she approached it was seen that she was flying the Red Ensign.

On being ordered to stop at 0619 the Italian ship which had claimed to be the British ship *Grosmont Castle*, lowered the Red Ensign, raised the Italian flag and opened fire with her 4·7-in guns. There seems little doubt that the Italian ship opened fire at a range of about 3,000 yards and she succeeded in hitting the cruiser on the funnel but by the time the *Leander* had fired five salvos from her main 6-inch armament, the enemy was ready to surrender and she lowered her flag. Boats were lowered and survivors left the ship very quickly. With a view to possible capture, the *Leander* sent across her motor boat with a boarding party but, fortunately before they reached her, the *Ramb I* erupted in a series of explosions and at 0718,

---

* *Supermarine Walrus* by G.W.R. Nicholl.
† *Well done Leander* by J.S. Harker (Collins NZ – 1971)

she sank in position 01°00'N.,68°30'E. Eleven officers and eighty-nine ratings were rescued and later transferred to the oiler *Pearleaf*.

Once again the difficulty of identification tempted a cruiser to come too close and it was fortunate that the *Ramb I* was lightly armed and had no torpedo tubes for otherwise the cruiser could have been disabled and overwhelmed. It is of interest to note that a sister ship of the *Leander*, the cruiser *Neptune*, also allowed herself to get too close to a suspect merchant ship. The late Paymaster Commander Vernon Gibbs, who served in *Neptune*, related that on one occasion, whilst operating off the West African coast in 1940, the cruiser came upon a suspicious merchant ship which was suspected of being a raider. She approached whilst the identification procedure was gone through and finally ended up steaming at '. . very slow speed almost alongside the suspect which turned out to be some sort of "Q" ship which finally identified herself to our Captain's satisfaction . . . ' This close proximity inspection according to the official historian was the subject of a critical report from the commanding officer of the 'Q' ship to the Admiralty but because of the need for secrecy it was never circulated. Certainly, Commander

*   *   *

Table 13
Summary of German Armed Merchant Raider Operations

Name	Fate	Date	Location
First Wave			
Atlantis	Sunk by *HMS Devonshire*	22.11.41	NW of Ascension Is.
Komet	Returned to Germany	30.11.41	
Orion	Returned to Germany	23.08.41	
Pinguin	Sunk by *HMS Cornwall*	8.05.41	North of Seychelles
Widder	Returned to Germany	31.10.40	
Thor	Returned to Germany	30.04.41	
Second Wave			
Kormoran	Sunk by *HMAS Sydney*	19.11.41	Off Shark Bay
Stier	Sunk by *USSS Stephen Hopkins*	27.09.42	Off Bahia
Michel	Sunk by torpedo from *USS Tarpon*	17.10.43	Off Bahia
First Wave – Second Voyage			
Komet	Sunk by *MTB 236*	13.10.42	Off Cherbourg
Thor	Burned out when supply ship *Uckermark* exploded in harbour	30.11.42	Yokohama

Gibbs never heard of any sort of adverse criticism levelled at his captain although later with the knowledge of later actions, it was accepted that *Neptune* had a lucky escape.

Effectively, 1941 saw an end to the activities of commerce raiders. That there were others both Germans and Japanese is not disputed but none achieved any worthwhile success and those that were sunk were not the victims of action with cruising ships. We have said earlier, that the activities of the raiders depended upon a well organised system of supply ships and it is perhaps appropriate at this point to summarise their activities and to consider the background which contributed to the successful elimination of these ships. (See Table 13.)

Operations Against Supply Ships and Blockade Runners

Writing about the loss of the *Atlantis* and the *Python* in late 1941, the German historian Vice-Admiral Friedrich Ruge was to comment ruefully: 'How the enemy managed to intercept two German ships in succession in waters remote from all shipping is a mystery which has never been cleared up.'*

No doubt he and his compatriots were equally puzzled by the clean sweep made by the Royal Navy in the aftermath of the *Bismarck* affair a few months earlier. The Official British Historian is almost as reticent when describing these successes in the Official British History;

> Though we never discovered the exact positions of the fuelling rendezvous used by raiders in the South Atlantic and Indian Oceans, evidence regarding the movements of the supply ships was slowly and patiently accumulated in the Admiralty, and when it had become sufficiently strong to justify sending out a search force-often to a considerable distance out in the remoter parts of the oceans-the Navy struck. . . . By the beginning of June it was clear . . . it was a favourable moment to sweep the waters which the enemy was likely to use . . . †

Both men of course were writing before the full extent of the way British Intelligence operated was revealed and then Ruge did not know, and Captain Roskill was not allowed to spell out, how these remarkable achievements were handled. Nowadays we have the benefit of hindsight to aid us and Patrick Beesly in particular has

---

* Ruge, Vice Admiral Friedrich, *Sea Warfare* (Cassell, 1957), p. 138.
† Roskill, Captain S.W. *The War at Sea, Vol 1* (HMSO, 1954), p. 542.

ETER 7

Cruiser losses were particularly heavy in the Mediterranean theatre. The 8-inch cruiser *York* was damaged by an explosive motor boat at Suda Bay Creek, and later received further damage from Stuka attacks.

The 6-inch cruiser *Achilles* was manned by the Royal New Zealand Navy and on her return to Auckland after the River Plate battle she received a tremendous welcome.

Originally armed with 7.5-
inch guns the *Effingham* was
re-armed just before the war
with nine 6-inch guns, but
saw only limited service
before she was wrecked on
an uncharted rock off Norway
and had to be destroyed.

Action was intense in the
Mediterranean Fleet in 1940,
and among the hazards
British cruisers had to face
was attack by Italian torpedo-
bombers at dusk. The *Liverpool* was one of three cruiser
casualties to such forms of
attack.

After her exploits at the River
Plate the 6-inch cruiser *Ajax*
went on to achieve even more
fame in numerous actions in
the Mediterranean. Here she
is seen weathering heavy
seas on a patrol in 1941.

given much fresh insight into this shadowy realm and the events that led to these crippling blows struck by British cruisers in the last part of 1941, both against blockade runners and supply ships.*

What is evident is that after the captured of material from the *U-110* enough data were interpreted to enable the whole support fleet of six tankers for *Bismarck*, plus two other supply ships, to be brought to book quickly. The difficulty was not so much in this as hiding from the enemy that we had cracked his codes after such a stunning coup. Operating in the Central Atlantic the heavy cruiser *London* quickly scooped up two of the tankers and a supply ship, the *Esso Hamburg* on 4th June, *Egerland* on 5th June and the *Babitonga* on 21st June. (Next day the *Atlantis* was snapped up by *Dorsetshire* as recorded and the *Python* further south in December.) At the same time far to the north the light cruiser *Sheffield* intercepted the tanker *Friedrich Breme* on the 12th and mixed forces caught three more the same month, while the tanker *Lothringen* was caught by the light cruiser *Dunedin* on the 15th, as recorded. A further victory was achieved in October when the light cruisers *Kenya* and *Sheffield* were sent from Gibraltar to search north of the Azores for a U-Boat supply ship. They were almost immediately rewarded with the interception of the *Kota Penang* on 3rd October.

Nor were the Germans the only ones to feel the effects of the British cruisers' ceaseless patrol work in this period. An attempt was made to run vital war material into Vichy France by the Pétain Government in November with a convoy of ships from Indo-China, and a special force was formed to intercept it. This force comprised the heavy cruiser *Devonshire*, light cruiser *Colombo* and two AMC's, *Carnarvon Castle* and *Carthage*. As a result of their work the Vichy ships *Bangkok*, *Commandant Dorise*, *Cap Padaran* and *Cap Touraine* were captured. Their escort, the sloop *D'Iberville*, was left unharmed and allowed to continue but Vichy submarines extracted cruel revenge by sinking the Norwegian freighter *Thode Fagelund* soon afterwards.

Other ships which fell to British cruisers during the June 1941 sweep, and associated operations, included the U-boat supply ship *Belchen* sunk off Greenland by the *Aurora* and *Kenya* on 3rd June, the *Gonzenheim*, torpedoed by the *Neptune* on 4th June. But throughout the war the interceptions continued. Of thirty-two German blockade

* Beesly, Patrick, *Very Special Intelligence*, (Hamish Hamilton, 1977), pps 88-92. This author is at pains to emphasise that not every success was the work of Ultra.

Table 14
German Supply Ships intercepted by British Cruisers

Name	Intercepted by	Date	Area
Belchen	Aurora & Kenya	3-06-41	Off Greenland
Coburg	Canberra & Leander	4-03-41	08°40' S – 61°25' E.
Egerland	London	5-06-41	07° N – 31° W
Emmy Friederich	Caradoc	23-10-39	Caribbean.
Esso Hamburg	London	4-06-41	07°35' N – 31°25' W
Friedrich Breme	Sheffield	12-06-41	44°48' N – 24°00' W
Gonzenheim	Neptune	4-06-41	North Atlantic.
Lothringern	Dunedin	15-06-41	19°49' N – 25°31' W
Regensburg	Glasgow	30-03-43	66°41' N – 25°31' W
Ketty Brovig	Canberra & Leander	4-03-41	South Atlantic.

German Blockade Runners intercepted by British cruisers

Name	Intercepted by	Date	Area
Olinda	Ajax	3-09-39	River Plate Estuary
Carl Fritzen	Ajax	3-09-39	River Plate Estuary
Cap Norte	Belfast	9-10-39	Northern Patrol
Bianca			
Biskaya			
Gloria		Between	
Gonzinheim	Delhi & Sheffield	12 & 26	Northern Patrol
Poseidon	with AMC's	10-39	
Rheingold			
Adolf Woermann	Neptune	21-11-39	Off Ascension.
Adolf Leonhardt	Shropshire	9-12-39	South Atlantic
Ussukuma	Ajax & Cumberland	5-12-39	South Atlantic
Dusseldorf	Despatch	5-12-39	Off Chile
Wahehe	Manchester	21-02-40	North Atlantic
Arucas	York	3-03-40	Off Iceland
Wakama	Dorsetshire	13-02-40	Cabo Fris
Troja	Despatch	1-03-40	Aruba
Heidelberg	Dunedin	2-03-40	Windward Passage
Wolfsburg	Berwick	2-03-40	Northern Patrol
Uruguay	Berwick	6-03-40	Northern Patrol
Hannover	Dunedin	8-03-40	Mona Passage
Idarwald	Diomede	5-12-40	Tampico
Rhein	Caradoc	11-12-40	Florida Strait
India (Italian)			
Piave (Italian)	Hawkins	-02-41	Off Massawa
Himalaya (Italian)			
Uckermark			

Ville de Tamatave (Vichy)	*Dunedin*	31-06-41	Off St Paul's Rocks
Ville de Rouen (Vichy)		22-07-41	East of Natal
Erlangen	*Newcastle*	25-07-41	Off River Plate
Norderney	*Despatch*	15-08-41	Off River Amazon
Rhakotis	*Scylla*	5-11-42	Bay of Biscay
Ramses	*Adelaide*	26-11-42	Off Diego Garcia
Hohenfriedberg	*Sussex*	20-02-43	Off Cape Finisterre
Irene	*Adventure*	10-04-43	West of Vigo.

runners which attempted the hazardous voyage no less than fourteen were intercepted in 1941 alone. Of the supply ships apart from those listed above, Table 14 summarises the successes of British cruisers on this routine, but essential work.

A study of these figures shows how the policy of the Germans in despatching their blockade runners in waves was followed by interceptions in similar waves. The initial success of the Northern Patrol in the first three months of the war is remarkable when it is considered that very few ships were at first available for this duty and these mainly of the older 'C' and 'D' classes under Admiral Max Horton. Their employment in this duty in the atrocious weather conditions of the Arctic in winter was brought about by the lack of larger ships and conditions aboard these small cruisers, built a quarter of century earlier for the waters of the North Sea, was far from a sinecure, as reports from the vessels themselves made clear at the time. The Northern Patrol had to guard some 435 miles of sea route north from Scotland with only eight ships in September 1939.

*   *   *

Table 15
THE NORTHERN PATROL – 1939

Commanded from the outbreak of war by Vice-Admiral Sir Max Horton flying his flag in *Effingham*. Flag later transferred ashore at Kirkwall.

At 3.9.39 the Northern Patrol consisted of:–

12th Cruiser Squadron – *Effingham* (**Flag**)
Emerald
Enterprise
Dunedin
Delhi
Cardiff

7th Cruiser Squadron – *Diomede*
                     Dragon
                     Caledon
                     Calypso

Partial blockade instituted on 6.9.39 between   Shetlands and Faeroes
                                              Faeroes and Iceland

SEPTEMBER
29.9.39 *Calypso* intercepted *Minden* – scuttled

OCTOBER
Effingham, Emerald and *Enterprise* detached for anti-raider operations 12th Cruiser Squadron disbanded and replaced by 11th Cruiser Squadron: –

                          Colombo (Brd. Pdt)
                          Cardiff
                          Ceres
                          Delhi
                          Dunedin

Supplemented by Seven Armed Merchant Cruisers:– *Asturias, Aurania, California, Chitral, Rawalpindi, Scotstoun, Transylvania.*

19.10.39   *Rawalpindi* intercepted *Gonzenheim* – scuttled
19.10.39   *Scotstoun* intercepted *Biscaya* – captured
20.10.39   *Transylvania* intercepted *Bianca* – captured
21.10.39   *Sheffield* intercepted *Gloria* – captured
21.10.39   *Transylvania* intercepted *Poseidon* – sunk
25.10.39   *Delhi* intercepted *Rheingold* – captured
 9.10.39   *Belfast* intercepted *Cap Norte* – captured

Seventy-three out of eighty-four eastbound neutral ships sent in for examination.

NOVEMBER
Northern Patrol reinforced by five AMC's:– *Andania, Forfar, Laurentic, Montclare, Worcestershire.*

On average the Patrol had: *2 ships south of the Faeroes*
                                       Four ships between Faeroes and Iceland
                                       Four ships in the Denmark Strait.

NOVEMBER

12.11.39   *Delhi* intercepted *Mecklenburgh* – scuttled
13.11.39   *Newcastle* intercepted *Parana* – scuttled
18.11.39   *California* intercepted *Borkum* – captured but torpedoed in prize
18.11.39   *California* intercepted *Eilbek* – captured
20.11.39   *Chitral* intercepted *Bertha Fisser* – scuttled
21.11.39   *Translyvania* intercepted *Teneriffe* – scuttled
22.11.39   *Laurentic* intercepted *Antiochia* – scuttled
23.11.39   *Calypso* intercepted *Konsul Hendrik Fisser* – captured

Sixty-six neutral ships intercepted of which fifty-five sent in for examination
After the loss of the *Rawalpindi* on 23.11.39, the Northern Patrol withdrawn and not reinstated until early December.
20.12.39 – Vice Admiral Horton relieved by Vice Admiral R.H.T.Raikes
During December, the constitution changed:–
    All 'C' and 'D' cruisers withdrawn and replaced by AMC's
New arrivals in December to give a total of 15 AMC's, were:– *Canton, Corfu,*
Derbyshire and *Maloja*

*   *   *

Just what this entailed can be glanced from a typical report that of the Commodore, 11th Cruiser Squadron, dated 13th November 1939:

> In all ships the conditions under which men are living are extremely bad. Due to their low freeboard upper decks are permanently awash in normal Northern Patrol weather . . . Sleeping accommodation is quite inadequate; men, most of whom have been living in their own homes, have to sleep on and under mess tables; every slinging berth is occupied. Mess decks are wet and drying room facilities are very poor (in the *Colombo* the drying room is always wet at sea) with the result that watch-keepers come down from their watch as lookouts, etc (often in northerly gales and blizzards) to great discomfort and little opportunity of drying their clothes.

What these conditions meant at sea can be shown by a report from the larger 'D' class cruiser *Dragon* on the 20th of the same month: 'Most electrical fittings exposed above the upper deck are water-logged, one magazine practically flooded, and a sea finding its way into the main W/T office had temporarily put out of action the main transmitter.'
Despite these considerable hardships their success rate was high

Berwick, 1943

Norfolk, 1943

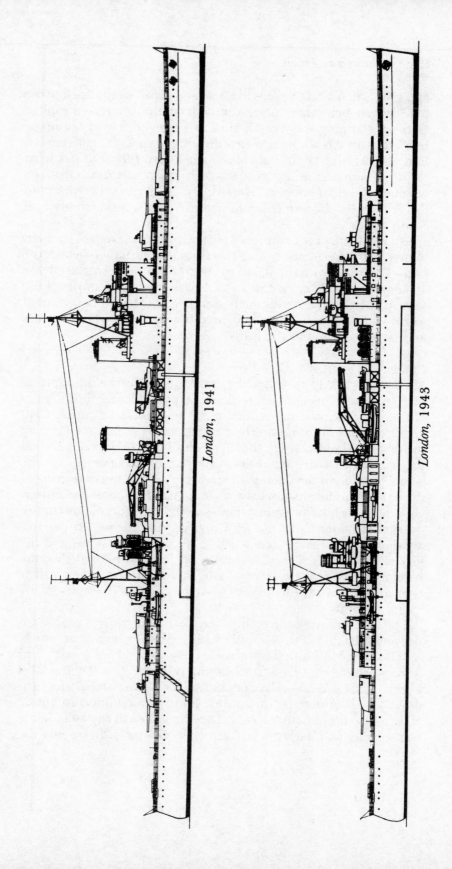

London, 1941

London, 1943

and grew when larger vessels like *York* and *Belfast* were added to the patrol when their other duties admitted. Off the Americas the toll of German shipping was even higher in 1940 and few of the many blockade runners who attempted the long sea passage got very far. Early in 1941 the fall of Italian Somalia forced *Il Duce* to risk what ships remained in an attempt to reach Japan and *Hawkins* had a windfall. A similar effort in reverse by Pétain to run in cargoes from the French Far-Eastern colonies likewise came quickly to grief off South Africa.

After 1941 blockade runners were few and far between. The main efforts by the Germans were to and from the Far East, of which the cruiser patrols took a small, but steady toll – so much so indeed that all attempts finally ceased in 1943. It was a telling example of the slow, painstaking, but ultimately completely successful exertion of world-wide seapower, mainly carried out by British cruiser forces and largely unsung in the press.

Operations Against Warship Raiders

Much more likely to catch the headlines were the attempts to intercept the main German raiders, the pocket battleships, battle-cruisers and heavy cruisers, that made several forays during 1940 and 1941 and did not end their threat until the famous *Bismarck* incident in May 1941. On these patrols of course the cruisers had the backing of every main fleet unit that could operate, but the actual location of the enemy, the tracking of him and delivering to the battleships for disposal always remained the job of the cruiser, with the odds heavily against them should they stumble by chance on such a raider alone. At least that was the theory. In practice although their chances seemed slim on many occasions (and the loss of the AMC's *Rawalpindi* and *Jervis Bay* emphasised this) the regular British cruisers were usually sufficient deterrent on their own to frighten off the largest German raiders. There are many examples of this.

The first serious sortie by the German battle-cruisers took place between 21st and 27th November 1939. The *Gneisenau* and *Scharnhorst* 31,000 ton battle-cruisers, carrying nine 11-inch guns and heavily armoured, sailed from Germany on the 21st. Their orders were to cause diversions by operating in the Faeroes-Iceland area to draw off our cruiser patrols so that homecoming liners might be able to slip through undetected. They were then to slip away in the bad weather and darkness and return to Germany. In essence the plan was followed almost exactly and, although not very ambitious, it was in fact the first time that German battle-cruisers had even succeeded in penetrating that far west in wartime.

Of the British cruisers at sea the *Caledon*, *Colombo* and *Cardiff* were strung across the Faeroes-Shetland gap, the *Ceres*, *Calypso*, *Delhi* and *Newcastle*, along with the AMC *Rawalpindi*, were covering the Faeroes-Iceland passage and the *Norfolk*, *Suffolk* and three more AMC's (*Transylvania*, *Aurania* and *California*) were covering the Denmark Strait. The *Glasgow* was north-east of the Shetlands searching for a reported German liner, the *Bremen*; one of the objectives of the German heavy ships' diversion was to enable her to slip through. In harbour or en route were the Northern Patrol ships *Sheffield*, *Dunedin*, *Dragon*, and *Diomede* at Loch Ewe, the *Devonshire* was with the Home Fleet on the Clyde, and the *Aurora*, *Edinburgh* and *Southampton* were at Rosyth. If these forces seem slender it should be remembered that at this time many cruisers, *Effingham*, *Emerald* and *Enterprise* among them, were being sent abroad on raider hunts which left home waters bare allowing for ships undergoing necessary refits.

At 1540 on the 23rd the two German giants stumbled on the weakest link in the patrol chain, and engaged the *Rawalpindi* in brief combat before they despatched her. She managed to score one hit on one of her opponents, which, although it did no real harm, was enough to persuade them to break off their sortie and seek sanctuary further north. She also got off two warning broadcasts at 1545, and at once the various British forces concentrated in order to close the net on the Germans, which *Rawalpindi* has described as the *Deutschland*. Only one of the British cruisers managed to get more than a fleeting glimpse of their true opponents. This was the *Newcastle*, northernmost of the Iceland-Faeroes patrol line. She steamed hard in atrocious weather for *Rawalpindi*'s last known position. After two hours she was rewarded by the sight of a searchlight on the horizon at 1735 and then at 1738 gunflashes appeared. It seemed as if action were imminent now. This light cruiser with her 6-inch guns had no hesitation in continuing straight for the 'pocket battleship', but in fact she was up against the two most powerful ships in the German fleet at the time.

The hope was that she might gain visual contact and hold it until the heavy ships of the Home Fleet, *Nelson* and *Rodney*, could come up from the Clyde, but they had a long hard journey in front of them. The *Delhi* was coming up from much closer to help *Newcastle* and, had they have been able to gain and hold contact, the other cruisers were also concentrating in order to intercept and track the German squadron. But it was not to be. Although extreme visibility was about eight miles the evening was a squally one, with rain clouds closing this in from time to time to next to nothing. Despite this, at 1815, *Newcastle* sighted first one, and then two, darkened ships at 070°, range 13,000 yards. At such ranges the eighteen 11-inch guns of the German battle-cruisers could have blown the cruiser out of the water with as little difficulty as they had *Rawalpindi*, but instead the German Admiral decided on on flight. By 1825 the range had come down still further and *Newcastle* was now in little doubt that she was up against two heavyweights. Accordingly she slowed down and steered to open the gap, while still retaining contact.

This was what the Germans had been waiting for and, taking advantage of a convenient rain squall that drifted between them and *Newcastle* at this vital juncture, they made off at high speed to the eastward. When *Newcastle* emerged from this area of mist, she sighted *Rawalpindi* for the first time heavily on fire at 1855. Owing to a faulty sighting report from a torpedo rating she went off on a false trail and lost eighteen precious minutes as a result. Nor did she ever succeed in regaining contact although, joined by *Delhi*, she searched diligently north-west and north-east from 1830 until dawn on the 24th. Had she been equipped with radar she would have been able to trail the Germans and guide the Home Fleet for a kill, but at that stage of the war, very few British ships were so fitted. It was a disappointment that was to be repeated, however. The Norwegian campaign and the resulting damage to many of their heavy ships meant that German attempts to break their heavy ships out into the Atlantic did not again take place until the autumn of 1940.

At this time both the pocket battleship *Admiral Scheer*, and the 8-inch cruiser *Admiral Hipper* were ready to sortie. When the *Scheer* left Brunsbüttel on 27th October she had a clear trouble-free run north about Iceland and through the Denmark Strait which she cleared on 1st November. She attacked convoy HX 84 on the 5th of that month, sinking the AMC *Jervis Bay* after a gallant defence and five of the convoy. This was the first time the British were aware that she was at sea. Moves to block her return to Germany included the despatch of the *Hood*, *Repulse*, *Bonaventure*, *Naiad* and *Phoebe*, to cover the approaches to Brest, *Formidable*, *Berwick* and *Norfolk*, from Freetown, *Cumberland* and *Newcastle* off the SE coast of South

America, *Hermes*, *Delhi* and *Dragon*, from St Helena and then *Hermes* with *Enterprise* to guard the Indian Ocean. These efforts were all fruitless however for the *Scheer* pressed on into the South Atlantic. Various moves to counter her presence included the setting up of further raider hunting groups *Norfolk*, *Cumberland* and *Newcastle* were all despatched thither to reinforce those cruisers already on watch. *Neptune*, *Dragon* and *Dorsetshire* all made fruitless attempts to bring her to book during December.

After a couple of false starts in September the *Admiral Hipper* refitted at Hamburg to remedy engine defects and sailed on 30th November. She cleared the Denmark Strait without detection by 7th December and came up on convoy WS 5A on the evening of 24th December. She at first withdrew being unable to assess the strength of the escort but, at 0153 on Christmas Day, she fired a spread of three torpedoes at a range within 5,000 yards. All missed their targets.

Later she came into action with the British escort. The gunnery duel commenced at 0638 between the German ship and the damaged *Berwick*, which was returning home after the Battle of Spartivento in November. It was a lively action. The *Berwick* received a hit on 'X' turret which was put out of action, another on one of the 4-inch gunshields and two hits on the waterline. The Walrus aircraft was jettisoned after being damaged by blast and *Berwick* had four Royal Marines killed and two wounded.

She, in return, fired forty-four salvos of 8-inch and hit the *Hipper* once abaft the funnel at 0707. The *Bonaventure* then came up and added 438 rounds of 5·25-inch shell which, although not hits, were enough to send the *Hipper* packing. *Hipper* had fired some 174 rounds of main and 113 rounds of secondary armament. The *Dunedin* was unable to get into the action and the carriers could not fly off their aircraft due to bad weather. The *Hipper* regained the sanctuary of Brest at 1600 on the 27th.

While operating in the Indian Ocean north of Madagascar the *Scheer* had a similar escape to those of the *Scharnhorst* and *Gneisenau*. On 20th and 21st February she sank three ships in this area, but not before two of them had got off raider reports. The *Glasgow* was some 140 miles north of her last sinking and promptly raced to the scene. Also in the general area, but much further away, were the *Hawkins* and *Australia* escorting a troop convoy; the light cruisers *Emerald* and *Enterprise*, and the *Canberra*, *Shropshire* and *Capetown* were also concentrating. Although these combined forces sound formidable it must be stressed that they were stretched over many hundreds of miles of ocean looking for the needle in the haystack. Nonetheless the net was cast though it needed a positive identification to draw it shut.

Hopes that this factor had been achieved came when, early on the 22nd, the scouting plane of the *Glasgow* actually sighed the *Scheer* in 8°30'S.,51°35'E. *Glasgow* instantly broadcast this to her compatriots on the hunt and announced that she intended to 'attack by night and shadow by day'. There was an air of hope and expectancy in the air for she had all day to close and mark the raider closely. But again the cruiser failed to do so; worsening visibility caused the shadowing plane to lose the *Scheer* before *Glasgow* herself could make visual contact, which once again was never regained. Nor did any of the other ships sight their elusive prey and *Scheer* made good her escape.

Nor was she ever brought to book. In early March she replenished and then steamed into the Atlantic passing undetected through the Denmark Strait again on the night of 22nd/23rd March and reaching Bergen on the 28th. The despatch of the *Fiji* and *Nigeria* to cover the area through which she passed came 48 hours too late. She was followed, equally easily, by the *Hipper* which had conducted a series of fruitless operations from Brest. She penetrated the Strait on the 23rd, sighting the two British cruisers but not being seen in return, and reached Kiel on 28th March.

Yet another close encounter was experienced by the *Gneisenau* and *Scharnhorst* when they sailed for a second attempt at breaking into the Atlantic on 23rd January 1941. This time British Intelligence suggested that an attempt was to made to the south of Iceland, and the Home Fleet and cruiser patrols were strengthened in anticipation. By this time many of the newer cruisers were fitted with radar, and again some justification could be held out for the hopes expressed that they would be caught. They almost were. As predicted the two battle-cruisers broke south of Iceland on the night of 27th/28th January. In the area were three British heavy ships, eight cruisers and eleven destroyers. Should they be sighted their doom seemed certain. And they *were* sighted, by radar, at 0640 on the 28th, by the light cruiser *Naiad*. She duly reported them and turned to shadow by radar. But the Germans radar was superior, for they had sighted *Naiad* six minutes earlier and were thus able to take avoiding action and shake her off instantly. She lost touch and the C-in-C concluded *Naiad*'s sighting was false. The battle-cruisers therefore broke free, although it was their closest shave yet.

When the *Scharnhorst* and *Gneisenau* were joined by the *Admiral Hipper* at Brest on 28th March, the British cruiser strength was stretched still tauter. While a blockade had to be mounted to cover the Bay of Biscay area in case this powerful squadron sailed again, the expected readiness of the *Bismarck* and *Prinz Eugen* at their home ports meant that the Home Fleet had two burrows to stop. The C-in-C organised his limited forces to cover the latter eventuality with the heavy cruisers taking turns to patrol the Denmark Straits in pairs while the light cruisers covered the Iceland-Faeroes passage. The position at the end of May was that the Home Fleet had on hand just two heavy cruisers and eight light cruisers to do this vital job.

In fact the two German ships sailed on the 19th May from Arkona to start their cruise but their absence was not reported until two days later than this. Not until the 21st did the C-in-C receive a sighting report that they were on their way northward. He had at Scapa Flow two battleships, an aircraft-carrier and a battle-cruiser, but his cruiser strength was divided. On patrol in the Denmark Strait was the *Norfolk*. Patrolling the Iceland-Faeroes gap were *Birmingham* and *Manchester*. *Arethusa* was en route to Iceland and *Suffolk* was refuelling there. *Hermione* was on passage to Scapa after repairs and at Scapa were the *Galatea, Aurora, Neptune* and *Kenya*. The only other cruisers in the general area were the *Exeter* and *Cairo* escorting convoy WS 8B to the west of Ireland.

It was at 1922 on 23rd May that the *Suffolk*, which had hastily rejoined her sister ship in the Denmark Strait, picked up the *Bismarck* and *Prinz Eugen* at a range of seven miles. The sighting was a visual one and *Suffolk* immediately took refuge in the mist to track the enemy by her superior radar set while signalling the *Norfolk* to join her. *Suffolk* confirmed visually again after an hour and *Norfolk*, with inferior radar, pounded up to join her, almost running into the German giant at six miles range. Three salvos from those huge and accurate 15-inch guns forced her hastily to make smoke and retire to a more respectable distance. Her sighting reports were picked up by the C-in-C who had failed to receive the earlier ones from *Suffolk*.

With what has been described as 'great skill and determination' the two 8-inch cruisers now shadowed the German squadron as it sped southward through the snow and rain of the icebound strait, with *Suffolk* on the enemy's starboard quarter and *Norfolk* her port quarter waiting for the *Hood* and *Prince of Wales* to close in and deliver the *coup de grâce*. For once the classic trap had been sprung and it now seemed mere formality for the finishing touch to be supplied

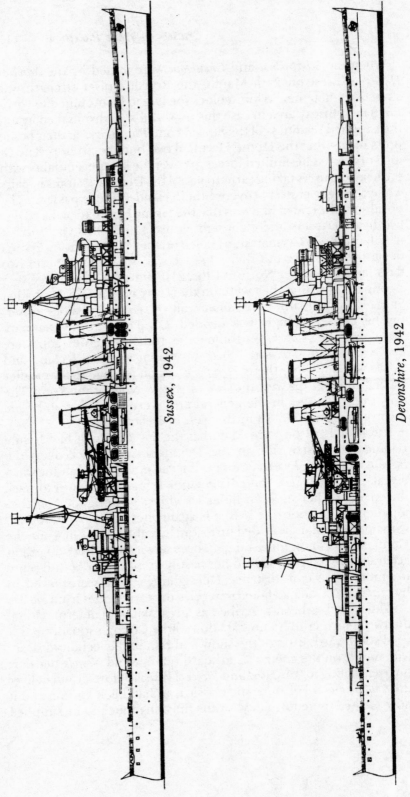

Sussex, 1942

Devonshire, 1942

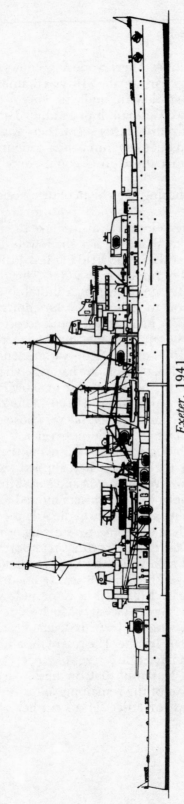

Exeter, 1941

by the British heavy ships. As everyone now knows, the result of that clash which took place early on the 24th was dramatic, but not in the way anticipated. *Hood* blew up and the *Prince of Wales* was badly damaged while the two German ships continued on their way. After being eyewitnesses to this ghastly scene there was nothing left for the two cruisers to do but to continue their patient shadowing once more in the hope that the C-in-C could come and do the job properly.

Now the *Bismarck*, having been hit in return, decided that her only hope was to make for a French port for repairs, while the accompanying cruiser slipped away to make the raid on her own. To do this she had to shake off her shadowers. For many hours now the two British cruisers had held her fast, losing her for a time but always picking her up again by radar. They had developed a pattern for this but the German Admiral outthought them. Meanwhile in an effort to slow the *Bismarck* down still further the untried carrier *Victorious* had been sent out escorted by the *Aurora*, *Galatea*, *Hermione* and *Kenya*, and she launched torpedo-bombers at the enemy giant at 1000 on the 24th, without success.

Even before this attack the *Bismarck* had fallen back on the British cruisers and engaged them with gunfire to allow *Prinz Eugen* to slip away unseen, which she did. Around 0100 on the 25th she repeated this tactic and after this, at 0306, the *Suffolk*, whose skill had held her for so long, lost contact and could not regain it.

Despite searches by both 8-inch cruisers to the west they never found her again for the *Bismarck* had slipped away to the south heading for St Nazaire. While *Norfolk* and *Suffolk* hunted to the west and south-west the four 6-inch cruisers hunted to the north-west, but all in vain. All other ships at sea in the Atlantic were called in to join the hunt, including the *Edinburgh* steering north in the central North Atlantic, the *Dorsetshire*, escorting an important convoy north in the same general area while the *Sheffield* sailed with Force 'H' from Gibraltar to cover the Bay of Biscay. For a time it was felt that *Bismarck* was heading back the way she came and sweeps were made towards the Iceland-Faeroes passage. Much valuable time was lost and precious oil fuel expended by this diversion and ships began to fall out of the chase one by one. The rest of the afternoon and night of the 25th and 26th passed in a fever of anxiety with the German ship still not located. Not until 1030 on the 26th was she re-sighted and the concentration of the remaining ships re-started.

The one hope was for Force 'H' to cut her off. Although the

The 8-inch cruiser *London* underwent a long refit during the early part of the war and emerged with an entirely new profile, not too unlike contemporary light cruisers of the 'Colony' class in many respects. Unfortunately her machinery was not modernised to the same extent, nonetheless she survived to fight on the Yangtse after the war in 'Amethyst Incident'. This photo shows her in 1941.

Among the many light cruisers that served briefly in the Mediterranean Fleet in 1941 was the *Glasgow*. Like her sister *Liverpool* she soon fell victim to Italian torpedo bombers, at Suda Bay, Crete, and was badly damaged.

The older cruisers served useful if mainly unspectacular lives on the traditional cruiser function of patrolling the distant sea lanes. Sometimes they were rewarded for their patient efforts as in this case as *Dunedin* intercepts the German supply ship *Lothringen* in the South Atlantic. This is the last known photograph of the cruiser as soon afterwards she fell victim to a U-boat attack.

One of the most famous cruiser/destroyer striking forces was the Malta-based Force 'K'. In the latter part of 1941 this small force played havoc with Italian convoys attempting to reach North Africa. *Penelope* is seen here entering Grand Harbour after another successful interception.

battle-cruiser *Renown* could not hope to engage the *Bismarck* on equal terms it was hoped that *Ark Royal*'s more experienced air group might score a torpedo hit and slow her down, and accordingly *Sheffield* was sent on ahead to gain visual contact and shadow. Unfortunately the first air strike attacked their companion of many months instead of the enemy and only by the most skilful handling did the British cruiser avoid the torpedoes aimed at her. A second strike was more successful against the correct target. By dawn on the 27th the final act of the drama was ready to unfold.

Among the ships that closed on the *Bismarck* that day were the cruisers *Sheffield*, *Dorsetshire* and *Norfolk*, but only the latter two got into the edges of the fight. It was particularly fitting that *Norfolk* should be present as she had been in on the hunt from the start, and it was equally apt that a cruiser, the *Dorsetshire*, should have finally despatched the *Bismarck* with torpedoes after she had been pummelled into scrap iron by the *King George V* and *Rodney*.* With the destruction of the *Bismarck* the most serious phase of the German surface attack on British trade came to a close. Although it was not the last time British cruisers tracked their enemy and delivered him to the guns of the battleships in the classic manner, it was the last time that the main Atlantic trade routes were threatened by such a force. Thus, by mid-1941, the latent threat of these giants had already been laid to rest in a fitting manner. Henceforth they rarely ventured far from shore-based air cover from bases deep within Norwegian fiords. With the sinking of the *Bismarck* therefore British cruisers can claim to have significantly brought about a victorious conclusion to one area of sea warfare. All the weeks and months of patient and arduous patrolling, often in unbelievable weather conditions, had come to fruition.

* Despite repeated German claims that *Bismarck* was scuttled rather than sunk by the British fleet, there is little doubt that *Dorsetshire's* torpedoes completed the job made almost perfunctory by the battleships' gunfire.

CHAPTER FIVE

Classical Roles and New Developments

Although in view of the diminished number of battleships in fleets it was obsolete, we have seen how between the wars the 'Battle Fleet Concept' dominated thinking in the Royal Navy and how that concept envisaged cruisers operating with the main fleets being used in much the same way as at Jutland in 1916: a distant screen of light cruisers extended before the fleet to locate and report on the enemy fleet's movements, strengths and dispositions, to maintain contact should the expected turn-away occur before the battle-lines became engaged, to support destroyer torpedo attacks by our own flotillas and help break up those of the opposing destroyers – all in the grand manner. Naturally, with the decline in numbers of all ships, by the outbreak of the second war battleships operated in single squadrons, usually never of more than three or four ships rather than in many squadrons of four, the whole ancillary display was similarly devalued to adapt to the changing conditions. Thus instead of several columns of light cruisers, usually one and never more than two were all there were available. Moreover the grave shortage of cruisers and the increased demands on those that remained meant that they, as much as the destroyer flotillas, were given little or no opportunity to operate as homogeneous squadrons for more than a few months at a time, if at all. Whereas the squadrons of Jellicoe's day would have been in each other's company for years, training and fighting as a unit with all the great advantage of such a system for smooth operating, the cruisers of the Second World War were rarely allowed such luxury.

It is fortunate then, that the rigorous training of the pre-war era should have imparted into the commanders of these ships an almost universal standard of excellence, so much so that units that had never worked together at all were able to come together in the heat of battle and operate as a single trained unit with very few failures. This is perhaps the biggest testimony to the much-criticised 'Battle Fleet Concept', and it has been much ignored. To our enemies the same concepts did not apply evenly. The Germans had too few ships to form a battle-fleet in the accepted sense of the word. They usually operated what heavy ships they had, when and where they could, to no overall plan. Thus their few 8-inch cruisers were treated in exactly the same manner as their battleships, battle-cruisers and pocket battleships, as commerce raiders operating in ones and twos or threes at most.

Perhaps the closest the Germany Navy came to forming a balanced fleet was during the escape of the *Scharnhorst, Gneisenau* and *Prinz Eugen* through the English Channel in February 1942, screened by destroyers, torpedo boats, E-boats and minesweepers in the grand manner. But this was a specialised operation and no major fleet action was expected from it of course. Had the *Bismarck* and *Tirpitz* sailed together, with *Prinz Eugen,* and joined forces at sea in the Atlantic with the *Scharnhorst, Gneisenau* and *Admiral Hipper,* it would have made a formidable force, which no British assembly at the time could have hoped to engage successfully, but this was never seriously contemplated by the Germans. The mere problem of keeping such a large number of huge ships supplied for any length of time would have been insurmountable, and there were no destroyers capable at that time of accompanying them into the Atlantic. They used their heavy ships as raiders and a general fleet engagement was always something to be avoided at all costs by them.

The Italians on the other hand had a balanced fleet and could operate it under the cover of their shore-based air power as and when they liked. Having the advantage not only of compactness, they had in addition central bases, short sea routes to control and could pick the time of their sorties to suit themselves. With all these aces up their sleeves they also had the supreme advantage of overwhelming numbers. It had been hoped therefore that general fleet actions would occur in the Mediterranean, but in fact only one took place. The results of this, the Battle of Calabria, were such that never again did the Italians willingly stand up to the British fleets, which were always inferior in numbers and operating thousands of miles from their bases. Although then the Italian fleet frequently put to sea in full battle array for specific operations the British were always hard-pressed to persuade them to make a stand-up fight and most actions ended unsatisfactorily with the Italian ships in full flight at top speed with the older British ships endeavouring to catch them up and falling behind: in other words a series of 'Stern Chases' from which no decisive result could be obtained. The Italian policy was known to one of limited tactical defence which led to an inbuilt reluctance to risk losses.

During late 1941 and early 1942 the British Battle Fleet in the Mediterranean suffered particularly heavy losses from torpedo, bomb and other devices with the sinking of the battleship *Barham*, the damage to the *Queen Elizabeth*, *Valiant* and *Warspite* and loss of the carriers *Ark Royal* and *Eagle*. This reduced the effective fighting strengths of the British in those waters to the handful of small cruisers of the 15th Cruiser Squadron but despite this convoys were still run in to Malta in the face of Italian battleship and 8-inch cruiser forces, a remarkable achievement. In these instances it was largely a matter of bluff and daring that carried the British cruisers through against seemingly hopeless odds, encumbered as they were by the convoys and without any form of air cover either.

The Japanese also used their Main Fleets sparingly. They had no hesitation in throwing in every ship when necessary, as at the Battle of Midway and at Leyte Gulf, but the very nature of the sea war as it developed in the Pacific ruled out major fleet actions of the classical type, which both sides had expected as avidly as had the British in the 1920's and 1930's. The elimination of the American Battle Fleet at Pearl Harbor in December 1941 by carrier attack made it inevitable the American response would be of a like nature and so the heavy ships rarely came into conflict. Again the cruisers were forced to take the predominant role, as at the Battle of the Java Sea and Savo Island already described. By the time the main fleets clashed in the series of titanic struggles in 1943 and 1944, the carrier-based bomber had so grown in numbers, range and striking power as to eliminate the scouting role of the cruiser in fleet action and at Leyte Gulf came the final battles in the old close-range slugging matches of history. But in these British cruisers played little or not part. When a fully balanced British Fleet returned to the Pacific in 1945 most of the Japanese units had been wiped out and our cruisers had to content themselves with the less spectacular roles of providing anti-aircraft protection against the Kamikaze and bombardment duties against the Japanese mainland.*

Yet if the cruiser's role in the classic main fleet action diminished, then that of spearheading special striking forces took on an increased importance in most theatres. The formation of the special

* The full story of the British Pacific Fleet is contained in Smith, Peter C., *Task Force 57* (Kimber, 1969).

'Hunting Groups' has already been analysed, but once the threat in distant waters waned the Admiralty increasingly utilised its newer cruisers in aggressive forces to strike hard at the enemy lines of communication, both in the central Mediterranean with the famous Force 'K' working from Malta, and in the Bay of Biscay against German convoys and blockade runners. It is both these uses of the cruiser that the following examples illustrate best.

The Battle of Calabria (9th July 1940)
This was the first major clash between the fleets of Italy and Great Britain and took place only a month after Mussolini had decided to throw in his lot with his Axis partner. The Italian Navy was at full strength, save for the fact that two of the brand-new 35,000-ton battleships were still not quite ready for sea although completed. On the other hand the Mediterranean Fleet under Admiral Cunningham had been much reduced between September 1939 and June 1940, as it was then a non-combat area, and only partially had this been redressed by the time the battle took place. Both main fleets had sailed to cover important convoy movements and the encounter took place in the central basin of the Mediterranean. The Italian admiral was placed close to the Italian mainland with his main ports and heavy bombers conveniently to hand, while Cunningham was one and a half thousand miles from Alexandria in Egypt, his fleet base, with only had the old carrier *Eagle* in company, with three obsolete biplane fighters aboard.

The British fleet had only five light cruisers in company, the *Orion* (flag of Vice-Admiral Tovey), *Neptune*, *Sydney*, *Gloucester* and *Liverpool*, which formed a force, Force 'A', placed out ahead of the main fleet. Moreover under the almost continuous bombing which preceded the actual battle one of these five, the *Gloucester*, had been badly damaged by a hit on her bridge which had killed her captain, and was thus in no state to engage in battle. She was, in fact, detached to guard the *Eagle* during the actual engagement and took no part.

The Italians however, were well served, having no less than six 8-inch and eight 6-inch cruisers at sea to oppose the four British ships. They were the *Pola* (flag of Admiral Paladini), with the *Fiume*, *Gorizia* and *Zara*, fine modern ships of 12,000 tons and the older *Bolzano* and *Trento*, all armed with 8-inch guns, and the modern light cruisers *Eugenio di Savoia*, *Duca d'Aosta*, *Attendolo* and *Montecuccoli* with 6-inch guns along with the older *Da Barbiano*, *Di Giussano*, *Cadorna* and *Da Noli*. The Italians also had twice the number of destroyers.

Despite the odds Cunningham eagerly accepted the chance of battle and steamed hard to cut off the Italian Fleet from its bases. Force 'A', probing out in front, was soon in contact with the leading Italian elements, and it was to the cruiser *Neptune* that the honour fell of signalling, for the first time in the Mediterranean in 150 years; 'Enemy battle fleet in sight.'* It had been the *Orion* that had first caught sight of of the Italians at 1452 that afternoon at a range of fifteen miles or more and, although they were heavily outnumbered with the *Warspite* some ten miles astern of them and the rest of the fleet even further away, the four British cruisers closed to ascertain the exact composition of the mass of ships ahead of them in the traditional manner. Quite naturally they were soon heavily engaged with the 8-inch cruisers of the enemy line but, despite some accurate shooting by the Italians, fortunately escaped any major damage.

It was perhaps fortunate that the *Warspite* was able to come up within range within the hour and a few salvos from her 15-inch guns made the Italian heavy cruisers turn quickly away under cover of a thick smoke screen laid by their accompanying destroyers. Meanwhile the four British ships had continued pressing ahead and at 1508 had sighted the two Italian battleships *Cavour* and *Cesare*. Guided by these reports *Warspite* was soon in action against these as well, and quickly scored a hit on the enemy flagship.

This was by no means part of the Italian Admiral's plans. He too turned quickly away and headed for port, sending in his destroyers to cover his withdrawal again with thick smokescreens. The British destroyers advanced to counter-attack supported by the four cruisers of the 7th Squadron but by the time they came clear of the smoke the enemy, well out of sight at full speed, had vanished from the scene. Attacks by Fleet Air Arm torpedo bombers and also by bombers of their own Air Force from Italy, failed to slow down the Italian Fleet, and although the cruisers probed further that was the end of the battle.

Although both inconclusive and, to both sides, a disappointment, the handling of the four light cruisers in the face of such heavy odds was another confirmation of the magnificent spirit of our cruiser captains and it was to be repeated unfailingly throughout the years in this area of operations.

* For the only fully detailed published description of this battle see Smith, Peter C., *Action Imminent*, (William Kimber, 1980).

The Battle of Spartivento (27th November 1940).

An even more striking demonstration of these qualities was shown at the Battle of Spartivento a few months later. A convoy to Malta from the west was given protection by the ships of Admiral Somerville's Force 'H' from Gibraltar.

This action had its origins in a complex series of movements which took place between 22nd and 30th November, known as MB9.

The operation involved the passage from Gibraltar to Malta and the Middle East of military and air force personnel and stores and the transfer to the Mediterranean Fleet of four corvettes. This aspect of the whole series of operations, was code-named Operation Collar.

Concurrently, the opportunity was taken of transferring the battleship *Ramillies* and the heavy cruiser *Berwick* which was suffering from turbine trouble, from the Eastern Mediterranean to the western basin where the latter with her speed restricted to 28 knots was considered more suitable for operation on the trade routes.

The preliminaries started as early as 9th November when the cruiser *Newcastle* sailed from Plymouth with RAF personnel and stores for Malta. She was to join Force 'H' at Gibraltar and, using the opportunities offered by an operation to fly aircraft off from the carrier *Argus* to Malta, she was to pass to the island. She duly arrived there on the 19th.

Meantime, two convoys had left the United Kingdom, one consisting of the *New Zealand Star* escorted by the cruisers *Manchester* and *Southampton* and the other consisting of the *Franconia, Clan Fraser* and *Clan Forbes*. These convoys rendezvoused some 650 miles west of Gibraltar and split again. The *Manchester* and *Franconia* made for Gibraltar but the *Southampton* and the two 16 knots Clan Line ships stayed in the vicinity of the rendezvous until joined by the cruiser *Sheffield* from Force 'H' on the 21st. Once *Sheffield* had taken over the two Clan Line ships, the *Southampton* was to proceed to Gibraltar and with the *Manchester*, take aboard 1,370 RAF personnel who had been disembarked from the *Franconia* and who were going on to Alexandria.

The forces that finally sailed from Gibraltar were split under the overall command of the Vice-Admiral, Force 'H', as follows:

FORCE 'B'	FORCE 'F'
Renown (Flag of SO Force 'H')	*Manchester*
Ark Royal	*Southampton*
Sheffield	1 Destroyer
Despatch	4 Corvettes
9 Destroyers	*Clan Forbes*
	Clan Fraser
	New Zealand Star

The two forces passed eastwards through the Straits of Gibraltar during the night of 24th/25th November.

The Mediterranean Fleet was then split into three forces:

Force 'A'	7CS	Force 'C'	Force 'D'
Warspite (Flag C-in-C)		*Orion* (Flag)	*Calcutta*
Valiant		*Ajax*	*Coventry*
Illustrious		*Sydney*	4 Destroyers
3 CS *York*		*Berwick*	*Breconshire*
Gloucester		*Malaya*	*Memnon* MW 4
Glasgow		*Ramillies*	*Clan Ferguson*
9 destroyers		*Eagle*	*Clan Macaulay*
		8 Destroyers	

Forces 'C' and 'D' left Alexandria on the 23rd and, after passing north of Crete, arrived at Malta on the 26th whereupon Force 'D' was reconstituted:

> *Ramillies*
> *Berwick*
> *Coventry*
> *Newcastle*
> 5 destroyers

Force 'A' left Alexandria at 0330 on the 25th and at 0230 on the following day when steaming along the north coast of Crete, the *Illustrious*, *Gloucester* and *Glasgow*, with four destroyers, were detached to carry out an air attack on Port Laki. Force 'A' entered Suda Bay at 0700 and the destroyers refuelled.

At noon on the 26th:

1. Force 'D' left Malta to meet up with Force 'B' off Galita Island in the morning of the following day.
2. Force 'A' sailed from Suda Bay and proceeded towards a position about 160 miles to the east of Malta.

In the afternoon of the 26th, Force 'C' now depleted by the transfer of *Ramillies* and *Berwick* left Malta as escort to convoy ME 4 consisting of five merchantmen with a close escort of *Calcutta* and three destroyers. Before arrival in Malta on the 26th, the *Eagle* launched a bombing attack on Tripoli.

Whilst these movements were taking place, Forces 'B' and 'F' proceeded on their eastward course intending to meet up with Force 'D' from Malta, at noon on the 27th, to the south of Sardinia. The combination of the three forces was then to make for a position between Sicily and Cape Bon by dusk. After dark, Force 'F', reinforced by the *Coventry* and destroyers of Force 'D', was to pass through the Narrows', into the Eastern Mediterranean to rendez-vous with Force 'A'. At the same time, Force 'B' now reinforced by *Ramillies*, *Berwick* and *Newcastle* from Force 'D', was then to turn back to the westward intending to arrive back in Gibraltar.

At 1000 on the 27th Forces 'B' and 'F' were in 37°41'N, 7°27'E steering eastwards and Force 'D' was some ninety miles to the east steering west towards the rendezvous. At 0920 aircraft from *Ark Royal* located an enemy force of five cruisers and five destroyers at a distance of 60 miles and another enemy force of two battleships and seven destroyers at a distance of 75 miles. This information reached Admiral Somerville at 0956 and he immediately detached the convoy to the south-east under the protection of the *Despatch* and two destroyers, *Coventry* was detached from Force 'D' to join the convoy escort and the remaining ships of Forces 'B' and 'F' made off at high speed to join Force 'D'.

At 1120 Force 'D' was sighted from the *Renown* and at the same time reconnaissance reports indicated that the enemy forces had altered course eastwards. Accordingly the *Ramillies* was ordered to steer a course of 045° in order not to lose ground as a consequence of her lack in speed.

All the cruisers were now united under the command of Vice-Admiral Holland and took their position in the van. With *Ramillies* now steering a course parallel to the *Renown*, there seemed a reasonable prospect of bringing the Italian forces to action with the intention of: ·

(a) Preventing the enemy force from obtaining a position from which they could attack the convoy and
(b) Within a tacit acceptance of some risk to the convoy, endeavour

to inflict loss on the enemy where hopefully two battleships might be very badly damaged or destroyed.

Of course, Admiral Somerville knew that Article 625 of Fighting Instructions made the safety of the convoy paramount but he hoped that if he could reduce the speed of the enemy ships to a level which matched that of his own ships, he might still be able to achieve his objectives.

At 1207 those in *Renown* saw smoke on the horizon, and at the same time the cruisers ahead sighted both smoke and masts over an arc of bearing from 346° to 006°. By this time the cruisers were in a line of bearing 075° to 255° in the order from west to east, of *Sheffield*, *Southampton*, *Newcastle*, *Manchester* and *Berwick*.

At 1220 the most westerly group of enemy ships opened fire and the British cruisers immediately replied. As soon as contact was made the Italian forces started to retire towards Sardinia in compliance with an order issued by Admiral Campioni at 1215 and the ensuing action was fought at extreme ranges between first of all the opposing cruiser forces and later, for a brief period, between the heavy ships, but without any tangible result. The cruiser *Berwick* received two 8-inch hits which put 'Y' turret out of action and the Italians later acknowledged that one destroyer, the *Lanciere*, suffered severe damage. Although their official communiqué stated that the *Fiume* was also hit and damaged, this did not later appear in their official report.

During the action, two strikes were mounted by Swordfish aircraft from the *Ark Royal* supported by Skua dive bombers but they caused no damage to the enemy and air attacks against the British forces were equally unsuccessful.

The British ships continued to chase their opponents but at 1310 when within thirty miles of the coast of southern Sardinia, Admiral Somerville decided that with no chance of bringing the enemy to further action, he had no option but to withdraw and course was set to rejoin the convoy by dark.

In explanation of his decision to break off the action, Admiral Campioni offered firstly the threat imposed by the fact that the enemy forces included an aircraft carrier and secondly, his lack of confidence in the ability of the shore-based Italian aircraft to inflict any damage on the British ships.

The course of the action conducted by Admiral Somerville was not altogether approved by the Admiralty and they went to the lengths of setting up a Board of Inquiry which sat at Gibraltar on 3rd December 1940. It lasted four days at the end of which the Board found that within the context of orders that were clear and concise the action that ensued was correct, spirited and achieved the purpose of protecting the convoy in face of a superior force. The only debatable point lay in the timing of the decision to withdraw which no one criticised in itself but which some thought might have been a little premature.

The Battle of Matapan (28th-29th March 1941).
The pattern set by Calabria and Spartivento was followed in the initial stages of the most decisive of the Mediterranean fleet actions at Cape Matapan in March 1941. It was clear that unless the Fleet Air Arm were able to hit and slow down Italian heavy units, the older and slower British battleships would never be able to bring them to battle. Fortunately in this instance, they were able to. Pressured by their German allies to use their fleet the Italian reluctantly and cautiously sailed to intervene in the waters south of Crete during the campaign in which the Axis crushed Greece and Yugoslavia. Shortage of fuel oil was the most pressing problem for the Italian Navy and lack of reliable air reconnaissance. The oil they obtained, the air reconnaissance the Germans promised to lay on for them and so they ventured out again with the battleship *Vittorio Veneto*, the heavy cruisers *Fiume*, *Pola*, *Zara*, *Bolzano*, *Trento* and *Trieste*, the light cruisers *Abruzzi* and *Garibaldi* and many destroyers.

Forewarned by special intelligence Cunningham put to sea to give battle with the battleships *Warspite*, *Valiant* and *Barham*, the carrier *Formidable* and a few destroyers. Against the six 8-inch and two 6-inch cruisers of the Italian fleet the British were again heavily outnumbered: Vice-Admiral Pridham-Wippell's Force 'B' consisted only of the 6-inch cruisers *Orion*, *Ajax*, *Perth* and *Gloucester*. The only 8-inch cruiser in the British fleet had been badly damaged at Suda Bay in Crete on 26th March which was a singular misfortune. This was the *York*, which was crippled by explosive motor-boats in a daring raid. Moreover the most powerful ship of Force 'B', the twelve-gun *Gloucester*, was herself damaged having run a plummer block bearing which restricted her top speed to a little over 24 knots in theory. Despite this Force 'B' refuelled at Piraeus and sailed to effect its rendezvous to the south of Gavdos Island, which lies off the south-west coast of Crete, by 0630 on the 28th March.

Table 16
Opposing Forces at the Battle of Cape Matapan

	Italian	British
Battleships:	*Vittorio Vento*	*Barham, Warspite, Valiant*
Aircraft Carriers:	—	*Formidable*
8-inch cruisers:	*Bolzano, Fiume, Pola, Trento, Trieste, Zara*	—
6-inch cruisers:	*Abruzzi, Garibaldi.*	*Ajax, Gloucester, Orion, Perth*
Destroyers:	*Alpino, Bersagliere, Fuciliere, Granatiere, Gioberti, Alfieri, Oriani, Carducci, Da Recco, Pessagno, Corazziere, Ascari, Carabiniere.*	*Ilex, Hasty, Hereward, Jervis, Janus, Mohawk, Nubian, Havock, Hotspur, Greyhound, Griffin, Stuart, Vendetta.*

*   *   *

The British cruiser force was detected by one of the floatplanes from the Italian fleet, and the 3rd Cruiser Squadron (the heavy cruisers *Bolzano, Trieste* and *Trento*) were sent to make contact with them and draw them towards the Italian flagship. Contact was made 0758 and, some fourteen minutes later, the Italians opened fire at a range of 25,000 yards, to which of course the smaller British ships were unable to make any reply. Pridham-Wippell therefore decided on the classic ploy as adopted by the enemy: to draw these ships to *his* battleships, and, despite his own orders, the Italian cruiser admiral, Sansonnetti, took the bait. Limited by *Gloucester*'s best speed the smaller British ships were in an unenviable position for the pursuing ships were at least eight knots faster.

Moreover it was the *Gloucester* at the rear of the British line on which all three Italian heavy cruisers naturally concentrated their salvos. Zig-zagging violently she managed to avoid being hit but not for a further fifteen minutes were her own rear turrets able to make reply and then her first salvos fell short of the enemy. Despite the fact that her shots were well short they were enough to dampen the temporary ardour of Sansonnetti and, at 0855, the big Italian ships broke off the action. This was in response to a recall order from the cautious Italian C-in-C, Iachino. Immediately Pridham-Wippell reversed his own ships' course and started to shadow the retreating 3rd Cruiser Squadron northward again, at a range of some sixteen miles.

Iachino, the Italian C-in-C, now arranged his forces to trap the British cruisers, hoping to sandwich them between the two heavy cruiser squadrons of Sansonnetti and Cattaneo's 1st Division while cutting off their retreat with his battleship. It was a trap that almost worked for just before 1100 the speeding light cruisers sighted an unknown vessel ahead of them on opposite course and the *Orion* flashed an identification signal. *Vittorio Veneto*'s 15-inch guns thundered their reply and the 8-inch cruisers turned in support. Pridham-Wippell's position was now unenviable to say least, but he did have one card up his sleeve – the battleships which, unknown to Iachino who thought they were still at Alexandria, were closing from astern. Once more the chase reversed with the four cruisers leading their even bigger opponent back to the south-east under heavy and accurate fire. By laying smoke they for a time avoided almost certain annihilation although again the *Gloucester*, the rear ship, being to windward of the smoke, was horribly exposed and drew the concentrated fire of the battleship for a long period. Despite her damaged 'A' bracket the *Gloucester* managed to work up to 31 knots and one of the destroyers, *Hasty*, covered her with a smokescreen of her own.

It was at this critical juncture that torpedo bombers from the *Formidable* made their first appearance and, although they failed to score any hits, they took the pressure off the cruisers just in time. This attack took place at 1127 and had the immediate effect of causing the Italian battleship to break off the pursuit and turn back to the north-west. Further air attacks by shore-based aircraft followed, equally without result other than reinforcing the Italians' decision to break off the sortie.

At 1230 the British cruisers rendezvoused with the battle fleet, reporting to Cunningham that when last seen the enemy had been on a bearing 312° on a course of 300° at 1116. This meant that the Italians had a fifty mile lead over the slower British battleships. Again all depended on the *Formidable*'s torpedo bombers.

They made a second strike against the *Vittorio Veneto* at 1510 and claimed three hits. In fact they had scored just one, and this was not serious enough to do more than reduce her speed for a time. It was clear that she could not be brought to battle before nightfall and Cunningham made his dispositions accordingly. At 1615 he formed his destroyers into divisions for night torpedo attacks and again despatched Force 'B', at 1651, with orders to push on ahead and gain contact with the enemy. Hopes were high after the reports

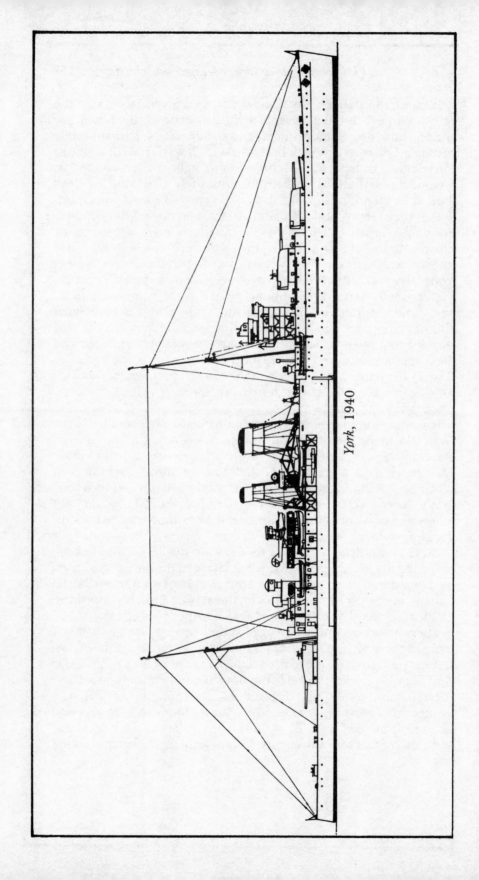

York, 1940

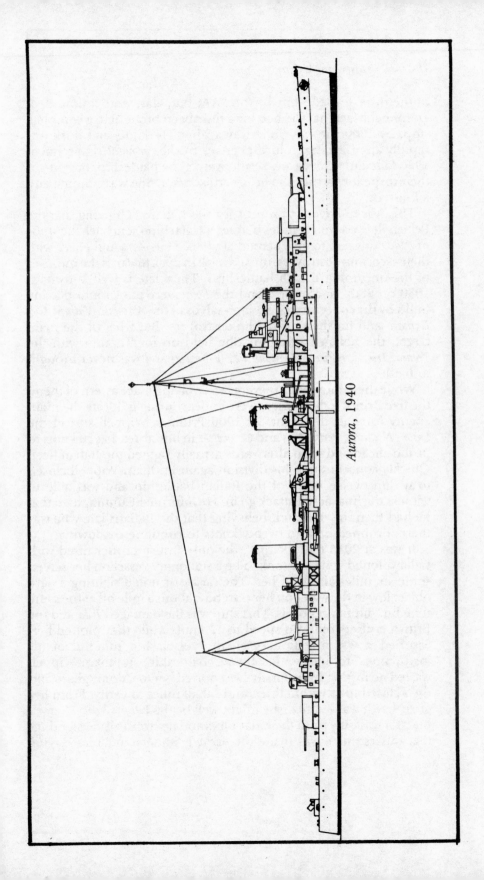

Aurora, 1940

of the three torpedo hits by the FAA, but, alas, were unfounded. Despite the fact that she had for a time been brought to a complete stop, by 1900 she was underway again at 19 knots and dusk was rapidly approaching. A further attack by the *Formidable*'s aircraft at 1930 failed to achieve any result against the battleship, but one of their torpedoes struck the heavy cruiser *Pola*. She was stopped and left astern.

This was to have fatal results for the Italians. Thinking that the British fleet was many miles behind him Iachino sent back the ships of *Pola*'s division to give her aid at 2030. Thus *Zara* and *Fiume* with their escorting destroyers, turned back in dusk towards the muzzles of the oncoming British battleships. Their fate is well known: at 1030 on 28th March they, and the *Pola*, were blown into blazing hulks by the concentrated 15-inch salvos of the *Warspite*, *Valiant* and *Barham* and finished off by the destroyers. But what of the main target, the Italian battleship? She held on for Taranto with the *Trento*, *Trieste*, *Bolzano*, *Garibaldi* and *Abruzzi* and was never brought to battle.

While these momentous events were taking place astern of them, the five British light cruisers were endeavouring to locate the main enemy force in the night. At 1906 Pridham-Wippell spread the *Orion*, *Neptune*, *Perth*, *Ajas* and *Gloucester* in line abreast at 30 knots to probe ahead and soon afterwards actually sighted the Italian fleet. Quickly concentrating his division again Pridham-Wippell closed to within twelve miles of the Italian battleship and was able to witness the final aerial attack go in. He informed Cunningham that he had them in view and, believing that the Italians knew he was there, dropped back to twenty knots to continue shadowing.

It was at 2015 that the *Ajax*, the only British cruiser fitted with radar, plotted what she took to be a stationary vessel on her screen some six miles ahead of her. The *Gloucester* noted sighting a dark object low in the water on her port bow about a mile off at the same time but did not report it. This ship was the damaged *Pola* and the British cruisers reduced speed to 15 knots while they plotted her. Satisfied it was a stationary enemy vessel, and mindful of his instructions to locate the Italian battleship, Pridham-Wippell wasted no further time. Firstly he reported her to Cunningham and then closed in to within three-and-a-half miles to verify. From her great size it was felt that she might well be the *Vittorio Veneto* herself but as it was only from the radar plots and not from visual sightings that this estimate was made the error is understandable. Having

Two of the 'Dido' class were hurried to sea without their proper armament due to delays and shortages early in the war. Armed only with 4.5-inch guns they were dubbed 'The Toothless Terrors' but soon earned themselves a grand reputation against Axis aircraft on the Arctic and Malta convoy routes. *Charybdis* herself, seen here in 1942, was later sunk by German destroyers in the Channel in an ill-conceived operation.

H. M. King George VI visits *Scylla* at Scapa Flow soon after her famous battle with Russia convoy P.Q. 18.

The *Exeter* was extensively refitted after her damage at the River Plate and sent east where she met a gallant end against overwhelming odds in the Java Sea in 1942. These photos show her last actions.

firmly obtain a fix on this immobile giant and given her position to Cunningham, Pridham-Wippell felt her fate was sealed and left it to the heavyweights to finish off the Italian 'battleship' while he took his small cruisers off in search of further prey.

The movements of the British cruisers were complicated by the fact that British destroyers were in the area and Pridham-Wippell expected them to mount torpedo attacks on the stationary Italian and any other ships they found, so to avoid any possible confusion he kept well clear and steered to the north. From the last reports he had received of the enemy cruisers he deduced they were making for Messina and he turned in that direction to catch them up. In fact *Vittorio Veneto* held on steadily to the north-west while the British veered off to the north-east, thus losing all hope of catching them.

This latter turn-away was in response to a signal from Cunningham, who, in the aftermath of the night battle, wanted all friendly ships to stay clear of the area while the destroyers mopped up. It was to have unfortunate results, for from 2112 onward the gap opened up and all hope of catching the *Vittorio Veneto* ended. The rest of the night and following morning were, for the five British cruisers, anti-climax. After steaming steadily towards the island of Kithera off the coast of Morea in Greece until 0430 they turned back along their tracks and rendezvoused with the destroyers and the Battle Squadron at 0700 before returning to Alexandria.

As to the effects of the battle, the main one was that the Italians became even more cautious, and never again ventured so far from their ports. For the British the succession of defeats on land that led to the evacuation of Greece and Crete was made bearable by the victory at Matapan, and the moral ascendancy maintained since June 1940 was reinforced and never lost.

The Second Battle of Sirte (22nd March 1942).

By the spring of the following year Britain's fortunes in the Mediterranean had reached an all-time low. The once dominant battle fleet of Admiral Cunningham had been reduced to a handful of small cruisers and destroyers while their duties had been extended by defeats on land in the Eastern Mediterranean, to which we only clung by our fingernails. Malta was more isolated than ever before and had been subjected to the most intense aerial attack to date. To keep this island supplied by sea was essential, even though we had neither the naval strength nor the air protection to do it. On the other hand the Axis, with the Luftwaffe heavily reinforced and the Italian Navy recuperated after a year of impotency, could both bring to bear their maximum strength.

It was under these circumstances that a supply convoy was sailed from the Eastern Mediterranean in late March bound for Malta. It consisted of the fast transports *Breconshire, Clan Campbell, Pampas* and *Talabot* and had a close escort which consisted of the anti-aircraft cruiser *Carlisle* and the escort destroyers *Avon Vale, Beaufort, Dulverton, Eridge, Hurworth* and *Southwold*. As 'heavy' cover Admiral Vian sailed with the 15th Cruiser Squadron, the 5·25-inch cruisers *Cleopatra, Dido* and *Euryalus,* with the destroyers *Hasty, Havock, Hero, Jervis, Kelvin, Kingston, Kipling, Lively, Sikh* and *Zulu.* They were to be joined by the 6-inch cruiser *Penelope* and the destroyer *Legion* from Malta on 22nd March to see the convoy safely in. All ships had to undergo heavy and repeated German air attacks throughout the whole of the passage but, up to the 22nd, no ship had been lost, although many were running low on anti-aircraft ammunition. No effective fighter cover was possible from the RAF to counter the enormous numbers of Axis aircraft on hand.

To deliver the *coup-de-grâce* against the British units the Italians sailed a overwhelmingly superior force from Taranto on 22nd March. Flying his flag in the battleship *Littorio*, sister to the *Vittorio Veneto*, was Admiral Iachino again. He had with him the 8-inch cruisers *Gorizia* and *Trento*, the 6-inch cruiser *Bande Nere* and ten destroyers as well as three German and three Italian submarines. This force sighted the British convoy at 1424 and a famous battle ensued. Again it should be noted that the captain of the *Penelope* had no time to study the intended fighting instructions of Admiral Vian before he joined forces with him and was almost immediately plunged into a confused and fast-moving battle. Nonetheless, as the Official Historian records: ' . . . so decisive was Vian's leadership that the *Penelope*'s captain was never in any doubt regarding what was required of him.'* Vian's plans in the likely event of such a confrontation were that the *Hunt* class ships should screen the convoy, while the *Carlisle* and *Avon Vale* covered them with smoke. The four light cruisers and the eleven 'Fleet' destroyers, in five divisions, were to act as a striking force and engage the enemy.

Three minutes after the Italian heavy cruisers sighted the convoy they in turn were spotted by the cruiser *Euryalus.* They at first were thought to be battleships; Vian immediately put his plans into effect

---

* Roskill, Captain S.W. *The War at Sea* (HMSO, 1958), Vol 2, op cit, p 52.

and *Cleopatra* and *Euryalus* led out to engage their armoured opponents with their little guns. The Italian cruisers turned to the right despite their superiority in firepower and a long-range gun duel followed with neither side scoring any hits. The intention of the enemy was to lead Vian's cruisers to the *Littorio*, but once the convoy was out of immediate danger the *Cleopatra* and *Euryalus* rejoined the other divisions north of it, satisfied to have driven off this initial threat.

Howerever at 1640 the enemy cruisers re-appeared and this time the *Littorio* was also sighted astern of them. Once more the British laid smoke and shielded the distant merchant ships, which were themselves undergoing heavy dive bombing though being defended by the *Hunt* class destroyers effectively. The sea was rising and a strong wind was spreading the layers of black and white smoke over a huge area. The Italians were exceedingly wary of entering this region for fear of torpedo attacks but their larger vessels were able to make better speed through the rough seas and fire more accurately outside the range of the effective response of the 5·25-inch guns of the *Didos*. They began working their way round the edge of the smoke to get at the convoy while the British responded with a series of point-blank charges at them, firing guns and torpedoes as they cleared the smoke, and then clawing round into its blanket before the 15-inch and 8-inch projectiles could smash through their own paper-thin armour.

At 1740 the enemy had only four destroyers between him and the convoy but, despite the fact that one was hit by a 15-inch shell, their torpedo attacks and bold front managed to hold them off until 1800 when the British cruisers re-emerged from the smoke and *Cleopatra* and *Euryalus* took on *Littorio* at the range of 13,000 yards. The Italian battleship drew off under threat of torpedo attack from *Cleopatra* and the destroyers but meantime contact had been lost with the three enemy cruisers. Accordingly Vian steered back eastward to try and find them again. Once more the *Littorio* almost broke through the thin screen, being sighted and engaged by the destroyers once more from 1808 onward, with ranges closing down to less than three miles at times. Another destroyer was hit by the battleship's great guns but the twenty-five torpedoes they fired in return sent their giant opponent scuttling back once more. The British cruisers again took up the contest, engaging all four Italian heavy ships between 1830 and 1840 while a third destroyer was hit by a 15-inch shell but all stayed afloat.

This final action was the last phase of the battle. Frustrated by the smoke, the threat of torpedoes and the aggressive tactics of the tiny cruisers the Italian heavyweights gave up the struggle and steered north to return to Taranto, losing two of their destroyers through bad weather on their return journey. It was *the* classic example of an inferior force holding at bay an enemy far stronger than itself and frustrating its every move. The Italians had no counter to Vian's tactics and left the field of battle absolutely defeated.

The Battle of North Cape (26th December 1943).

Although the Germans had carefully husbanded their remaining capital ship strength since the early days of North Atlantic raiding that had ended with the return of the *Scharnhorst* and *Gneisenau* to Germany in February 1942, the situation on the Eastern Front towards the end of 1943 caused them to re-think their policy in a belated attempt to stop the flow of munitions and vehicles from America which was turning the tide against them there. Dönitz had fought against the premature scrapping of the big ships after a series of defeats had exhausted Hitler's patience with his Navy and plans were afoot to take advantage of the long Arctic nights to sortie the *Scharnhorst* against the next Russia convoy.

On 20th December the opportunity was provided with the sailing of two convoys, one from Lock Ewe to Russia, JW55B, and another from Kola to United Kingdom, RA55A, each of which had an escort of ten destroyers. As had been the usual pattern for Arctic convoys since their earliest days, a British cruiser squadron was over the horizon to provide close cover for both these convoys with the Battle Fleet some distance away ready to intervene. This had been the formula for two years and only once had the trap almost worked when the *Tirpitz* narrowly escaped destruction in 1942. The risk to the cruisers from U-boat and air attack always meant that they had to patrol out of sight to the north of the convoys though they would be on hand if needed. The force involved for this operation consisted of the 8-inch cruiser *Norfolk* and the 6-inch cruisers *Sheffield* and *Belfast*, with Rear Admiral Burnett flying his flag in the latter vessel. With the C-in-C, Admiral Fraser flying his flag in battleship *Duke of York*, was the 6-inch cruiser *Jamaica* and four destroyers. Fraser had a 'strong hunch' that this time *Scharnhorst* would sail and had made detailed plans to cope with such an intervention. His hunch was correct for *Scharnhorst* and five destroyers, under Admiral Bey, actually sailed to intercept the convoys on Christmas Day and headed north from the North Cape to head them off east of Bear Island.

On the 26th the *Scharnhorst* was still steering north on her interception course in heavy weather which had forced her destroyers to turn back. The C-in-C, with the *Duke of York* and *Jamaica*, was steering eastward to get in position behind her to cut off her retreat and the three cruisers under Burnett were steaming steadily south-west directly for the oncoming German battle-cruiser and about 150 miles east of convoy JW55B, her target. At 1601 all three British forces broke wireless silence and reported their positions, thus clarifying the plot aboard the flagship and showing that the trap was well and truly set this time.

At 0815 the British cruiser force increased speed to 24 knots and steered north-west to close the convoy and, at 0840 the radar plot aboard the *Belfast* picked up a large vessel only 25,000 yards distant through the murk and blackness, some thirty miles from the convoy. The trap was sprung.

The range rapidly decreased until, at 0921 the *Sheffield* had the *Scharnhorst* in sight at a range of 13,000 yards. *Belfast* fired star-shell and, at 0929, the three were ready to fire on their completely surprised opponent as ordered by Burnett. Because the British ships were disposed in quarter-line formation however, only the heavy cruiser *Norfolk* was actually able to commence salvos at this time. The *Scharnhorst* made no answer to these first shots but instead put her helm about and headed south for safety. The cruisers immediately responded but in the huge seas the big battle-cruiser was able to maintain thirty knots and the British ships fell behind rapidly, but not before *Norfolk* had landed one or two 8-inch shells on her German target.

Although his instructions were to avoid combat with superior forces Bey had not yet given up his attempt to strike a blow for the soldiers on the Russian Front. He turned north-east again at 0955 in an attempt to come round behind the cruisers and close the convoy from ahead and above. But, tracking him by radar, Burnett was not deceived and, to cut the corner and make up for his lack of speed, he hauled his cruisers round to the north-east to place himself between the convoy and the enemy in good time. For a time then contact was lost. Some criticism was levelled at Burnett for failing to comply with the primary duty of a cruiser force, that of holding the enemy at all costs until the heavy ships came up. Had the *Scharnhorst* escaped because of this, such criticism might have been more widespread but in view of the superior speed of his larger opponent and the need to protect the convoy his decision to take that risk was justified by subsequent events.

Joined by four destroyers from the convoy Burnett in fact accomplished his purpose by 1040, being some ten miles ahead of the convoy ready to defend it against the next probe. The C-in-C meanwhile was steadily closing the gap from the south-west. He was anxious for further news of the enemy but Burnett had read the Germans' intentions correctly and was rewarded when, just before noon, *Belfast* again picked up the enemy on her radar, and, at 1221, *Sheffield* was again able to signal 'Enemy in sight'.

Both sides opened fire at a range of 11,000 yards and the action continued for twenty minutes with blows being given and received by each other. An 11-inch projectile from *Scharnhorst* hit *Norfolk* hard, putting one turret out of action and knocking out all her radar sets, and the *Sheffield* was slightly less damaged, but in return they scored several hits on the battle-cruiser which turned sharply away to the south-east, frustrating attempts by the destroyers to get in on the action. The enemy was now heading for home, with all further thoughts of attacking the convoy gone; but she was now steering-straight for the *Duke of York* and *Jamaica* and so Burnett contented himself with shadowing her by radar outside the effective range of her main armament and all firing had ceased by 1242. This cat-and-mouse game continued for the next three hours with the British cruisers holding the *Scharnhorst* steadily and making no attempt to divert her from her course.

At 1617 the reward for their persistence was the sighting on *Duke of York*'s radar of the oncoming battle-cruiser, blissfully unaware of the British battleship's presence. By 1650 the German ship was surrounded, the C-in-C's plan being to close within 12,000 yards of the smaller enemy ship and pound her with his own 14-inch guns. The *Belfast* illuminated her by star-shell and *Duke of York* and *Jamaica* opened fire together.

There could only be one outcome to such a battle. With British ships all around her, caught by surprise for the third time with her turrets fore-and-aft when first seen, The *Scharnhorst* could do nothing but sell her life as dearly as she could. She turned north away from the pulversing fire of the *Duke of York*, then east, but it was no use. Although the *Sheffield* had been forced to drop out of the chase due to shaft trouble, the *Norfolk* and *Belfast* now opened fire, pinning the German giant in a mesh of armour-piercing shells.

Both groups of British ships, one to the north and one to the south, continued to pour salvos on their stricken opponent to which she soon ceased to make effective reply. At 1850 four of the British destroyers closed to within 3,000 yards of the enemy and fired torpedoes, several of which hit, sealing her fate.

At 1900 the *Duke of York* and *Jamaica* re-opened their fire at 10,400 yards, and *Belfast* and *Norfolk* joined in ten minutes later. Torn apart by this merciless hail of shells the *Scharnhorst* was little more than a floating wreck by 1930 when both *Belfast* and *Jamaica* closed in to finish her off with torpedoes, joined in this by the remaining four destroyers. By 0745 she had sunk along with most of her 2,000 man crew. Thus by brilliant teamwork of all arms, battleship, cruisers and destroyers, the last classic surface engagement, fought without the participation of any aircraft whatsoever, was brought to a splendid finale.

Never again were British cruisers allowed the opportunity to track down and deliver German heavy ships to their fate, but throughout the war they led many special striking forces against lesser targets. Perhaps the most successful of these was the famous Force 'K', based at Malta during the dark days of 1941-42.

Force 'K' (9th November 1941)
Churchill had long been goading the Admiralty to base surface striking forces at Malta from the earliest days of the Italian entry of the war. With the extremely tight situation prevailing in numbers of available ships and, equally important although overlooked by the impatient Premier, the lack of sufficient oil stocks on the island, this did not at first prove practicable. Finally, though, enough ships were scraped together to set up such a force. For a time the 14th Destroyer Flotilla operated against Italian convoy routes to Tripoli and Benghazi and in the spring of 1941 these were replaced by the 5th Destroyer Flotilla from Home. All these vessels were needed desperately at the time of the evacuation from Crete in May of that year and suffered grievous losses; thus for a while, the Italian convoys were unmolested.

With the advance of the Axis on Cairo that autumn pressure was again exerted from Whitehall for the Navy to do something to halt this supply and, on 22nd August 1941, a typical 'Action This Day' type memo passed from the Prime Minister's office to the Admiralty which read: 'Will you please consider the sending of a flotilla, and, if possible, a cruiser or two, to Malta, as soon as possible.'

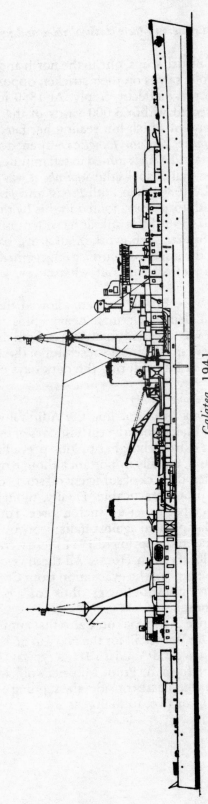

Galatea, 1941

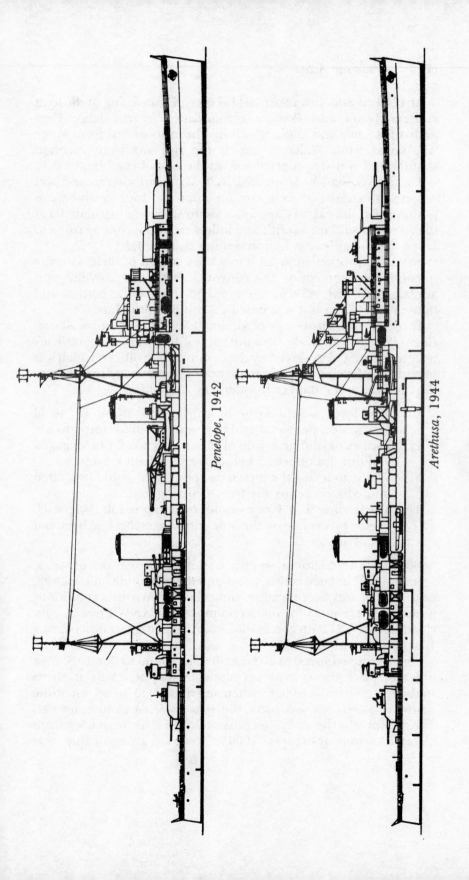

Penelope, 1942

Arethusa, 1944

At 1730 on 8th November 1941, Force 'K' consisting of the light cruisers *Aurora* and *Penelope* accompanied by the large Fleet destroyers *Lance* and *Lively*, which had been seconded from Force 'H', sailed from Malta to search for and attack an escorted southbound convoy reported well to the east of the island.

The convoy had been sighted by a Maryland aircraft and was reported to consist of six merchant ships and four destroyers in position 40 miles east of Cape Spartivento and it was calculated that the enemy would turn south and follow the usual convoy route to Libya passing at least a hundred miles east of Malta.

Force 'K' proceeded at 28 knots on a course of 064° with the intention of intercepting the convoy at 0200 and a Wellington aircraft fitted with ASV was sent out to shadow the convoy and home Force 'K' in but it suffered an equipment failure.

Force 'K' was formed in single line ahead of the order *Aurora, Lance, Penelope* and *Lively*, at a distance of four cables apart. They were to follow a plan agreed by the commanding officer, which was intended to develop the maximum power of attack and to reduce to the minimum, the danger from enemy torpedoes:

1.   The force would keep in single line ahead to avoid recognition problems and to give freedom for torpedo fire
2.   Escorts on the near side of the convoy would be engaged and put out of action before the merchant vessels
3.   Whilst attacking the merchant vessels, fire would be shifted immediately on to any frest escort sighted.
4.   The leading ship *Aurora* would so far as possible, keep each enemy escort fine on the bow until that escort had been put out of action

At 0040 on 9th November, when in position 180 miles east of Malta, a group of darkened ships was sighted about nine miles away, bearing 030° and steering approximately 170°. Weather conditions prevailing were ideal for interception – wind NNW force 3, light cloud, sea state 21 with good visibility under a bright moon bearing 100° at an elevation of 45°.

Aurora reduced speed to 20 knots and led round to port to 350° in order to place the convoy up moon, before attacking from its starboard quarter. At 0050, when nearly abeam of an escorting destroyer astern of the convoy, the *Aurora* steered straight for her. The convoy was then seen to consist of eight large merchant ships escorted by four destroyers. At 0052, a second group of ships was sighted bearing 330° at a distance of 6 miles and steering a southerly course. This group appeared to consist of two large vessels and two destroyers.

In fact, the second group consisted of the heavy cruisers *Trento* and *Trieste* with four destroyers and the first group consisted of seven merchant ships: *Rina Corrado* (5180), *Sagitta* (5153), *Maria* (6339), *Conte Di Misurata* (tanker 5014), *Minatitland* (7599), *San Marco* (3076) and *Duisburg* (7389) escorted by six destroyers.

The *Aurora*'s main armament trained on the radar bearing, was ready to open fire on the escort destroyer and the port side 4-inch guns controlled from aft, on the northern group. At 0057, seventeen minutes after the first sighting, fire was opened on both targets at a range of 5,700 yards. The first three 6-inch broadsides hit the rear destroyer, the *Fulmine* which sank almost at once. The action then became general; the *Penelope* engaged a destroyer, which was probably the *Grecale*, and the two British destroyers both fired at merchant ships.

At 0059, the *Aurora* hauled round to starboard and led Force 'K' up the starboard side of the convoy, each ship engaging targets in succession, with gunfire or torpedoes as they passed. At 0125, the *Aurora* led round to port, by which time all the merchant ships were on fire. From time to time, enemy destroyers appeared through the smoke and were fired upon. About twelve torpedo tracks were sighted on occasion, by the British cruisers.

At 0145 course was altered westward to pass round the convoy and to search for any ships which might still be undamaged. None was seen and at 0206 Force 'K' increased speed again to 25 knots and shaped course for Malta where it arrived at 1305, having suffered neither damage nor casualties.

Between 0835 and 0920, four attacks were made on Force 'K' by torpedo aircraft but a combination of strong AA gunfire and the presence of fighter escort made the attacks abortive.

Italian losses amounted to:

Seven   merchant ships totalling some 40,000 GRT sunk
One   destroyer (*Fulmine*) sunk
Two   destroyers (*Grecale* and *Euro*) damaged

Later in the morning of the 10th, the destroyer *Libeccio* was torpedoed by the submarine *Upholder* and sank whilst on tow in the *Euro*. Her crew were transferred to the *Euro* and the *Fuciliere*. Personnel casualties amounted to 12 killed and 46 wounded.

It had been a truly remarkable engagement. Every one of the merchant ships had been sunk and one destroyer. Several others were badly damaged and one of these was finished off by a British submarine next day. On the British side casualties were put at ' . . . five canaries, thought to be yellow', which died from the concussion of the gunfire aboard *Penelope*. She also made the famous signal to *Aurora*:

'Congratulations on your magnificent borealis.'

Bay of Biscay (28th December 1943).
Equally as impressive in its way was the engagement fought by the light cruisers *Enterprise* and *Glasgow* against a powerful squadron of no less than eleven German destroyers on 28th December 1943 in the Bay of Biscay.

The Germans had attempted to bring home some blockade runners through the Bay at this time and sail others. Close watch was kept by aircraft on the Bay ports and the C-in-C, Plymouth, Admiral Leatham, held in readiness the *Glasgow* and *Enterprise* to back them up. Attacks by RAF torpedo bombers caught one enemy ship, the *Pietro Orseolo*, off Lorient and sank her on the 18th, and a homeward-bound ship, the *Osorno*, was attacked unsuccessfully until she ran aground whereupon she was attacked from the air again, though again without success. The third blockade runner was the *Alsterufer*, which was located and sunk by aircraft on the 27th. A strong force of German destroyers and torpedo boats (escort destroyers) had put to sea to escort her in and these were considered ripe pickings for the two Plymouth-based cruisers.

The German ships comprised the 8th Destroyer Flotilla (Captain Erdmenger) with the large destroyers *Z23, Z24, Z27, Z32* and *Z37* which displaced some 2,600 tons and were powerfully armed with five 5·9-inch guns and eight 21-inch torpedo tubes, and the 4th TB Flotilla (Captain Kohlauf) with the *T22, T23, T24, T25, T26* and *T27*. These latter were the same displacement and had a similar armament to British destroyers, carrying four 4·1-inch guns and six 21-inch torpedo tubes on a displacement of 1,300 tons. The odds were highly stacked in favour of the German flotillas, both in numbers and weight of gunfire, without their added bonus of heavy torpedo armaments, but when they were sighted by American aircraft at 0920 on the morning of the 28th the two British cruisers were already on their way.

The *Glasgow* and *Enterprise* were south of the enemy when these reports came in; the German flotillas were in two groups heading westward. At once the cruisers put on extra speed, working up to 28 knots and steering to close the gap. By 1100 the shadowing aircraft reported that all eleven German ships had joined forces but had now reversed course and were steering east back towards the French coast.

Although the sea was rising in the Bay any British flotilla would have welcomed the chance offered by the two isolated British cruisers. At 1335 they came in sight of the enemy at a range of some 18,000 yards and immediately opened fire with their forward mountings. There was some distraction when German bombers arrived overhead and carried out attacks with glider-bombs but these were all avoided without harm to either cruiser. The Germans then tried a half-hearted torpedo attack from two directions which was not very well carried out. All their torpedoes were avoided by the cruisers and, on seeing they had failed to deter the British duo, the German ships split up again and endeavoured to escape at their best speed.

Here the weather conditions favoured the larger cruisers for the German destroyers were always bad sea boats being overloaded with guns and equipment.

Four destroyers fled to the north-west and the rest laid a thick smoke-screen and turned south. Rather than split their fire the *Enterprise* and *Glasgow* concentrated their efforts on tracking down the first group and a long-range gun duel followed in difficult conditions. This continued until 1600 by which time the German flotilla leader, *Z27* and two of the smaller destroyers, *T25* and *T26* had been sunk.

Both British ships were now running low after so much long-range shooting and decided to call off the pursuit at that point. Furthermore the older *Enterprise* had begun to develop defects through the high speed of the chase and the conditions of the sea. The German bombers returned but were again ineffective and both cruisers returned to Plymouth intact on the evening of the 29th. Of the rest of the German force, four reached Brest, two the Gironde and two took refuge in St Jean de Luz. 230 survivors of the three sunken vessels were later picked up from a complement of over 600.

The table below gives some idea of just how splendid an achievement this little skirmish was for the two cruisers.

Table 17

Comparison of armaments in the Bay of Biscay action.

Type of Armament	British	German
6-inch guns	19	–
5·9-inch guns	–	25
4·1-inch guns	–	24
4-inch guns	13	–
21-inch Torpedo tubes	16	76

CHAPTER SIX

Cruisers against Aircraft

On the outbreak of war the cruisers of the Royal Navy were generally equipped with what was thought at the time to be fairly adequate, and even substantial, gunnery defence against enemy aircraft. Unlike the destroyer flotillas, in which even the most modern vessels of the 'J' and 'K' classes had virtually no anti-aircraft defence at all, the modern cruisers, constructed since the late 1920's, usually featured batteries of 4-inch HA guns from eight to ten in number. For firing long-range, controlled barrages at altitude bombers flying at steady courses which could be plotted and laid, these guns could be said to be somewhat effective, although they were never as great a deterrent as had been expected pre-war, even in these cases. For close-range work the Royal Navy relied almost totally on the re-vamped pom-pom, a multi-barrel 2-pdr gun of good hitting power but with a very restricted range and zone of fire. The main purpose of these weapons was to lay down a 'wall of explosions' in front of low-flying torpedo aircraft at a distance through which it was expected they would have to fly before releasing their missiles. Again it was a good weapon in such circumstances, but it proved of strictly limited value.

The rejection pre-war of the foreign-built light automatic cannon, the 20-mm Oerlikon and, more important, the 40-mm Bofors, proved to be one of the biggest errors the pre-war planners of Britain's defences committed. Although most foreign navies were similarly to bewail the absence of such guns in large enough numbers, and all nations under-estimated just how *many* would be required, many had made provision for these weapons, or similar ones, in their warships early on in the 1930's and were therefore much better equipped in this respect, the Germans in particular with their batteries of 37-mm cannon. A cruiser captain wrote that, pre-war, he visited the pocket battleship *Deutchland*, in the company of Admiral Sir Roger Backhouse:

... we immediately noticed the very large number of close-range weapons with which that ship was fitted. Admiral Backhouse was a gunnery officer, and he at once realised that the German Navy had a different conception of defence against air attack from that current in the Royal Navy, and he drew the Admiralty's attention to this. But war arrived before his recommendations could be fully implemented.*

The dangers inherent in the British policy were doubled by the fact that by the two Continental Axis powers initially, and later by Japanese Naval air power, it was the aircraft that was used as the weapon of attrition against the superior sea power of the Royal Navy. Thus the force the least well equipped to deal with air attacks was the same force that had to bare the brunt of such attacks against warships between 1940 and 1942. This factor was accentuated by the very nature of naval operations conducted by British forces during those three years of combat. Owing to an equal lack of appreciation of just how effective the dive bomber was against warships, British cruisers and other smaller ships were time and time again forced into the close proximity of enemy-held coasts from which these aircraft, relatively short-ranged as they were, could attack them virtually non-stop. The Royal Navy soon learned this lesson; the politicians whose decisions continued placing them in such an unenviable position, were much slower to learn, and even in 1943 in the Aegean political decisions thrust British cruisers into the same impossible situations as in 1940, and with the same fatal results.

We have seen how the arming of some of the old 'C' class cruisers was a positive step in the right direction of providing adequate anti-aircraft protection at sea, but in these cases it was mainly the provision of such defence for convoys and main fleet units that was behind the idea. Again, although the principle was sound enough, the weapons that had perforce to be used were mainly obsolete 4-inch guns left over from the first war, supplemented by pom-poms. Equally important as the weapons themselves of course was their direction, and here too the Royal Navy lagged behind the world in this crucial field. Radar, to give early warning of approach of enemy air formations, was to help later in the war, as were close-proximity fuses and the fitting of large numbers of light automatic weapons, but these most desirable features did not come until 1942 onward

* B.B. Schofield, *British Sea Power*, (Batsford, 1967), p 156.

Table 18

REPRESENTATIVE CHANGES IN CRUISER ARMAMENT – 1939 TO 1945

Armament

Ship	1939	1945
Colombo	Five 6-in (5 × 1) Two 3-in AA (3 × 1) Two 2pdr (2 × 1) Eight 21-in TT (4 × 2)	Six 4-in AA (3 × 2) Four 40mm (2 × 2) Eight 20mm (4 × 2) Two 20mm (2 × 1)
Emerald	Seven 6-in (7 × 1) Three 3-in AA (3 × 1) Two 2pdr (2 × 1) Sixteen 0·5-in (4 × 4) Sixteen 21-in TT (4 × 4)	Six 6-in (6 × 1) Three 4-in AA (3 × 1) Eight 2 pdr (2 × 4) Twelve 20mm (6 × 2) Six 20mm (6 × 1) Eight 21-in TT (2 × 4)
Cumberland	Eight 8-in (4 × 2) Eight 4-in (4 × 2) Eight 2pdr (2 × 4) Eight 0·5-in (2 × 4)	Eight 8-in (4 × 2) Eight 4-in (4 × 2) Eight 2pdr (2 × 4) Ten 20mm (5 × 2) Six 20mm (6 × 1)
Devonshire	Eight 8-in (4 × 2) Eight 4-in (8 × 1) Eight 0·5-in (2 × 4) Eight 21-in TT (2 × 4)	Six 8-in (3 × 2) Eight 4-in (4 × 2) Twenty Four 2 pdr (6 × 4) Thirty Four 20mm (17 × 2) Six 20mm (6 × 1) Eight 21-in TT (2 × 4)
Norfolk	Eight 8-in (4 × 2) Eight 4-in (4 × 2) Sixteen 2 pdr (2 × 8) Eight 0·5-in (2 × 4) Eight 21-in TT (2 × 4) Eight 6-in (4 × 2)	Six 8-in (3 × 2) Eight 4-in (4 × 2) Twenty Four 2pdr (6 × 4) Nine 40mm (9 × 1) Twenty Two 20mm (11 × 2) Eight 21-in TT (2 × 4)

Leander	Eight 4-in (4 × 2) Twelve 0·5-in (3 × 4) Eight 21-in TT (2 × 4)	Six 6-in (3 × 2) Eight 4-in (4 × 2) Eight 40mm (2 × 4) Six 20mm (3 × 2) Four 20mm (4 × 1) Eight 21-in TT (2 × 4)
Arethusa	Six 6-in (3 × 2) Four 4-in (4 × 1) Twelve 0·5-in (3 × 4) Six 21-in TT (2 × 3)	Six 6-in (3 × 2) Eight 4-in (4 × 2) Eight 2pdr (2 × 4) Eight 20mm (4 × 2) Three 20mm (3 × 1) Six 21-in TT (2 × 3)
Sheffield	Twelve 6-in (4 × 3) Eight 4-in (4 × 2) Eight 2 pdr (2 × 4) Eight 0·5-in (2 × 4) Six 21-in TT (2 × 3)	Nine 6-in (3 × 3) Eight 4-in (4 × 2) Eight 2 pdr (2 × 4) Sixteen 40mm (4 × 4) Twenty 20mm (10 × 2) Six 20mm (6 × 1) Six 21-in TT (2 × 3)

Note

Although these figures are extracted from Admiralty records, the discerning reader will know that on occasion, figures were published which did not always match up with the weapons actually fitted and furthermore, ships did undergo armament changes after publication and the only real check on accuracy is by reference to photographs printed from untouched Admiralty (MOD) negatives.

*   *   *

in most ships, far too late to prevent grievous losses in the early years of the war. Adequate fighter cover was a luxury indeed in those years, depending on both sufficient numbers of aircraft carriers, and on those carriers being equipped with high performance aircraft of the interceptor type to enable him to deal with modern land-based aircraft.

Both factors were notably absent in the early years. Six new carriers were being built, but carriers without high performance aircraft are merely large and vulnerable targets, as was shown by the crippling of the *Illustrious, Formidable* and *Indomitable,* all by Ju87 Stukas and all in the constricted waters of the Mediterranean in 1941-42. The Fleet Air Arm aircraft of the day were called upon to perform several roles in one airframe. For example the Skua was designed as a dive bomber first and a fighter second; the Fulmar was a two-seater also for navigation purposes and so on. Naturally then they could not catch, let alone cope with, modern single-engined fighters like the German Me109, the Italian Reggiane 2002 or the Japanese Zero. Even the more modern bombers of the enemy air forces such as the Junkers Ju88. could outpace them. It was not until the arrival of good and correctly designed interceptors for naval use from America, like the Grumman Hellcat and the Vought Corsair, that our naval pilots could take on the enemy in anything like equal terms. Likewise the provision of escort carriers filled the gap of the shortage of proper carriers after 1943.

Yet another factor that played its part in ensuring the combat between bomber and cruiser was a one-sided affair was the lack of adequate fire control and fire prevention facilities aboard British ships. Damage control was by no means universally efficient and it took the loss of several fine cruisers to bring this home.

Attacks on the Home Fleet (September-December 1939)

Early German aerial excursions took the form of strictly limited air attacks against Home Fleet units at Scapa Flow and in the Firth of Forth. Limited though these actions were they immediately illustrated that, even in the safety of their own harbours, British cruisers were vulnerable.

The first such raid took place on 16th October 1939 when Ju88's of I/KG 30, led by Captain Pohle, were despatched against a target in the Firth of Forth. The battle-cruiser *Hood* had been reported off Rosyth and they were to cripple her if they could. However at this early stage of the war both the British and German air forces were strictly bound by their political leaders to avoid causing civilian casualties if they could and Pohle was instructed not to attack any ship in harbour. They found the *Hood* was in dry-dock and therefore turned their attentions to the 2nd Cruiser Squadron which was anchored in the Firth itself, even though the battle-cruiser *Repulse* was present, and a more worthwhile target.

The German pilots had also been informed that no British fighters were based in the area, but, in fact, no less than three squadrons of Hurricanes and Spitfires were based nearby and warning should have been given by radar of the approach of the bombers in time for them to intercept. In the event the radar failed, the Ju88's arrived over the anchorage and commenced their 80 degree dive bombing runs before the alarm was sounded. The fighters scrambled away and eventually shot down three of the attackers but not before they had made their attacks. The AA defences destroyed a fourth.

Pohle himself dived against the *Southampton* and scored a direct hit with his 1,000-lb bomb from a release height of 3,000 feet. This bomb hit the cruiser amidships on the starboard superstructure and penetrated obliquely, cutting through three decks and emerging just above the waterline, sinking the Admiral's barge tied up alongside. The hit should have been devastating, but the bomb failed to detonate. It was an extremely lucky escape. The *Edinburgh* was near-missed by another heavy bomb and suffered splinter damage, as did the destroyer *Mohawk*.

On 16th March 1940 Scapa Flow was attacked again by three bombers. The heavy cruiser *Norfolk* was hit at 1952 in a diving attack from 7,000 feet. The bomb struck her on the port side of the quarterdeck abaft 'Y' turret, passed through three decks and exploded near 'Y' shellroom blowing a hole in the hull below the waterline and flooding both after magazines. She was under repair for three months.

These warnings were further reinforced by a similar experience which overtook the AA cruiser *Coventry* at Sullom Voe on 1st January 1940. The cruiser was anchored at the time and, initially, the German Do217 appeared harmless as it was engaged by the ship's array of 4-inch guns. But then it went into a dive and things changed rapidly, as witness this account:

Flying high and on steady course, the Dornier came in from astern, and the gunnery staff were anxious to get a convincing hit. Petty Officer Goldring, Quarters Officer of No 5 and 6 guns, situated on the raised deck in the ship's waist, was intoning the essentials of good shooting as if at a special parade on Whale Island, improving the effect with a honeyed voice that radiated encouragement. Then the enemy's nose dipped and Goldring ejaculated 'Blimey, he's going to bomb us.' Just before this, many guns had made successive reports that they were 'not bearing'. This skilful attack could now he met only by the multiple O·5 Vickers machine guns aft.

All 4-inch guns crews stood idly gaping as the grey attacker dived, watching his projecting machine guns and waiting for the Vickers to beat them to it. The Vickers spat a short burst, Chief Petty Officer Davenport saw tracers stream into the fuselage. Then two barrel-like objects, apparently chained together, left the aircraft and hurtled towards us. In my ears sounded confident voices of gunnery officer lecturers with their convincting argument about the near impossibility of a bomb hitting a moving ship. Fortunately I did not reflect that anchored, *Coventry*'s movements were restricted to slow short swings in alternative directions. Spellbound I watched the falling objects slowly nearing us, and was just conscious of the odd crouching postures assumed by idle gunners trying to use any possible cover. The chief ordinance artificer, oil can in hand, stalked as rapidly forward as his dignified status allowed. With relief I saw the falling objects splash into the Voe a few yards from the ship's side. I was about to rejoice, when *Coventry* was flung violently upwards. The deck seemed to rise and hit me in the face. Next there was a nauseating drop which tumbled me on deck. After this a deluge of salt water.*

The Norwegian Campaign (April-May 1940)

But if such attacks perturbed the Admiralty their experiences off Norway a few months later shook them badly. Here the anti-aircraft cruisers were utilised as floating AA batteries in support of the troops ashore, not their proper role, but one forced upon them by lack of proper equipment ashore. Hemmed in by the narrow sheer sides of the Norwegian fiords, miles from the sea, and with little room to take evading action, the cruisers once again had to sit and take it. Under such limitations the cruisers fired off prodigious amounts of 4-inch ammunition for little or no result, for their sighting of the enemy was only brief. On 24th April the *Curacoa* was hit and badly damaged in such an attack off Andalsnes, while on the 26th the *Curlew*, operating off Skanland, received a lethal blow when two bombs exploded below her stern knocking out her bottom. Rudderless she slewed around out of control, ran around, riding up bows high and was abandoned.

However perhaps the greatest shock came with the ordeal of the heavy cruiser *Suffolk*. She had been sent from Scapa Flow with an

* G.G.Connell, *Valiant Quartet*, (William Kimber, 1979), pp 54-55.

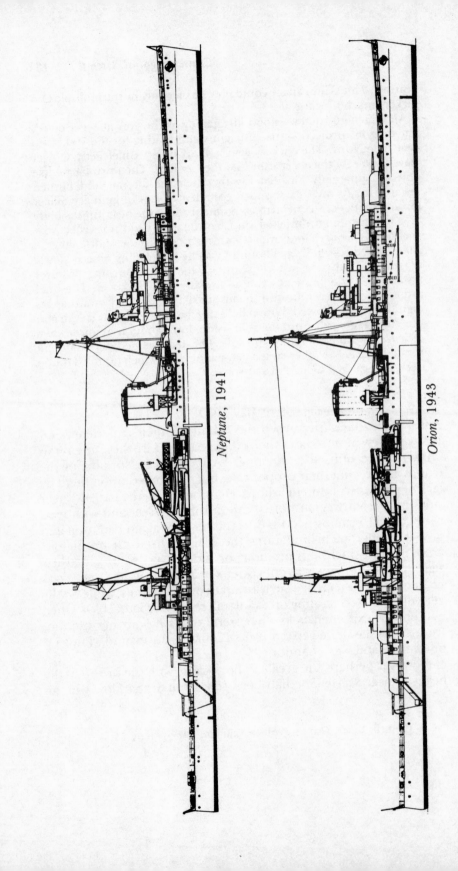

Neptune, 1941

Orion, 1943

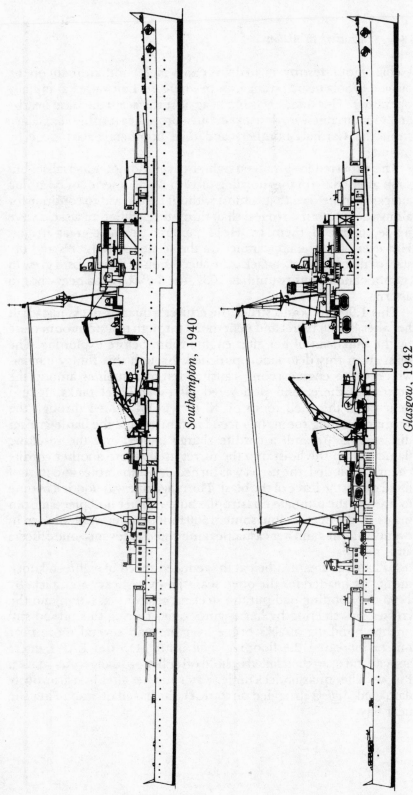

Southampton, 1940

Glasgow, 1942

escort of four destroyers, to deliver an 8-inch bombardment on the airfield of Sola near Stavanger from where the Luftwaffe was initially operating. This attack was made against the seaplane base nearby and four aircraft were destroyed, but it brought a terrible vengeance from the German bombers and dive bombers based close by inland.

The expected long-ranged fighter cover did not materialise, but soon after 0825 on the morning of 17th April, a series of bombing attacks commenced that, almost without pause, was to continue for almost seven hours. No less than thirty-three different attacks were made, many of them by He111 aircraft from a great height. However, with the appearance on the scene of the Ju88's and the start of dive bombing attacks, the succession of near misses grew in number and intensity until, at 1037, the *Suffolk* took a heavy bomb astern.

This 1,000-lb bomb struck the cruiser's quarter-deck, just abaft her after 8-inch turret and penetrated through to a storeroom close by the bulkhead of her after engine room before exploding. The blast from this detonation punched through this flimsy barrier, wrecked the engine room, causing severe casualties among the personnel there, and perforated all the oil-fuel tanks. It also penetrated the shell room of 'X' turret and vented through the cordite handling room. In a scene reminiscent of the battle-cruiser distasters at Jutland, a cordite charge ignited and the resulting flame ran up the hoist into the turret itself where another cordite change exploded; the turret was turned into a shambles and its roof lifted off by the force of the blast. The magazine was flooded in time to prevent the ultimate catastrophe but, with her hull pierced from inside by the devastation, some, 1500 tons of water were shipped in twenty minutes and her casualties amounted to seventy-one officers and men.

Still able to steam, albeit at the reduced speed of eighteen knots, the *Suffolk* headed for the open sea, still under heavy air attack. By 1305 the flooding had put the steering gear out of action and the cruiser was steering by her engines only. During this period still further bombing attacks broke over her and several more near misses increased the flooding. Not until 1415 did RAF fighters appear and even then failed to hold off still more dangerous attacks. But, with her quarter deck under water and her after hull grievously damaged, *Suffolk* struggled on to reach the haven of Scapa Flow the next day.

It was the most clear indication yet that ships designed to resist the pounding of 8-inch shells in surface actions were no match, and carried completely inadequate armour protection horizontally, for bombers with any sort of sporting chance. Nor was the *Suffolk* the only cruiser victim to fall foul of the Luftwaffe while at sea and with room to take evading action. On 19th April Ju88's from the same unit that had crippled her, II/KG.30, hit and damaged the French cruiser *Emile Bertin* off Namos.

The fact that heavy cruisers were as vulnerable as the small and old 'C' class ships and the new *Town* class 10,000 tonners when it came to air attack had already been indicated a month earlier when, in yet another raid on Scapa Flow on 16th March, the *Suffolk*'s sister ship, *Norfolk*, was damaged as described earlier, albeit by no means as seriously.

The Mediterranean Theatre (1941)
Norway taught the Royal Navy to have a healthy respect for the dive bomber, a feeling reinforced by the events off France and the Low Countries during the evacuation of the Continent, and by experience in the English Channel during July and August when many destroyers and the auxiliary AA ship *Foylebank* were summarily despatched by the short range Ju87 dive bombers. The immediate cure was to keep warships of cruiser size and upward well clear of enemy coastal waters unless heavy fighter cover could be provided, although this was by no means always possible. Nonetheless further heavy losses of the nature taken off Norway were for a time avoided in Home Waters.

Unfortunately the lessons of Norway seemed not to have been taken sufficiently to heart by other commands. In the Mediterranean area there was no place beyond the range of the Italian heavy bombers at all, but Admiral Cunningham was determined not to allow this to restrict his freedom of action, and, to his eternal credit, despite the bleatings from other officers who counselled crippling caution at all times, nor did it. Nonetheless an early indication that the massed waves of high level bombers of the *Regia Aeronautica* were well trained soon came his way.

During the operations in the central Mediterranean that led to the Battle of Calabria in July 1940, the Mediterranean Fleet was subjected to almost a week's non-stop altitude bombing. Despite a considerable expenditure of anti-aircraft gunfire, very few of these high flying bombers were damaged, let alone brought down, nor did it seem to impair their accuracy much. Fortunately this form of bombing rarely if ever achieved hits on steaming ships, but such was the scale of the attack that, if only due to eventual odds, the odd hit *was* made; in this case a direct hit was made on the bridge of the cruiser *Gloucester* on 8th July. The bomb actually hit on the cruisers compass platform, being the last one of a stick that had crept up her wake; it caused severe damage to her bridge structure and the heavily armoured Director Control Tower, killing her captain (Captain F.R.Garside), seven other officers and eleven ratings and wounding nine others. Although the *Gloucester* stayed with the fleet she had to be conned from her emergency steering position aft, and, when the surface battle commenced the next day, had to be withdrawn from taking an active part.

While it could be said that this was an isolated case the situation took on a more serious outlook with the arrival of the first German dive bomber squadrons in Sicily in January 1941. Although once more Cunningham refused to be overawed by this, his experiences in the Sicilian Channel and the near loss of the *Illustrious* to Stuka dive bomber attack on the 10th of that month reinforced the lessons of Norway very harshly indeed. During subsequent attacks on Malta harbours the light cruiser *Perth* was damaged, but again a more serious loss at sea proved to be the real turning point here as in the North Sea.

The light cruisers *Gloucester* and *Southampton*, with two destroyers, were steering eastwards on 11th January after seeing the crippled carrier safely into Valletta, and their crews were relaxed in what was assumed to be an area well out of range of the Ju87's. Thus they were caught completely by surprise when a formation of these dive bombers appeared from out of the sun and commenced their dives on both ships. The *Gloucester* was hit again in this attack, although, again fortunately, the bomb which hit her failed to explode. Her sister ship, *Southampton,* was not so lucky.

There were twelve Ju87's of II/StG2 led by Major Enneccerus, and they attacked from out of the sun. The *Gloucester* was struck as before on the bridge structure; the Director Control Tower roof was hit fair and square and the ship suffered nine killed and fourteen wounded. *Southampton* was hit twice in this attack: one bomb penetrated the officers' wardroom, the other the petty officers' messdeck; both were crowded with these valuable personnel at tea and losses were severe. The explosions soon started raging fires which could not be brought under control and just after 1900 the order was given to abandon ship. The blazing wreck was sunk by torpedoes at 2050 by *Orion*.

Quite why the cruisers imagined themselves to be in a relatively safe zone is hard to understand. The Ju87 dive bombers that attacked them were fitted with long-range fuel tanks to be sure, which extended their area of operations somewhat, but these self-same aircraft had used them freely in the Norwegian Campaign; so their attack should not have been unexpected, especially as the *Southampton* herself took part in that campaign. Whatever the reason it was a shock that such a modern vessel could succumb so easily to air attack. Neither cruiser was fitted with radar at the time.

The most feared and expected form of aerial attack, mass attacks by torpedo bombers, fortunately did not feature much in the initial stages of the war. Although the ships themselves were better equipped to deal with such low-flying aircraft than the plunging dive bombers, the effect of torpedo hits below the waterline was obviously feared as more likely to be fatal than bomb hits in the superstructure. The reason this form of attack did not cause more damage than it did was that the Axis airmen had very few of these types of aircraft on hand in 1940-41. Indeed the Luftwaffe was almost totally deficient save for a few floatplanes. The *Regia Aeronautica* had devoted more study to the problem, of course, and the Royal Navy was obviously one of their main opponents, but even so had only relatively few of their most modern bombers, including the three-engined Sm79's converted for this purpose in the summer of 1940. Intense training took place as squadrons were adapted for this work, and indeed some of the most famous Italian air aces made their reputations and names from subsequent missions against the Mediterranean Fleet. The Germans were forced to follow much of the Italian methods adapting them to their own requirements with their He111 and Ju88 aircraft similarly adapted, and, by 1942, the Luftwaffe had at its disposal a most formidable torpedo bomber force.*

What they lacked in numbers in 1940-41 the Italian torpedo bomber pilots made up for in skill and daring. The operations of such aircraft obviously required careful organisation, and thus dusk attacks were particularly favoured, with the aircraft creeping in low over the sea to surprise the ships and then dropping at long range before being sighted. It required especial vigilance to detect

*; See *Arctic Victory*, Peter C Smith (William Kimber, 1975) for the full story.

such aircraft and, all too often, that vigilance was not exercised. The tally of British cruisers damaged by Sm79 attacks soon grew to quite large proportions, and has been largely ignored to date.

The first victim was the heavy cruiser *Kent*, which had only just joined Cunningham's command, having been detached from the main fleet to carry out a shelling of Bardia after an attack on Benghazi. She was attacked by Sm79's and hit in the stern by one torpedo. Only with the greatest difficulty did her escorting destroyer tow her back to Alexandria on 15th September 1940. The attack had taken place by moonlight and the cruiser's propellers were completely wrecked.

The next victim was the *Liverpool* which was returning to Alexandria after operations against the Italians in the Aegean with the main fleet. On the evening of the 14th October 1940, in the twilight, Sm79's approached the fleet and were met by a heavy barrage. Despite this the *Liverpool* took a torpedo hit right forward in her bows. Although the damage was slight the explosion triggered off a fire which spread first to a petrol tank, then to the foremost magazine. The resulting explosion tore a huge gash in her hull foward and her bows were left hanging from just before the bridge. For a time it seemed as if she must be lost for, presenting as she did a sitting target to the other torpedo bombers roaming around, she seemed doomed. Fortunately she escaped further damage and, taken in tow by the stern by the *Orion,* and protected by the *Calcutta* and *Coventry*, she was brought safely home, despite anxious moments as the towline parted and her bows finally fell off. She left for repairs in America much later.

Last was her sister ship, *Glasgow*. She was anchored in Suda Bay, Crete, on 3rd December 1940. Two Sm79's attacked down through the entrance of the bay and achieved complete surprise. They dropped their torpedoes at a range of some three thousand yards, and not until they had done so did any gun aboard the ships open fire. Two hit the *Glasgow* and damaged her badly. Fortunately the cruiser was still able to steam at sixteen knots, and she too was brought back to Alexandria, patched up, and sailed for more permanent repairs in February 1941.

Serious though the damage to these three fine ships was, no further losses took place from air attack until political circumstances again thrust the cruisers close inshore to enemy held-territory and forced them to battle it out with the dive bombers once more, again completely unsupported from the air. This took place in May during the evacuation of Crete and this time casualties were far more severe. In fact, for a time, the cruiser force of the Mediterranean fleet was almost totally decimated.

The evacuation of the British Army from the beaches of Crete was a very different affair from the Dunkirk episode of 1940. There the destroyers had done the bulk of the work and the beaches were larger and the distances to convey the troops small. Almost constant air patrols could be provided, even if in some instances they were inadequate to prevent heavy losses. But at Crete the distance from Alexandria was formidable, no smaller vessels in any numbers were available to supplement the lift from the beaches to the larger ships and the cruisers were not only called upon to embark the troops, but initially to provide striking forces to intercept Axis convoys. This meant operating north of Crete, within easy range of the Ju87's and the fighter bombers of the Fw190 type, as well as the long range aircraft, and during daylight hours almost non-stop bombing took place against every force involved. Such was the scale of air attack that could be mounted that anti-aircraft ammunition was soon used up and cruisers were sent in practically defenceless against a non-stop shuttle of bombers.

Under such impossible circumstances then, it is hardly surprising that the cruisers took such heavy punishment. Although not denying the achievements of the German dive bomber crews, who grasped this heaven-sent opportunity with vigour, the odds were very much against the cruisers in this disastrous encounter.

It was on 21st May that the first full-scale confrontation began. A striking force under Admiral Glennie, consisting of the *Dido* (flag), *Ajax, Orion* and four destroyers had swept north of the Antikithera Channel the previous night and was withdrawing towards Canea and rendezvous with the battleships under Admiral Rawlings. A second striking force, Force 'C' under Admiral King, the cruisers *Naiad* (flag), *Carlisle* and *Perth*, with four destroyers, had made a similar foray in the Kaso Strait towards Heraklion, while Force 'B', the cruisers *Gloucester* and *Fiji*, were on their way from Alexandria to join the main force under Admiral Rawlings. With the approach of daylight these groups were all quickly located by the Luftwaffe and the attacks began in earnest, but initially the only cruiser casualty was the *Ajax* which was near-missed and took some casualties from splinters.

Thus the two cruiser striking forces moved back north of Crete that night still relatively unharmed, but with stocks of AA ammunition

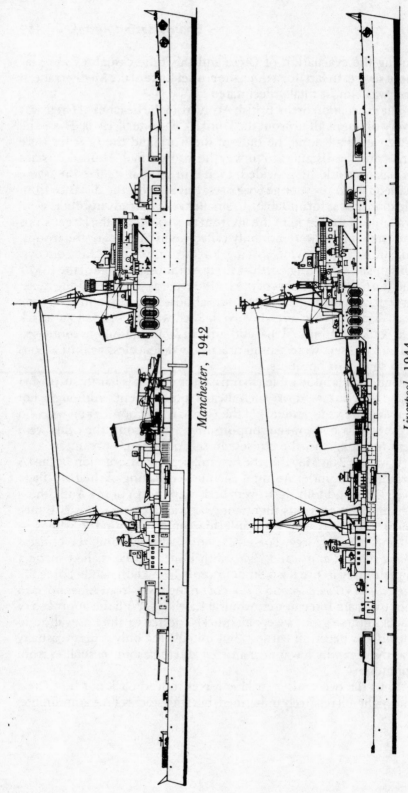

Manchester, 1942

Liverpool, 1944

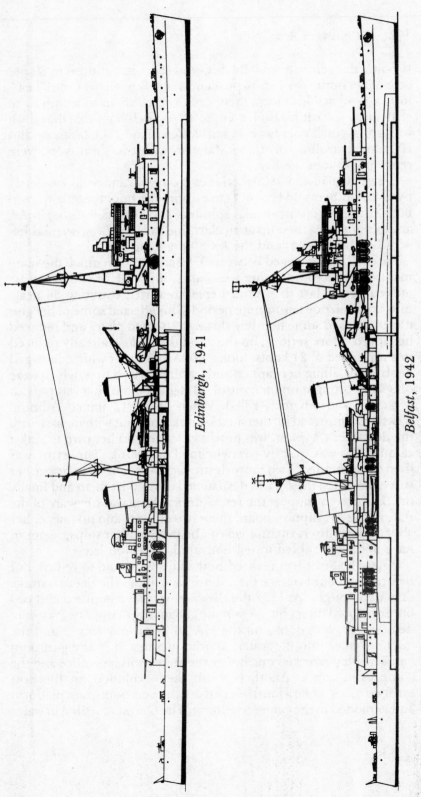

Edinburgh, 1941

Belfast, 1942

running dangerously low. By this time *Dido* was reduced to 30 per cent of her outfit, *Orion* to 38 per cent and *Ajax* to 42 per cent. The C-in-C ashore at Alexandria therefore ordered them to withdraw to replenish. The withdrawal of Force 'C' was delayed while they dealt with some small enemy vessels off Milos island. The *Gloucester* and *Fiji*, after patrolling off Cape Matapan with two destroyers, were returning to join the flag.

Between 0630 and 0800 this latter group was attacked ceaselessly by dive bombers and was lucky to escape with but minor damage to both cruisers from near miss splinters and concussion. Again AA ammunition was used up at an alarming rate; the *Gloucester* was left with but 18 per cent and the *Fiji* 30 per cent.

Force 'C' was engaged between 0700 and 1335 in much the same manner while withdrawing westwards, the scale of which can be judged by the fact that *Naiad* herself reported counting 36 near-misses within one ten-minute period. This affected some of her gun turrets, caused some flooding through strained plates and reduced her speed. More serious, on the 22nd the *Carlisle*, already reduced to a top speed of 21 knots, took a heavy bomb hit which damaged her bridge, killing her captain and starting serious fires, which were only later brought under control. 'B' 4-inch mounting was put out of action and ten men killed. When Force 'C' joined Admiral Rawlings command further attacks took place but with no loss until the destroyer *Greyhound* was unwisely sent off on her own to sink a caique. She was quickly overwhelmed and sunk. This error was then compounded. Two more destroyers were sent off to rescue her survivors. Then the *Fiji* was despatched to support them and finally the *Gloucester* to support the rest. Admiral King was unaware of the state of the AA supply aboard these two cruisers and no one, either aboard the cruisers themselves or aboard the other ships, seems to have initially troubled to tell him until it was too late.

When the error was realised both ships were told to return, but before they could retrace their steps back under the fleet's barrage they were caught. At 1527 the *Gloucester* was dive bombed and two bombs scored direct hits. Again the gallant ship's upperworks were demolished; one bomb hit the HA Director knocking it and the main topmast into the water, another detonated in the gunroom flat. The blast wrecked one boiler room, the wireless office and the compressor room. Another bomb then exploded on the port torpedo tubes while a fourth wiped out the port pom-pom platform and exploded in the canteen below it. The *Gloucester* settled in water ablaze and a series of explosions around 1545 marked her end. She took on a heavy list to port and was abandoned. After lying over at an acute angle for some time and still subjected to further attacks, she turned turtle at 1715 and went down by the stern. There were very few survivors.

The *Fiji* did not long outlast her. Closing the battle fleet at 27 knots she was still some thirty miles away when a solitary Me 109 *Jabo* (fighter bomber) hit her close alongside to port amidships. The explosion blew the bottom out of the ship and as the water flooded into her boilers, she too, heeled over to port with a 25 degree list, her speed reduced to 17 knots. For half an hour she stayed thus, then a passing Stuka put her out of her misery with a three-bomb salvo, all of which hit her, bringing down her foremast. The list increased another ten degrees and she was abandoned, finally rolling over and going down at 2015.

When the decision was taken to evacuate the Crete garrison, the surviving undamaged cruisers were again sent in to face the dive bombers alone. First to feel their fury was Force 'B' under Admiral Rawlings, with the *Orion*(flag), *Ajax* and *Dido,* with six destroyers. They were ordered to sea on 28th May to pick up the Heraklion soldiers and bring them away to Egypt. While still some ninety miles from Scarpanto they were caught by the Luftwaffe, who attacked them until nightfall. Ten attacks were made, of all kinds. The *Ajax* was the first casualty; a near miss bomb damaged some side plates and started a small fire. Despite the fact that this was not too serious, *Ajax* was sent back to Alexandria.

The rest of the force continued under cover of darkness to carry out the evacuation, and then, with their 'tween decks crowded with troops, steered back to Alexandria and awaited the coming of daylight and the renewed enemy assault they knew must come. It did. Attacks started as early as 0600 and continued almost without a break for nine hours. At 0735 Ju87's machine-gunned the *Orion*, killing her captain, and scored a near miss which reduced her speed to 21 knots. At 0815 another Stuka attack resulted in eight near misses which shook the *Dido*'s hull and these were followed by a ninth bomb which hit her atop 'B' turret. This hit was described by an observer in one of the escorting destroyers:

A great sphere of black smoke burst out from ahead of her bridge and a single stick-like object curled up into the air and dropped smoking into the sea. It was one of her guns from a fore turret. Then she seemed to come steaming out of the blackness like a miracle and she was engaging aircraft with her after guns, and one gun missing from B turret with its twin bent nearly double.*

The Royal Marines' mess deck was wrecked by this explosion, and, crowded as it was with soldiers, the carnage was ghastly: 27 sailors and 19 soldiers killed, 10 sailors and 28 soldiers wounded.

The Ju87's were back at 0900 and this time it was the *Orion* which took a direct hit, this time atop her 'A' turret. The armoured top was peeled back and the turret wiped out while 'B' turret was also severely damaged. A near miss followed half an hour later, and then at 1045 a Stuka planted another bomb in her bridge structure. This bomb carved through her upperworks, sliced through the sick bay bathroom and exploded deep inside her in her packed stokers' mess deck. In that crowded confined space the carnage was indescribable. 107 sailors and 155 soldiers were killed and 84 sailors and 216 soldiers were wounded, some horribly, by this one bomb. Wreathed in smoke and flame, her bridge decimated, three of her boilers out of action, steering gear damaged and out of control, the *Orion* slewed round back towards Kaso for a time before her course to safety was resumed.

The battered squadron finally reached Alexandria at 2000 that evening. *Orion* had two rounds of her 6-inch ammunition left to her and ten tons of oil fuel. As Admiral Cunningham was later to record: 'I shall never forget the sight of those ships coming up harbour, the guns of the fore-turrets awry, one or two broken off and pointing forlornly skyward, their upper decks crowded with troops, and the marks of their ordeal only too plainly visible.'†

A second force was despatched to Crete despite this carnage: Force 'D' under Admiral King comprised the cruisers *Phoebe* (flag), *Perth, Calcutta* and *Coventry,* with a personnel ship and three destroyers. They picked up troops from Sfakia on the night of the 29th/30th and left for Alexandria. They were joined by three more destroyers at 0645 that morning. The Luftwaffe were not long in arriving.

At 0930 the *Perth* was hit by a heavy bomb just abaft her bridge. This bomb penetrated down to her foremost boiler room before detonating, killing four seamen and nine soldiers. Another attack

* Hugh Hodgkinson, *Before the Tide Turned* (Harrap, 1944).
† Cunningham of Hyndhope, *A Sailor's Odyssey* (Hutchinson, 1951).

resulted in a near miss on the same ship, but that was the limit of their ordeal.

The next night another force was sent out, the cruiser *Phoebe* and the minelayer *Abdiel* with three destroyers. On their return they were met by the AA cruisers *Calcutta* and *Coventry*. At 0900 radar detected incoming enemy formations and at 0913 two Ju88's dived out of the sun on the two cruisers. Both ships were taken by surprise by these attacks, which is inexplicable, and *Calcutta* was sunk. Two bombs struck her in the after boiler room and engine spaces and blew out the bottom of the ancient little vessel. She sank at 0920; 23 officers and 232 ratings were rescued by *Coventry*.

Loss of Dorsetshire and Cornwall, (April 1942)

It hardly needed the tragic losses off Crete to reinforce the fact that dive bombers could sink cruisers, even the most modern ones. In the Mediterranean as in the North Sea, the choice was, while the RAF did not provide air cover and the Fleet Air Arm was unable to do so, either to accept the risks or to stay clear of them. In the Central Mediterranean certain areas were labelled 'Stuka Sanctuaries', areas thought to be beyond the range of the Ju87; they were very limited indeed however and to supply Malta cruisers had to run the gauntlet along with their merchant ship charges and the destroyer escorts, and sometimes even the heavy ships were risked. In the North Sea and Atlantic most cruisers operated out of range of these aircraft. But what could you do if you came up against an enemy fleet that brought its own dive bombers with it? And dive bombers as well trained and accurate, if not more so, as the German Stukas? The answer to that question was found almost one year exactly after Crete, in the warm and hitherto little troubled waters of the Indian Ocean.

Here a scratch fleet had been built up to counter the Japanese expansion which had followed Pearl Harbor and the loss of the *Prince of Wales* and *Repulse*. With the bulk of South-East Asia lost as a result of this, India itself seemed under threat and Admiral Somerville was given five old battleships, two carriers with a complement of obsolete and outdated biplanes as their striking force, and an assortment of cruiser and destroyers with which to stop them if he could. In April the Japanese Admiral Nagumo sortied into the Indian Ocean to smash this force and damage its bases at Trincomalee and Colombo in Ceylon (Sri Lanka). He had six big carriers filled with modern aircraft and a balanced and completely integrated backing force with which to do it. Fortunately Admiral Somerville's main fleet never came into contact with this powerful array of naval power, but two of his heavy cruisers, *Cornwall* and *Dorsetshire*, were not so fortunate.

Admiral Somerville had deployed his fleet early to counter the expected Japanese incursion into the Indian Ocean, but, after waiting for several days and using up fuel and water, he was forced to withdraw to Addu Atoll, his secret fleet base, to replenish. Unfortunately for him no sooner had he begun to do this than the Nagumo force appeared and inflicted heavy casualties on dockyard installations and ships at Colombo and Trincomalee. Seldom has a fleet commander been caught more on the wrong foot than Somerville was in April 1942. He hastily sailed his fast ships leaving the slower group to follow. It was perhaps fortunate for him that he again failed to make contact for he could have thus been destroyed piecemeal. But this did not stop further heavy losses. He had already divided his command further, despatching the small carrier *Hermes* to ferry aircraft to Australia, and his only two 8-inch cruisers, *Dorsetshire* and *Cornwall* to Colombo.

The *Dorsetshire* badly needed refitting. She had commenced this at Colombo at the end of March but had hurriedly ceased when the first alarm had been raised. Now that it was felt that alarm might have been false, she was sent back there to re-commence this at once. The *Cornwall* accompanied her as she was allocated as convoy protection for a troop convoy, SU4, carrying Australian soldiers back to their homeland from the Middle East. The two cruisers arrived at Colombo on the afternoon of 4th April. No sooner had they commenced to refit and were ready to embark additional anti-aircraft guns and other equipment than the warning was again raised and they were once more told to drop everything and rejoin Somerville at top speed. By 2000 they had cleared harbour once more and headed towards the rendezvous which was expected at 1600 next day.

Early on Easter Sunday both ships detected shadowing aircraft on their radar plots but were not unduly concerned at this. In the first instance they felt themselves to be beyond the effective range of any Japanese carrier aircraft and in the second they hoped that fighter cover from Somerville's carriers would be over them by at the latest, 1400 that day. Nonetheless both ships went to action stations with gun crews closed up in readiness.

In fact they were under an illusion. Some eight Val dive bombers had been launched from the Japanese carriers against them, under the command of Lieutenant Commander Takashige Egusa, the dive bombing ace who had led the attack on Pearl Harbor the previous December. So confident were the Japanese that no fighters were sent to escort them. This great mass of aircraft was picked up on the cruisers' radar screens soon after 1300, with more than an hour before the expected Fleet Air Arm protection was due to arrive. A wireless report was made to Somerville warning him of the fact that the cruisers might be attacked soon from the air, but it was never received.

There then followed a brief, and totally efficient demonstration of the effectiveness of the dive bomber at sea. Splitting into two groups Egusa's aircraft attacked both cruisers with overwhelming force and incredible accuracy. From the outset the ship's gunners had no chance; the Japanese dive bombers attacked from ahead in an endless line, on which bearing of course most of the broadside mounted AA weapons were 'wooded' and unable to take any effective part in protecting the ships.

The first bomb struck the *Dorsetshire* (Captain A. Agar, VC), on her aircraft catapult, destroying the nearby pom-pom mounting. Successive hits followed almost immediately and without pause; the cruiser took bombs on her W/T hut and bridge, in her engine room and boiler rooms. The ship's steering was jammed hard to starboard by these hits and numerous near misses and she circled until she ran to a halt. A further hit penetrated one of the ship's magazines which detonated. Within a mere eight minutes of the commencement of the attack the *Dorsetshire* was sinking by the stern.

Nor was the *Cornwall* (Captain P.C.W.Manwaring) to survive her by any length of time. It was at 1340 that the first wave bore down on her and immediately she was hit by a large bomb on her port side astern. This hit was quickly followed by others despite a violent turn to starboard. Many of her anti-aircraft guns were destroyed by hits and near misses in these terrible moments. In all the *Cornwall* was hit by about fifteen bombs in the space of seven minutes, such was the precision of the Japanese airmen. She listed hard over to port and sank, bows first. The survivors from both ships spent many ghastly hours in the water before rescued by the *Enterprise* much later.

The Japanese later noted that the destruction of these two cruisers was much simpler to effect than their pre-war training attacks against the old target ship *Settsu*! And it was achieved without the loss of a single dive bomber. It is interesting to note that although much time and effort had been put into the 8-inch gun pre-war to give it an elevation capable of engaging aircraft at long range, and although *Dorsetshire* had an additional nine single 20-mm Oerlikons fitted, all seemed equally unavailing against dive bombing from ahead. This was such a common feature (the Ju87's in the Mediterranean used the same technique) that later in the war a few of the *Dido* class had one forward turret removed and a multiple pom-pom or 40-mm mountings in its place which combated just this threat.

Other losses

Three more British cruisers were to be sunk by dive bombers before the war ended despite such improvements and the mounting of further 20-mm cannon as they became available; two of them were specially converted AA ships. The *Trinidad* was sunk by Ju88's in the Arctic, after being damaged in action against German destroyers earlier during a convoy action. One of the *Fiji* class, her AA weaponry consisted of the standard eight 4-inch and eight pom-poms, which had been supplemented by no less than sixteen 0·5-inch machine guns and two 20-mm Oerlikons by the time of her loss of 15th May 1942, barely a month after the two County ships had gone.

A factor in the loss of such modern ships by bombing was thought to have been their lack of reserve stability to compensate for damage in action. In *Trinidad*'s case she did not sink right away but after many hours of struggle she had to be abandoned and was put down by a torpedo from one of her escorting destroyers. Since her designed features consisted of a light displacement of 8,668 tons on completion, itself well over the original specification of 8,130 tons, and this had been increased by the many additions since then to a standard displacement of 8,821 tons and a deep displacement of 11,086 tons, it is easy to see that this could be so.

The next loss was also in 1942 and rounded off an appalling year at sea. The *Coventry* was sent to support an ignominious failure at Tobruk, was pounced on by Stukas and was sunk very quickly indeed, on 14th September of that year. The *Coventry* (Captain R.J.R.Dendy) had shipped an additional five 20-mm Oerlikons the previous May to add to her already formidable AA weaponry. She also had fighter direction facilities and radar warning of the attack.

Beaufighters were overhead. Despite this the fifteen dive bombers of III/StG3, under Leutnant Göbel, achieved a quick and clean-cut kill before most of the guns even opened fire. Attacking from out of the sun, the Ju87's scored hits which blew off the cruiser's bow as far as 'A' gun while other hits wrecked the engine and boiler rooms. Another attack scored a direct hit under the bridge which destroyed the W/T and radar offices and the lower conning position. She was abandoned and sunk by a torpedo from the *Zulu*, which was herself attacked and sunk a short while later.

The Aegean Campaign (September-October 1943)
Much the same fate overtook the *Carlisle* more than a year later during the Aegean campaign. Despite the elapse of thirty months during which time AA weaponry, radar and fighter direction had improved beyond anything known by the Navy at the time of Crete in those self-same waters, the results of the self-same kind of duel-cruisers against Ju87's – were almost the same. During this campaign the cruiser *Penelope* was damaged by a direct hit which failed to explode and by several near-misses on 7th October, after an attack by eighteen Stukas. Two days later the *Carlisle* was set on by dive bombers of the same unit, based on Rhodes, II/StG3, which again achieved complete surprise. How could this be?

USAAF Lightning fighters were patrolling overhead in waves, but one wave failed to arrive at this critical juncture. Their display of their identifying IFF (Identification Friend or Foe) signals had been intermittent, which led to some confusion aboard the ships of whether approaching formations were in fact fighters come to guard them or enemy bombers. The radar screens were playing up, for the nearby land masses of the islands were interfering with the display and causing blurring echoes. All this led to a fatal delay in identifying the Stukas for what they were and the dive bombers made quick use of it.

Quickly going into their attack dives, they sank the destroyer *Panther* with direct hits that cut her in two, but the bulk of attackers concentrated on *Carlisle*. Two bombs hit her close together on, or close by, her number four mounting, wrecking it and distorting her quarterdeck. Two more bombs with delayed action fuses then hit her in almost the same spot, plunging right through the ship and detonating under water, blowing in her starboard side plating and framing, fracturing her stern casing and flooding the after magazines, oil fuel tanks and steering compartments. Two more bombs were near misses on the starboard side abreast Number Three gun and the after boiler room. The starboard tail shaft and propeller were blown off and the port shaft bracket was buckled. The HA Directors and W/T equipment was damaged by the shock, there was extensive splinter damage on her upperworks and a cordite fire was started aft. Only two guns were left in action.

She was finally towed into Alexandria but was considered to be beyond repair. However this was not the end of the matter. For every cruiser sunk by air attack many more were damaged and the Aegean debacle was no exception. On the 17th the *Sirius* was caught by Ju88's of LG1 and a 250-lb bomb hit her quarter deck abaft 'Y' gun. It blew a hole twenty feet in diameter in her upper deck and started a fire in the Oerlikon magazines. One 20-mm mount was destroyed and the two after 5·25-inch turrets damaged. The rest of the four bomb stick were near misses along her port side, throwing her over on her side and putting out of action her main aerials, torpedo tubes and radar sets.

The *Aurora* suffered the same fate on 30th October. Again it was the Ju87's of II/StG3, reported decimated in the earlier attacks, that did the damage. Fourteen Stukas broke through the air patrol over the ships and made no mistakes. The *Aurora* was hit by a 500-lb delayed-action bomb just abaft her after funnel on the after conning position, which was destroyed. Her main battery of 4-inch AA guns took the full blast effect from this bomb; P1 mounting was wrecked and the other three mountings, both funnels, the port pom-pom, three Oerlikon mountings, the after Director, the port torpedo tubes and the radar sets and aerials were all put out of action. Ready-use ammunition and Oerlikon ammunition ignited and under a heavy pall of smoke all the after guns, including the 6-inch mount, fell silent. 46 officers and men were killed and 20 wounded. She reached Alexandria but was out of action for many months.

The sinking of the Spartan (29th January 1944)
Perhaps the worst form of attack from the air that the cruiser had to face was the guided missile which made its debut during the latter years of World War II. The weapon first appeared at the Salerno landings in September 1943; it was a radio-controlled bomb, the FX-1400, or *Fritz X*.

A specially converted unit, *Kampfgeschwader 100,* commanded by Major Bernhard Jope, was formed. They used converted Dornier bombers, the Do217K-2, to carry two of these stubby little missiles under the wings. The modified bomber had a longer wingspan to enable it to climb above 20,000 feet. At such heights the bombers were immune from AA fire, and even at bomb release height (18,000 feet) only the Lightning aircraft of the USAAF had the ability to catch them. Once launched the bomb was controlled straight to its target, reaching a terminal velocity of 800 feet per second and making any attempt at avoidance useless. They naturally had great penetrating power and the armour of even the most modern and well-built battleships was no proof against them at all. This was proved by the sinking of the Italian battleship *Roma* by one such weapon which penetrated a magazine. The battleship *Warspite* was hit by one which penetrated every deck and went out through her keel. She took on 5,000 tons of water and was towed out of action. The wonder is that cruisers hit by this weapon survived at all. Off Salerno the US cruisers *Philadelphia* and *Savannah* were both hit and seriously damaged and, on 11th September, the British cruiser *Uganda* was hit by one. So badly was she damaged by it that she had to be towed to Malta. Repairs in the USA and Britain followed but she was out of the war, for she was not completed and ready for sea until June 1945.

All that could be done by way of defence against such weapons was to fit out special ships with equipment to listen in on the enemy wavelengths and hope to jam the transmissions of the controlling aircraft. Three ships of this type were included in the Anzio invasion fleet but they were not yet efficient enough to guarantee success. Thus it was at dusk when Jope's crews made their attacks they were able to score a direct hit on a Liberty Ship, *Samuel Huntington*, which blew up, and the light cruiser *Spartan*. Roger Hill in the destroyer *Grenville* had come up against these weapons in the Bay of Biscay and his answer was to go to full speed directly 'Tiptree' was signalled, which meant radio controlled bombs were being used. He had every radio set switched on to full power with a special signal being sent continuously on the main set, 'the Chief Gunner's Mate hammering out "Bollocks" . . . '* Such tactics might have helped save his ship, but the *Spartan* was at anchor and stood no chance. She was hit and capsized with heavy loss of life.

Another destroyer skipper has described her last moments:

We were only a few cables away from *Spartan* when she was hit; it was a

* Hill, Roger, *Destroyer Captain* (Kimber, 1975)

glider-bomb, and I watched it descend like a comet relentlessly guided onto its target by the parent aircraft. It hit the cruiser amidships, and at once a large fire broke out. I could hardly believe it, yet the next morning it was only too true. There she lay, keel up in shallow water like a great stranded whale. It seemed astonishing that a single bomb amidships could have sunk her so quickly. I felt sick and angry at the enemy's success.*

Apart from the losses, the list of cruisers damaged by air attack is a long one: *Aurora, Birmingham, Cleopatra, Coventry, Delhi, Dido, Manchester, Norfolk, Orion, Penelope, Sirius, Suffolk,* and *York.* Unluckiest perhaps was the heavy cruiser *Sussex* which was in dock at Glasgow undergoing a refit on the night of 18th September 1940; she was hit in the blitz of that city by the Luftwaffe and was two years under repair. *Delhi* was hit and damaged in a similar way on 20th November 1942, while at Algiers. *Manchester* was hit by a torpedo bomber while covering a Malta convoy from Gibraltar on 23rd July 1941. She was repaired only to be torpedoed by an E-boat covering another Malta Convoy in August 1942, when she had to be scuttled. *Penelope* was so covered with plugged up holes from bomb splinters while operating from Malta in 1942 that she was dubbed HMS 'Pepperpot' by her crew. *York* had already been damaged badly at Suda Bay, Crete, by an Italian explosive motor boat and was already a wreck, but could have been salvaged given time. The invasion of that island denied her that and the Stukas finished her off with bombs.

So far we have only examined the debit side of the coin. All warships suffered heavily from lack of sufficient AA guns during the early years of the war. Whereas battleships could rely on their heavy armour protection to save them and destroyers on high speed and zig-zagging, cruisers were in the middle. They had better defence than the destroyers, but less speed to avoid attacks; they had a smaller target area than a battleship, but lacked protection and resilience. Considering how they were used in the face of over-whelming enemy air strength it could be considered that they stood up well and the surprise may be that losses were not heavier.

And they were not completely defenceless. Many gave as good as they got. The little 'C' class AA conversions were in the thick of the fight, especially in the Mediterranean and certainly earned their keep. The deterrent effect of their guns almost certainly saved many

* Donald, William, *Stand by for Action* (Kimber, 1956)

a merchantman under their care. Likewise the *Didos* with their dual-purpose guns were indispensable in that area and for a period, constituted the Royal Navy's heaviest ships against the full strength of the Italian battle-fleet and the Luftwaffe combined. Most of the modern cruisers had good long-range AA capability, and, once they learned to watch for it, could stand up to orthodox torpedo bombing with a good chance of success. What no cruiser could cope with was dive bombing.

Improvements were constant to both short-range AA weaponry, radars, damage control and other relevant equipment, but such improvements paid the price in decreased stability, which became critical when the ship was damaged and led to unnecessary losses. Fighter cover from carriers was the most desirable protection and, with it, things improved. Shore-based protection from RAF fighters was not much use, as proved by *Suffolk* early on, reinforced by such actions as Operation Pedestal in 1942, and emphasised by the Aegean Campaign in 1943. RAF pilots just did not have the expertise to operate over ships at sea. Fighters overhead are useless if they do not intercept the bombers and improved fighter-direction equipment was mounted on cruisers during the war in an attempt to overcome this.

The torpedo bomber could be defeated by heavy barrages, as the *Scylla* proved during Arctic Convoys like PQ18. Blind, fixed barrages at night defeated many later attempts in the Mediterranean in 1943 and 1944 and this threat was made almost impotent by the loss ratio of the aircraft involved. Altitude bombing was never very effective, although the *Gloucester* suffered severely, but no solution that was one hundred per cent effective was ever found against determined dive bombing. The ultimate in manned bombing attack was the Kamikaze; fortunately for the Royal Navy the brunt of these attacks fell upon the American Navy, who, although far better equipped than Royal Navy ships to withstand them, suffered heavily indeed. The *Australia* was the main victim of these manned-missiles. Against the true missiles like *Fritz X*, there was little or no defence.

The introduction of the proximity fuse made all anti-aircraft fire far more effective of course, but for most of the war a direct hit was necessary to bring down an aircraft and to achieve this was very difficult, given the primitive HA/DF equipment of the time. Even so some ships made a good showing. How to compute which ship from a fleet of fifty or so all firing at the same group of aircraft brought down an individual aircraft is impossible to state with any accuracy. But conservative estimates *were* made. In all British cruisers were credited with the destruction of 97 enemy aircraft in World War II. By far and away the most accurate cruiser in terms of planes knocked down was the old *Carlisle*, which was credited with the destruction of no less than eleven aircraft. As a group the 'C' class conversions were given a total of 31, almost a third of the whole total of cruiser kills, while the *Didos* had fifteen between them, seven being the highest score, while among conventional cruisers *Penelope*'s seven was the best result.

One of the problems was AA ammunition stowage aboard these relatively small vessels. Supply was always exceeded by demand and many ships loaded far more than designated capacity before major operations and accepted the risks.

Perhaps the most telling thing about the many cruisers versus aircraft duels that punctuated World War II was the enormous effect of just one bomb burst compared with that sustained by a shell hit. Cruisers were manifestly unable to absorb the damage wrought by a single 500-lb bomb exploding topside even though they were designed pre-war to take 8-inch shell hits and go on fighting. The crews of the open-shielded 4-inch AA batteries were particularly vulnerable to splinters and blast, as in the case of the *Aurora*. One cannot help but feel that the fully-enclosed 5-inch mounts featured by the US Navy gave their crews far more protection in this area than the Royal Navy's standard weapons. On the other hand the completely open mountings, like the old 4-inch that equipped the early 'C' class conversions, were often preferred by the gunners themselves as they had greater fields of fire and gave the feeling that at least one gun would be able to shoot back no matter what angle the enemy approached.

All-in-all though, remembering that anti-aircraft defence was almost always the *secondary* consideration of most British pre-war cruiser designs, the cruisers of the Royal Navy came through an intensive period of attrition creditably, although it must be remembered that their deadliest opponents, the Ju87 dive bombers of the Luftwaffe, were themselves not specially trained anti-shipping units like the Japanese Navy pilots, but included warship busting merely as one of their many roles, the chief of which was always close support of the Army ashore. Such specialised units as were later formed, like the Ju88's of LG1 in the Mediterranean, were formidable opponents for any cruiser to take on unaided.

CHAPTER SEVEN

Cruisers and Army Co-Operation

It is doubtful whether much consideration, if any, was given before the war to the usefulness of the new multi-gunned cruisers in the role of supporting the army ashore. Yet shore bombardment in support of troop landings had long been a recognised skill. The maritime strategy of the Napoleonic Wars had seen frigates, the lineal forebears of cruisers, often engaged in this vital work. In Victorian days and the era of gunboat diplomacy, supporting landing detachments of Royal Marines and seamen with light weapons, like Gatling guns, to subdue the enemy. Typical examples of this type of support can be found in the Suakim Expedition and the Nile Campaigns of 1884-5 and, on the more normal smaller scale, the Peking Uprising and the Benin Expedition of the early 1900's. More heavy support could be provided, many hundreds of miles from salt water, with the landing of naval guns, as in the Boer Wars when the Navy's guns were sometimes the only decent artillery our forces possessed in out-of-the-way places.

The more traditional gunfire support given direct from the warships themselves anchored at sea had taken place in the same period. The bombardment of Alexandria is the best-known example of this, and the Navy had followed this type of work up in the Great War at the Dardanelles and off the Flanders Coast. But there had not been a great demand for it. This is not surprising when it is realised that the war of 1914-18 saw the abandonment of traditional maritime strategy and the adoption of the Continental type of warfare, resulting in millions of dead and wounded. Nonetheless as the most powerful warships on most minor stations it had usually been the cruisers, that had provided the calming influence of their guns to terminate many a threatened revolt or massacre, as was the case during the massacre of Europeans at Nanking by the Chinese in 1927. Only the bombardment by the *Emerald* prevented further horrors being perpetuated upon innocent civilians.

Norway: (April-June, 1940)
The first instance of the Royal Navy becoming embroiled in Army business in this way was probably the Norwegian Campaign, and an unhappier debut could hardly have been dreamed of. Just about every mistake that could be made was made, and everything that could go wrong did go wrong. Neglect and indifference in inter-service co-operation pre-war was matched and magnified by the totally irrelevant and often highly misleading intervention of Winston Churchill, often by-passing the C-in-C, Home Fleet, with resulting chaos everywhere.

On the neglect of combined operations, one distinguished historian had this to say:

> In the twenty years between the wars, Combined Ops took a back seat. The Dardanelles were fought all over again, in printer's ink and at the Staff Colleges, in Britain, the United States and Australia. Churchill and Keyes remained unrepentant and defiant apologists for the attempt; but on the whole people remembered the carnage on the beaches to the exclusion of all else... Most people, even the sanguine Keyes, reckoned that daylight assaults against a defended shore were suicide and folly. Everybody was looking at the past rather than the future; money was tight, and what there was had to be spent on needs more obviously urgent than experiments in Combined Operations.*

At the beginning of the Norwegian fiasco, troops were waiting ready to descend on the coast fully equipped and embarked in the cruisers of the Royal Navy at Rosyth, *Berwick*, *Devonshire*, *Glasgow* and *York*, bound for Stavanger and Bergen. When the balloon went up on 7th April, the C-in-C sailed with the Home Fleet from Scapa and the orders for the 1st Cruiser Squadron to disembark the troops hastily and sail to join him were telephoned through to the C-in-C Rosyth to their commanding officer, Admiral J. Cunningham, by the First Sea Lord himself later that evening. The opportunity to thus land troops to forestall the advancing Germans was lost and was never regained.

On 13th April, however, opportunity was taken to order Captain Pegram of the *Glasgow* that *Glasgow* and *Sheffield* should land an advance force of 350 Royal Marines sailors to take Namos, in order

---

* Fergusson, Brigadier Bernard, *The Watery Maze; the Story of Combined Operations*, (Collins, 1961)

to forestall the Germans and hold it until reinforcements arrived. This was done the next day. On the 17th another cruiser trooping run took place when Admiral Edward-Collins left Rosyth with the *Carlisle*, *Curacoa*, *Arethusa* and *Galatea* with 1,000 troops of the 148th Infantry Brigade. These were landed at Andalsnes on the 18th without loss, there and at Molde.

Support for the Army was extended here to AA protection, as we have noted, and two AA cruisers remained off those ports under continuous air attack on this duty until the *Curacoa* received a hit which badly damaged her on the 24th. This set the pattern for the ensuing days. On 22nd April *Arethusa* landed personnel and supplies for the setting up of an RAF base there, Edward-Collins returned with *Galatea*, *Glasgow* and *Sheffield* on the 23rd with part of the 15th Infantry Brigade and the next day *Birmingham*, *Manchester* and *York* disembarked the rest.

Bombardment of Narvik in readiness for an assault took place on 24th, with the cruisers *Effingham*, *Aurora* and *Enterprise* among these ships taking part. There was much to be learnt. Although the sight of the huge shells ploughing up and down the snowbound landscape looked spectacular enough, little actual harm was done to the enemy and there was no ashore direction to home the ships in on worthwhile targets in the largely featureless landscape. The landing did not take place and, '... poor visibility entirely prevented any estimate being made of the effect achieved ... '

Almost as soon as they were ashore the British troops, bombed mercilessly without fighter protection and outclassed on the ground by specialised German troops, were clamouring to be lifted again. On 29th April the Norwegian Royal Family was picked up at Molde and transferred to Tromso by the *Glasgow*, the first of many such transportations on HM cruisers of fleeing European monarchy. On the night of 30th April/1st May the *Arethusa*, *Sheffield* and *Southampton* were part of an evacuation force that lifted 2,200 troops from Andalsnes and Molde. Next night the *Birmingham* and *Manchester* lifted 1,500 more while the *Calcutta* lifted the 1,000-man rearguard. *York* was among the ships that lifted the 5,400 Allied garrison from Namsos on the 2nd/3rd May.

Off Mo a German battle group took to the water, but the Norwegian steamer *Nord Norge* was intercepted by the *Carlisle* and sunk soon after they landed. The Guards Brigade was taken into Bodo to block the southern approaches to Narvik by the *Cairo*, *Enterprise* and destroyers the same day. As part of the build-up for

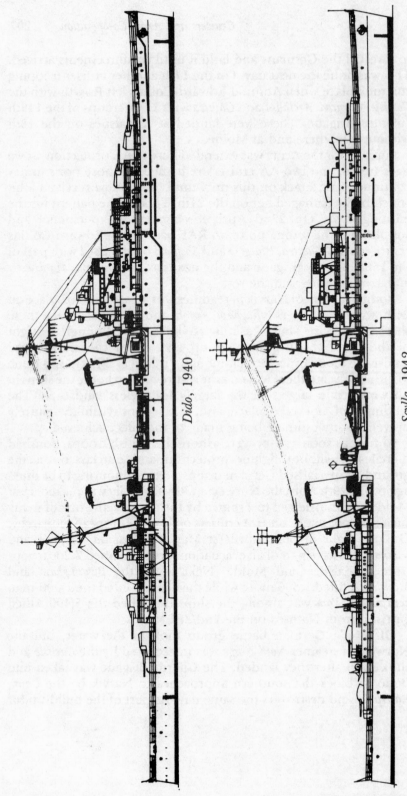

Dido, 1940

Scylla, 1942

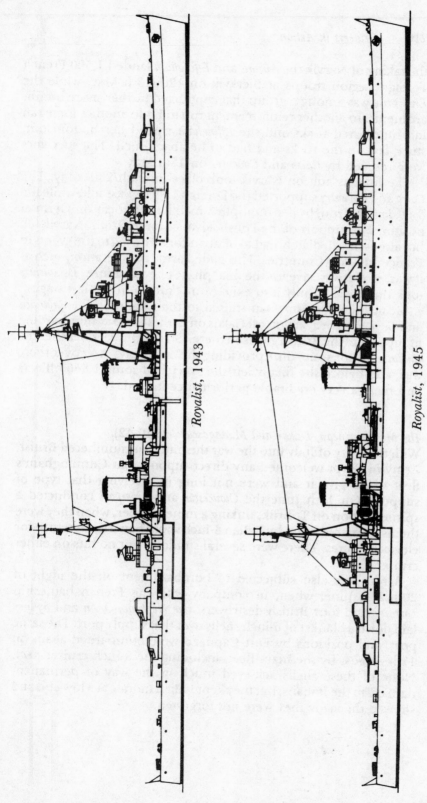

Royalist, 1943

Royalist, 1945

the taking of Narvik the *Aurora* and *Effingham* landed 1,500 French Foreign Legion troops at Bjerkvik on 12th/13th May, while the *Enterprise* was among a group that conducted further shore bombardments. In another reinforcement run to Bodo another force ran into uncharted rocks and the *Effingham* ripped her bottom out, stuck fast on the rocks and had to be abandoned. The survivors were rescued by *Cairo* and *Coventry* on 17th May.

The final assault on Narvik took place on 26th/28th May. The *Cairo* and *Coventry* supported the Foreign Legion's assault, while the *Southampton* brought her multiple 6-inch guns to bear on German positions in support of the Polish advance on the 28th. Narvik fell but almost immediately had to be abandoned owing to the events in France and Low Countries. This ended army co-operation, such as it was, in Norway save for the final phase of evacuations. *Devonshire* took the Royal Family into exile from Tromso in the last stages.

Meanwhile attention had shifted to the Channel. The *Arethusa* and *Galatea* were in action off Calais on 24th/26th May bombarding in support of the British garrison there. Off the Dunkirk beaches the *Calcutta* lay for some time providing the only heavy AA cover there was, and before she finally left she evacuated some 1,856 officers and men, a very creditable performance indeed.

The Mediterranean, Dakar and Madagascar: (1940-42).

With the entry of Italy into the war the much-outnumbered British Army in Egypt welcomed any direct support that Cunningham's fleet could give it and were not long in receiving that type of support. On 12th June the *Gloucester* and *Liverpool* conducted a spirited action off Tobruk, sinking a minesweeper, when they were themselves fired upon by Italian 8-inch shore batteries in return for eleven minutes. There were several straddles but no hits on either cruiser.

Bardia was also subjected to bombardment on the night of 20th/21st June, when, in company with the French battleship *Lorraine* and four British destroyers, the *Neptune*, *Orion* and *Sydney* laid down a blanket of 6-inch shells over that supply port. The same port, and positions by Fort Capuzzo were bombarded again on 17th August by the main fleet, including the 8-inch cruiser *Kent*. None of these shells achieved much in the way of permanent damage to the Italians, but they kept Italian morale at a low ebb and showed the army they were not forgotten.

Bombardment was still very much in the 'Heath Robinson' stages at this period of the war of course, a fact emphasised by the dreadful fiasco at Dakar between 23rd and 25th September. Among the British ships engaged with the Vichy-French shore batteries and warships there were the 8-inch cruisers *Australia*, *Cumberland* and *Devonshire* and the 6-inch cruiser *Dragon*. The results were far from auspicious for the ships, for they achieved little. In return the French gunners hit two British destroyers and the *Cumberland* on the 23rd. The 9·2-inch shell hit *Cumberland* at 1129, striking her port side amidships above her armoured belt and exploding above her lower deck. The engine-room was badly damaged, the main switchboard wrecked and the big cruiser had to withdraw at her best speed of ten knots to Bathurst after this solitary knock. She was out of action for thirteen days.

Against shore batteries then British cruisers did not shine initially. It is very interesting to notice that against ship targets, which they had been trained and designed to fight, they did much better, both in the Mediterranean where several Italian destroyers were sunk in this period, and also at Dakar, where the Vichy destroyer *L'Audacieux* which tried to attack *Australia*, received her just deserts in very short order indeed. Taking full salvos of 8-inch shell at a range of 4,000 yards, she was quickly reduced, with her bridge demolished.

Army co-operation in the field of limited Combined Operations was of necessity on a small scale at first, for there were no spare ships, men or expertise. A step in the right direction was the raid on the Lofoten Islands off Norway, Operation Claymore. The heavy cover for this raid included the cruisers *Edinburgh* and *Nigeria*. It took place on 4th March 1941.

More than a year later a more ambitious operation, the capture of the Vichy French naval base of Diego Suarez in Madagascar before the Japanese took it over, showed some limited advances over what had gone before. The *Devonshire* and *Hermione* joined in a brief ten minute bombardment of the defences before the port fell on 7th May 1942.

By the time of the North African landings in November of that year, cruisers had begun to play a much more prominent part in the softening up of enemy shore batteries and defence works by bombardment, and were increasingly called upon to maintain a standing patrol off the disputed beachheads on call for any request from the Army ashore to lay down blanket fire from their multiple fast-firing guns to repulse any attempt to mount counter-attacks against the vulnerable Allied troops. The technique and the growing skill being acquired soon began to have their effect, and thereafter no major landing was complete without its offshore cruiser support. This made a welcome change from the endless evacuations that had punctuated most of the fighting ashore hitherto; Greece and Crete followed Norway and Dunkirk as examples of cruisers lifting enormous numbers of troops to safety from under the noses of the victorious enemy, as we have seen.

The Mediterranean Theatre: (1942-44)
Among the cruisers in action off Tunisia and Algeria during November 1942 were the *Aurora*, which sank and damaged several Vichy destroyers, the *Bermuda*, which carried out some invaluable bombardments in support of US troops ashore by the *Argonaut* and *Sirius*. But this was just the beginning, although a far cry from September 1939 when, Rear-Admiral Maund says, the Inter-Service Training and Development Centre was disbanded with the words, ' . . there would be no combined operations in this war.'*

One of the old maxims re-learnt at Dakar was that warships could never take on forts on equal terms. Admiral Sir William James wrote at the time that, 'Pitting ships against forts is always hopeless, if the forts mean business.'† General Irwin's own report of the operation agreed, stating that one weakness of the plan was 'the continued adherence to the hope, in spite of all historical examples, that ships can reduce forts'. Churchill, of course, would have none of it. Not so, he cried. Under certain circumstances ships could do so. Yet at the Dardanelles long bombardments had made little or no impression on the old Turkish forts. Only direct hits on the guns themselves was any use in silencing them for long. He had not learnt anything from this early fiasco; however he did have a point, for in *some* cases, if only as a diversion, cruisers took on the heaviest forts.

At the Sicily landings in July 1943 Admiral Harcourt had a special force of four cruisers *Mauritius*, *Newfoundland*, *Orion* and *Uganda*, with the AA cruisers *Carlisle*, *Colombo* and *Delhi* and other vessels, to work close inshore with the assault forces, providing both initial gun support as they hit the beaches and acting as their flank

* Maund, Rear-Admiral L.E.H., *Assault from the Sea*, (Methuen, 1949).
† James, Admiral Sir William, *The Portsmouth Letters*, (Macmillan, 1946)

guards against counter-assault from both land and sea. This succeeded admirably.

At Anzio Rear Admiral Mansfield utilised the *Orion* and *Spartan* in the same role; the latter fired off some 900 5·25-inch shells on the night of 18th/19th January 1944 to excellent effect. In the American sector the *Penelope* performed the same function. The original intention that the ships should leave this vulnerable area after the troops were established was frustrated by the quick reaction of the Germans, and continual demands were made on cruisers throughout that protracted period of desperate defence, to supply gun support for the hard-pressed troops, more even than at Salerno earlier. *Orion* fired on an enemy radar station on the first day of operations, while *Dido* was engaged in counter-battery work on 29th January. For three months, their fire control directed from special Head-quarters Ships, the cruisers played a vital role in holding off the enemy thrusts.

It had been at Salerno in September that shore observers had taken over control of cruiser bombardments with much success. Air spotting was also tried, but a centralised offshore control was found from experience to be best for accuracy and precise co-ordination, and this was to become a regular job for cruisers. The expenditure of ammunition was large during the worst assaults; *Mauritius* fired over 1,000 6-inch shells on 13th September alone at Salerno. A constant turn-around of cruisers was needed while replenishment took place. Also, exposed as they were, casualties were heavy; we have seen how the *Uganda* (damaged) and the *Sparton* (sunk) paid the price during these operations. Yet others replaced them. The *Aurora* and *Penelope* were in hot action at Salerno, and the *Dido* at Anzio. The *Penelope* came to the end of her proud and eventful career on her way back from Anzio to replenish and must be counted as the second loss of this action. She was hit by three torpedoes from the *U-410* on 18th February, a sad end to such a fine fighting ship.

It was on 3rd February that the main German assaults broke over the Anzio beachhead. The crisis lasted almost a fortnight during which every available cruiser was in action. Admiral Mansfield had at his disposal the *Mauritius, Orion, Phoebe* and, until her loss, the *Penelope*. Between them the four cruisers fired off 7,800 rounds of 5·25-inch and 8,400 rounds of 6-inch shell by the end of the month. Captain Roskill records that: ' . . . the enemy's War Diary makes it plain that their harassing fire on his concentrations of troops and tanks, and their engagements with his mobile batteries, contributed greatly to halting his drive towards the beaches.'*

In May the *Dido* took up the battle, and in eighteen days she alone carried out seventeen bombardments and fired 1,865 5.25-inch shells in direct support against shore targets.

Normandy Landings: (June 1944)
The lessons drawn from the three major combined operations in the Mediterranean between November 1942 and March 1943 were applied to the ultimate test: the Allied landings in Normandy in June 1944. Only the scale of the enemy defences and expected opposition differed in that it was expected to be a far tougher nut to crack. Germany had four years to ready her defences on the Channel Coast as against weeks, or even mere hours, at Salerno and Anzio. What were the main lessons of the Mediterranean successes passed on? Captain Roskill lists the following aspects which affected British cruiser deployment for D-Day:

> Of all the lessons learnt perhaps the most important concerned the need to neutralise the enemy's defences by heavy bombardments before making an opposed landing. Every important combined operation so far carried out, from the failure at Dieppe to the successful assault on Sicily, had re-affirmed that principle. In his report on 'Avalanche' Admiral Hewitt strongly criticised the decision to sacrifice preliminary air and naval bombardments in the interests of achieving surprise. He pointed out that, because the assembly of the assault convoys was bound to be noticed, and Salerno was an obvious choice for their destination, we were in any case unlikely to surprise the enemy; and today it seems undeniable that to land the assault troops in the face of prepared and intact defences was to accept avoidable hazards. The emphasis placed on preliminary bombardment in the reports on Operation Avalanche did, however, ensure that they would be fully employed in the future.*

With regard to the efficiency of such bombardments a great deal of thought and preparation went into this facet of the operation also. Haphazard bombardment had shown itself to be a waste of effort at

* Roskill, Captain S.W., *The War at Sea, Vol 3, Pt. 2* (HMSO, 1960)

Bardia and Dakar. For Normandy detailed plans were drawn up to ensure that accurate and precise air and ground observation was carried out and the necessary communications equipment was available afloat to direct these reports quickly to the ships concerned. Any delay in transmission of such data in a rapidly changing situation such as was likely inland of the beachhead, would make the information valueless. Equally important it was necessary to ensure that any rapid movement inland by our own forces would not bring our troops under fire by friendly ships in error.

The RAF therefore provided a total of 104 specially trained fighter aircraft, of the latest marks of Spitfire and Mustang. These worked in pairs over their assigned sectors, one plane acting as observer, the other guarding it against enemy fighter assault while thus engrossed. Ashore the rapid deployment of highly trained Forward Observers Bombardment (FOB's) was given high priority. These men were trained specifically to work in close harmony with their assigned warships and practised with them beforehand to the nth degree. This ensured the minimum misunderstanding when the time came for the real thing. Thirty-nine FOB's landed with the forward troops at Normandy ready to report on the ships' fall of shot against assigned and targeted opposition, like forts and gun emplacements, and ready also to convoy the Army's requests for targets of opportunity as and when they arose. Not only were they trained to work with individual ships, but all such groups were given basic training in working with other ships, including foreign warships, so that interchangeability was obtained with the minimum of delay should events move swiftly ashore from one ship's sector to another's.

The long haul from the Anzio beaches to Malta during the Shingle operation, which the huge expenditure of shell necessitated, was another lesson learned. Great care was taken that a huge reserve of all types of shell used was readily available in the ships' base ports across the Channel so that replenishment was made simply and quickly. The turn-around of ships was thus expedited to a great degree. Fortunately the distances involved were far less arduous than at Anzio.

As for bombardment practice itself, Scapa Flow in the months before Normandy became the busiest it had been since 1918 with whole squadrons of battleships and cruisers and flotillas of fleet destroyers busy exercising gunfire, while the Home Fleet units went about their own usual business as well. In knocking out the huge forts that the Germans had constructed the heaviest shells were essential, and this was mainly battleship work. Their 15-inch and 16-inch shells were the only ones capable of cracking such stoutly built emplacements. They also had the longer range (twenty miles) to prove more enduring in support as the fighting swept inland. The bursting power of their one-ton projectiles also had an inestimable effect on the morale of the troops, lowering that of the enemy who found themselves under attack far from the sea, and raising that of the Allies. But for targets like mobile field batteries, tank concentrations and troops in the field, the much more rapid fire of the modern multi-gunned light cruisers was far more effective. The crushing effect of such a barrage of 5·25-inch or 6-inch shells bursting on such targets, relatively unprotected, was stunning and the cruisers had the added mobility their speed and shallower draught gave them so that they could be more rapidly switched from one danger sector to another. A modern cruiser armed with nine 6-inch guns could deliver seventy shells a minute into such a concentration, with the usual result of total annihilation of the target up to a depth of ten miles inland.

The importance of Command ships, fitted out with all the latest radar and communications equipment, was also not forgotten and the *Scylla*, as Admiral Vian's flagship, was specially suited to this role. She was fitted out at Chatham with all these extra electronics and served not only to co-ordinate events ashore but as the organiser of the offshore patrols each night against expected German naval intervention. She also took the opportunity to get in some bombardment work of her own with the eight 4·5-inch guns; the 'Toothless Terror' had something of a reputation to maintain after her work against German torpedo bombers on the Arctic Convoys in 1942-43. Unfortunately she was mined on 23rd June, and the damage was so extensive that her machinery was completely wrecked and she had to be towed to England. Although she remained in Reserve at Chatham for many years, the money to repair her was never forthcoming and in May 1950 she was towed to Barrow for scrapping.

D-Day finally took place on 6th June after a 24-hour postponement but long before then the ships of the Bombardment Squadron had assembled in the Clyde and at Belfast and were moving south to take up their initial bombarding positions off the Normandy coast. On the night before these huge ships slipped quietly into their assigned anchorages and prepared themselves for the eventful days ahead of them, some twenty-three in all. Here, behind thick concrete embrasures up to seven feet in depth and surrounded by minefields, trenches and barbed wire, the thick noses of the guns, ranging from 6·1-inch to 4·9-inch in calibre, covered all the seaward approaches. All had long ago been 'ranged in' to cover every area of the surface of the quiet water immediately to their front. Secondary defence works consisted of field guns and immediately to their front. Secondary defence works consisted of field guns and howitzers on wheeled mountings, of similar calibres to the batteries, but mounted in reinforced casemates. These were more open to destruction by cruiser fire than the coast defence batteries and were cruiser targets in the main.

The bombarding forces were divided into five groups corresponding to the five beaches and their dispositions and targets are contained in Table 19.

* * *

Table 19   Cruisers at the Normandy Landings 6th June, 1944

Cruiser	Force	Beach	Target Batteries.
Mauritius	S	Sword.	As required.
Arethusa	S	Sword.	Le Mont. Merville.
Frobisher	S	Sword.	Riva Bella.
Dragon	S	Sword.	Colleville sur Orne
Danae	S	Sword.	Ouistreham.
Scylla (Flag)	S	Sword.	As required.
Diadem	G	Juno.	Moulineaux.
Belfast	G	Gold.	Ver sur Mer.
Orion	G	Gold.	Mont Fleury.
Emerald	G	Gold.	Arromanches.
Argonaut	G	Gold.	Vaux sur Aure.
Ajax	G	Gold.	Longues.
Glasgow	O	Omaha.	Omaha Beaches then as required.
Hawkins	U	Utah.	Maisy.
Enterprise.	U	Utah.	St Martin de Varreville.
Black Prince.	U	Utah.	Morsalines.

* * *

It was at 0530 on 6th June that the cruisers opened fire along with the battleships and destroyers along the whole fifty mile arc from Barfleur to Le Havre. The scale of the bombardment was crushing, its accuracy devastating and the enemy was overwhelmed completely.

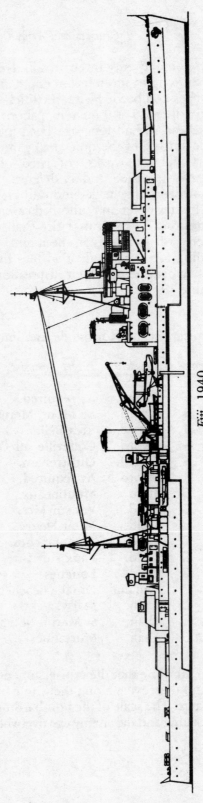

Fiji, 1940

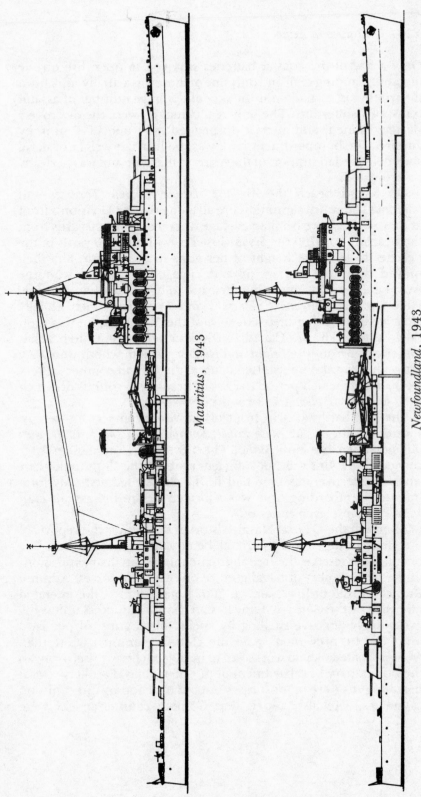

Mauritius, 1943

Newfoundland, 1943

Only a few of the coastal batteries survived to open fire on the incoming landing craft and only one of these was actually sunk from the whole vast armada nor did any of the huge number of assault transports suffer hits. The only real casualties were the destroyers *Wrestler* (mined) and *Svenner* (torpedoed) and one LCT sunk by gunfire. The bombardment itself was the heaviest weight of naval shell delivered in support of the Army to that date and was perfectly co-ordinated.

On Sword beach the *Arethusa*, *Danae*, *Dragon*, *Frobisher* and *Mauritius* laid down saturation fire all along the 3rd Division's front as they went ashore from an average distance of 14,000 yards from the beaches. At 0700 the *Scylla* closed to within 5,500 yards of the beaches to lend the weight of her guns to the assault. She then moved over to Gold sector and engaged in a duel with the Arromanches guns, diverting their fire to herself with no damage. Here the *Ajax*, *Argonaut*, *Emerald* and *Orion* had been equally effective in silencing their targets and the 50th Division was soon safely ashore. The 3rd Canadian Division went in on Gold beaches under cover from the *Belfast* and *Diadem*, both of whom were very active this day and intermittently up to the 14th in counter-battery work, during which period the *Belfast* fired 1,996 rounds of 6-inch shell and the *Diadem* 1,748 round of 5·25-inch.

The bombardments in front of the American sectors were of shorter duration. The *Black Prince*, *Enterprise*, *Glasgow* and *Hawkins* did not open fire until 0550. The US Army Commander later conceded that this was not sufficient time for the ships to do their work as effectively as they had in the British sectors; only forty minutes bombarding time was allocated before the assault craft went in from eleven miles out.

Although the Official Naval Historian deprecates the reports of the German defenders ashore as being extravagant and needing treating with reserve, they are almost unanimous in their expressions of the effectiveness of naval gunfire on their own forces. Admiral Krancke wrote in his Diary on 20th June that '... the intended offensive by the German Army has no chance of success unless the exceedingly effective shelling by enemy naval guns, of our land units can be prevented.' And the C-in-C, Rommel, wrote that, 'Weapons sited in field works had to be dug out before use, owing to the preliminary bombardment of the enemy naval artillery. Coast defence guns were in most cases put out of action by direct hits on casemates.' He also added that German counter-attacks were broken up and ' . . . suffered heavy casualties in the neighbourhood of the coast through naval artillery fire'.

At Longues, for example, it was found that two 6-inch shells actually passed through the embrasures and scored direct hits on the guns inside. Not surprisingly the ship concerned was the famous *Ajax*, which fired, along with the *Argonaut*'s 5·25's, some 179 rounds at this target. Such accuracy has been dismissed as 'perhaps luckily' able to score such hits, but the overall standard of precision is surely something that should arouse admiration rather than criticism. In all events the Allied soldiers themselves were full of praise for the job the Navy did for them.

The Mediterranean Theatre: (1944-45)
The last major landings in Europe were the invasion of the south of France in August 1944. Neglected by British historians because the troops set ashore were mainly American, the bombarding forces were chiefly British warships, although under American admirals. They were equally as effective, in fact more so for the lessons learned at Normandy were applied to Dragoon a few months later. It had been found at Normandy, for example, that the bombarding ships sometimes lost touch with the ground observers ashore in the confusion that followed the actual landings. To mitigate this flaw some landing craft were equipped as control ships to direct the ships' fire from close inshore and this proved most effective. Some of the bombarding ships were those that had gained invaluable experience at Normandy and these added their expertise to those from the Mediterranean Fleet ships involved. Among the cruisers that served to cover both landings were the five British cruisers *Ajax*, *Argonaut*, *Black Prince* and *Orion*. The others bombarding were the *Aurora*, *Dido*, *Sirius* and the old *Caledon*, while the *Royalist* acted as flagship of the offshore escort carrier group to which the AA cruisers *Colombo* and *Delhi* added their protection. The *Argonaut* alone fired some 394 shells on D-Day alone in this operation. The operation was crowned by the liberation of the French naval base of Toulon on 13th September, The occasion was handed over for ceremonial purposes to the French, but Admiral Cunningham was there flying his flag aboard *Sirius* as representative of those who had done the fighting in the years between 1940 and 1944 which had made it possible.

Although large-scale bombardments had ceased in the Mediterranean British cruisers still found work to do in support of the Army and our allies in those waters as the Germans retreated toward their homelands. With the departure of the German Army the Communists were quick to see their chance to substitute their own form of dictatorship on the freshly liberated nations. In Yugoslavia their leader, Tito, already had the full backing of the Churchill administration in his aims, but, although nominally allies, the crews of the *Colombo* and *Delhi* were treated more as bitter foes when they tried to help in the Adriatic that winter. In Greece the Moscow-inspired revolution almost took the country in its grip and only swift action by the British, which the Americans scorned to help with so blind were they, foiled this coup which came to a head in December 1944. Fortunately the 15th Cruiser Squadron under Admiral Troubridge was on hand when needed. It included among its number the *Ajax* and *Orion* who had last served in those waters three-and-a-half years before when we were bombed out. Now they helped restore freedom and democracy to the cradle of civilisation again.

The Far East Theatre of Operations (1944-45)
In the Pacific and South-East Asia landings of vast scale and magnitude were taking place at this period, but the weight of the bombardments for these was almost exclusively born by the US Navy who had assembled a mighty array of fighting power, comprising a dozen different Task Forces, any one of which was the size of a main British Fleet. Nonetheless some British cruisers did manage to make very meaningful contributions in this vast arena, initially mainly the ships of the Australian and New Zealand navies, although later joined by the more modern vessels of the British Pacific Fleet under Admiral Fraser.

Among the first of these was the seizure of the island of Morotai, northernmost island of the Halmahera Group that lay between the north-west tip of New Guinea and the north-east tip of Celebes. As such it was a natural stepping stone for the planned invasion of the Philippines. The assault went in on 15th September 1944, and, unusual for Japanese-held-territory, it was only lightly defended. Among the ships providing covering fire for the landing were the 8-inch cruisers *Australia* and *Shropshire*; the latter had been handed over by the Royal Navy to replace the lost *Canberra*.

In the Indian Ocean limited offensives were at last begun and the first of these was the naval bombardment of Sabang, at the northern tip of Sumatra. This took place on 25th July 1944, and among the cruisers carrying out a heavy bombardment of Japanese military installations on the island were the heavy cruiser *Cumberland* and the light cruisers *Ceylon*, *Gambia*, *Kenya* and *Nigeria*. In all they delivered 134 8-inch and 324 6-inch shells onto the Japanese emplacements with satisfying results.

When the invasion of the Philippines got underway with the initial landings at Leyte, the *Australia* and *Shropshire* were again among the covering warships, the former feeling the wrath of the new Japanese suicide aircraft, the Kamikazes, first of all. On the 21st she was hit in her bridge by one of these 'missiles' and her captain was among those killed; she had to withdraw to Manus to effect repairs.

The Third Arakan Offensive which took place in the early part of 1945 involved some substantial cruiser-Army co-operation as combined operations were mounted to clear the coast ready for the assault on Rangoon in Burma. In particular the occupation of the strategically important island of Ramree, which took place between 17th and 19th January, was heavily supported by the Royal Navy, and the *Phoebe* carried out bombardment work with the battleship *Queen Elizabeth*. In a follow-up operation some 500 Royal Marines were landed from the cruisers *Newcastle*, *Nigeria* and *Kenya* on Cheduba island farther south on 26th January and later these ships carried out fire support duties against the Ramree defences. These cruisers were joined by the *Royalist* in March, in her role as Task Force Command Ship of the escort carrier groups and further sorties were planned. Early in May the *Phoebe* was among the warships which prepared to liberate Rangoon from the sea to re-establish the British rule in Burma and the Japanese were in full flight.

All this time the struggle for control of the myriad islands of the Philippines Group had continued. *Australia*, her damage made good, returned to the fight early in 1945 only to be hit by Kamikazes yet again on 5th January 1945; she was hit yet a third time, and twice more by these same weapons, suffering over 100 casualties. She remained afloat despite all this punishment but once again had to pull out to refit.

With the Okinawa landings in April and May 1945, the British Pacific Fleet finally came to the fore. Although initially it was confirmed to air strikes against Japanese islands containing airstrips through which the enemy were ferrying planes to the battle, and the cruisers' main duties were AA protection of the carriers, on 4th May they had the opportunity to have a crack at themselves. Admiral

Rawlings took his two battleships and the cruisers *Black Prince*, *Euryalus*, *Gambia*, *Swiftsure* and *Uganda* in towards the island of Miyako in the Sakishima group to deliver an accurate bombardment of the airfields, which aircraft bombs had failed to put out of action. Although this was successful, the absence of the heavy ships AA batteries left the British carriers totally reliant on their own fighters to ward off the Kamikazes; this proved insufficient, and two of them were hit and badly damaged. The cruisers returned to their protection and were joined by the *Achilles* on the 23rd.

For the assault on Rangoon meanwhile, Operation Dracula, powerful Royal Navy forces had assembled, including the *Phoebe* and *Royalist*. On 1st May this was achieved, the sailing into that great river port and capital on the 6th. The East Indies Fleet then went on to deliver a heavy bombardment of the Japanese bases at Cap Nicobar and Port Blair where the 8-inch cruisers *Cumberland* and *Suffolk* and the 6-inch cruiser *Ceylon* contributed their quota of shells to the enemy's discomfiture. When the Japanese decided to evacuate the Nicobars soon after, both the *Ceylon* and *Phoebe* took part in patrols to intercept them.

Meanwhile another Australian cruiser, *Hobart*, supported Allied landings at Tarakan in Borneo on 27th April 1945, on the north-east coast, and in follow-up assaults further down the coast at Balikpapan in the Macassar Strait in June further firepower was added by the arrival of the *Shropshire*. Both Australian ships took part in numerous bombardments, which, because of the grave danger of minefields, had to be carried out with the cruisers at anchor. Fortunately shore battery and aerial attacks were not severe enough to take advantage of this dangerous situation.

In the Pacific freshly arrived reinforcements for the BPF were blooded by an attack on the old Japanese base at Truk in the Carolines. Although now mainly abandoned and a backwater it provided invaluable combat experience. The cruisers *Achilles* and *Uganda* shelled the island of Dublon, the *Newfoundland* Uman and the *Swiftsure* pounded Moen on 14th-15th June.

The war in the East was now approaching its climax. In the Indian Ocean the heavy cruiser *Sussex* took part in bombardments of the Kra Isthmus under Kamikaze attack on 24th-26th July. In the Pacific the BPF was working off mainland Japan with immunity and on 9th August the *Gambia* and *Newfoundland* turned their 6-inch guns on the city of Kamaishi on Honshu itself. At the final surrender ceremony in Tokyo Bay British cruisers were represented

Cornwall and *Dorsetshire* served with distinction against German raiders in 1941 but in the Indian Ocean in 1942 they were left alone and unsupported when attacked by eighty Japanese naval dive bombers from the Nagumo Task Force. They were soon overwhelmed by the sheer scale of the attack and its accuracy.

The new light cruisers were in the thick of the fight as soon as they joined the fleet. In the hard fought Malta convoy 'Pedestal' the *Kenya* was soon damaged but kept with the convoy. On her return to Gibraltar she was subjected to further heavy air attacks.

Of the older light cruisers many were converted to anti-aircraft ships and performed very useful roles in the war. The only 'D' class cruiser to be so converted was the *Delhi*, and she was unique in that she was re-armed with the superior American 5-inch D.P. gun.

by the *Gambia*, *Newfoundland*, *Shropshire* and *Hobart*. In the Indian Ocean similar ceremonies were watched over by the *Ceylon* at Penang, the *London* at Sabang and the *Sussex*, *Cleopatra* and *Nigeria* in Singapore. The liberation of Hong Kong took place on 30th August, and in the Task Force assembled off that great harbour were the cruisers *Black Prince*, *Euryalus* and *Swiftsure*; Shanghai was occupied by a force that included the *Argonaut* and *Bermuda*, and Djakarta was taken by the *Cumberland* on 15th September.

Trooping: (1945-46)
There were no more bombardments, but Army co-operation took on a new meaning for British cruisers in the immediate post-war months as, being comparatively large ships, they were pressed into service by a desperate Labour administration, as troopships to bring home first the wounded and the POW's and then the troops from the Far East. It is perhaps fitting to end this chapter of the Royal Navy cruisers' role in aid to the brothers-in-arms of their sister service, which had taken part in the adverses of Norway, Dunkirk and Crete and the triumphs of Salerno, Anzio, Normandy and South France, with such a peaceful and happy role.

Losses in fulfilling the Navy's obligations to the Army had been heavy over the years of war, both directly and indirectly. From the *Effingham* running aground with troops aboard off Norway, the loss of the *Curlew* trying to give AA support in the same campaign, through the sacrifice of the *Fiji* and *Gloucester*, the loss of the *Coventry* covering Army disasters in the Mediterranean, the sinking of the *Spartan* off Anzio, the torpedoing of the *Penelope* stemming from the same operation, to the ultimate self-sacrifice of the old cruisers *Durban* and *Dragon* at Normandy, scuttled as breakwaters to aid the Army's supply problem in the face of storm damage, the roll-call was a long and worthy one.

Table 20
British Cruisers used for Trooping Duties 1945-47.

Ship	Period of Duty
Cumberland	July 1945–March 1946
Berwick	July 1945-February 1946
Suffolk	August 1945–March 1946
Devonshire	July 1945–March 1946
London	November 1945–March 1946
Enterprise	May 1945–January 1946
Newcastle	October 1945–February 1946

CHAPTER EIGHT

Cruisers at War: An Assessment of Their Role and Final Days

By the end of the war in 1945 the role of the British cruiser was completely different from the one envisaged for it in 1939. Instead of patrolling the distant oceans and convoy routes and scouting ahead of the main battle fleets, they found themselves bombarding shore installations and acting as anti-aircraft warning pickets, command ships for specialised Task Groups and troopships. We have examined in some depth all these roles and how well the cruisers, designed pre-war, coped with them. Let us now examine some of the changes and why they came about and look at the successes and failure of the British cruiser as a type of fighting ship for World War II.

One thing is immediately apparent in studying the Second World War by comparison with the Great War, and that is that the cruiser attained greater prominence in the Royal Navy in the second struggle than it had in the first. This was inevitable because of the great cut-back in battleship strength that followed 1918. The whole of the Royal Navy's capital ship strength never amounted to much more than half the strength of just the Grand Fleet on its own during 1914-18, let alone other battle squadrons. In the place of the vast array of squadrons steaming in majestic splendour across the North Sea, battleships had to act in small Task Groups, rarely exceeding three ships, assembled according to current needs and availability. Cruiser strength, in proportion to the total, although smaller, was not so much affected, and cruisers frequently had to substitute for a proper battle fleet, as in the Mediterranean in 1942. It was not a job of which they were really capable but one they performed with amazing success, though if the Italian or German battle fleets had been commanded with a little more flair and élan than they were, the bluff could have been called at any time. Luckily it was not in European waters, although the Japanese exposed it often enough in the Pacific and off Java etc in their hey-day, against the Americans whose own battlefleet had been put out of action at Pearl Harbor and against the British who lost theirs off Malaya three days later.

During the six years of intensive sea warfare there were many brilliant episodes in full keeping with the Royal Navy's long tradition of victory. Overall the standard both of individual command and general leadership seems to have been high. It may merely be the fact that opportunities were more than in the Great War, but the overall impression of keenness to engage the enemy no matter what the odds seemed to come to the fore more than in the First World War. There was less hanging back and waiting for superior decisions before commitment. This may only be a false picture, but the aggressiveness of cruiser commanders did much to mitigate some adverse situations that were thrust upon them by the political decisions over which they had no control, or bad policy decisions by their admirals.

Let us look at the successes and the failures.

Almost the first cruiser action of the war showed the good qualities of British cruisers. The River Plate battle was something of a classic in how an inferior strength squadron of light ships could, by determined action, defeat a vastly superior enemy commanded with timidity. It set the standard for similar actions, some as brilliant in their conclusion, others not so, but all of a common policy of not evading the odds. The cruisers represent good examples of this with the actions of Force 'K' at Malta in 1941, by the brilliant handling of the 15th Cruiser Squadron at the battles of Sirte in 1942, the Bay of Biscay action in 1943 and the tactical handling of these ships during the destruction of the *Scharnhorst*. But there are a host of lesser examples.

Opportunities to engage enemy warships proved rare, owing to enemy policy of generally avoiding action even in the most favourable circumstances. Nonetheless when the chance presented itself British cruisers got in some heavy blows. One of the most interesting took place on the night of 11th/12th October 1940 off the island of Malta. A convoy was being brought out from the island to Alexandria and one of the covering cruisers, the *Ajax* (Captain E.D.B. McCarthy) was attacked by two flotillas of Italian destroyers.

All the odds were in the Italian ships' favour; the British cruiser was caught by surprise. The Italians were heavily armed with torpedoes against which the British ship had no defence, and they were firing flashless ammunition with tracer which was of great value in night attacks, whereas *Ajax* had her gunners partially blinded by her own gunflashes in the darkness. There was bright moonlight which also aided the Italian flotilla vessels. There were seven enemy destroyers, the *Airone*, *Alcione* and *Ariel* of the 1st

Flotilla and the *Artigliere, Aviere, Camicia Nera* and *Geniere* of the 11th Flotilla which were well aware of the British dispositions in advance. Despite all this *Ajax* was handled brilliantly and, after the initial surprise, she took the offensive.

With the ranges coming down at times to less than 4,000 yards she took on all comers and with fast salvos of her 6-inch turrets she quickly smashed up the *Airone* and *Ariel* and severely damaged the *Artigliere*. The remaining four Italian vessels scored in return some seven direct hits on *Ajax* at close range which damaged her bridge and radar and caused a fire in a storeroom. Nonetheless she continued to chase the fleeing enemy who retired quickly behind a smokescreen and took no further part in the action. Admiral Cunningham praised the 'resolution and skill' with which this famous ship was handled.

Nor was the enemy's discomfiture over yet. The *Artigliere* was taken in tow by *Camicia Nera* and was spotted next day. The 8-inch cruiser *York* (Captain R.H. Portal), was sent off 'hot-foot' to finish her off and came upon the two destroyers next day. While her consort slipped the tow and vanished at high speed the *York* dropped floats for *Artigliere's* crew and then blew her out of the water with controlled salvos, putting the seal on a good night's work.

On the same night as the Taranto attack took place, 11th/12th November 1940, a cruiser striking force under Vice-Admiral Pridham-Wippell, consisting of the *Ajax, Orion* and *Sydney* and destroyers *Mohawk* and *Nubian*, made a daring foray into the enemy's backyard by striking at the convoy route between Albania and Italy in the Straits of Otranto. It was very much like a German naval force based at Kiel, making a raid on British shipping in St George's Channel with immunity. At around 0115 on the 12th this force came upon an Italian convoy. There were four merchant ships escorted by an auxiliary cruiser and the destroyer *Fabrizi*. These took the unique action of defending their charges by making off at their best speed when fire was opened on them and the *Fabrizi* was hit. The cruisers then enjoyed what Admiral Cunningham described as a 'riotous night' among the unhappy merchantmen and quickly reduced the convoy to a shambles; all four were hit and left on fire, and all subsequently sank; the victims were the *Antonio Locatelli, Capo Vado, Catalani*, and *Premuda* totalling some 17,000 tons. The British ships were unscratched. This brilliant little action was on par with the best of Force 'K's' exploits but is overshadowed by the greater victory at Taranto.

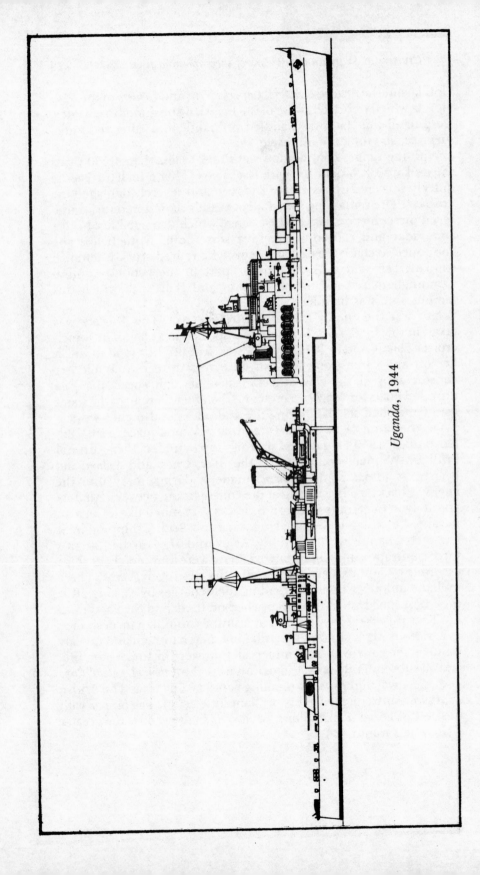

Uganda, 1944

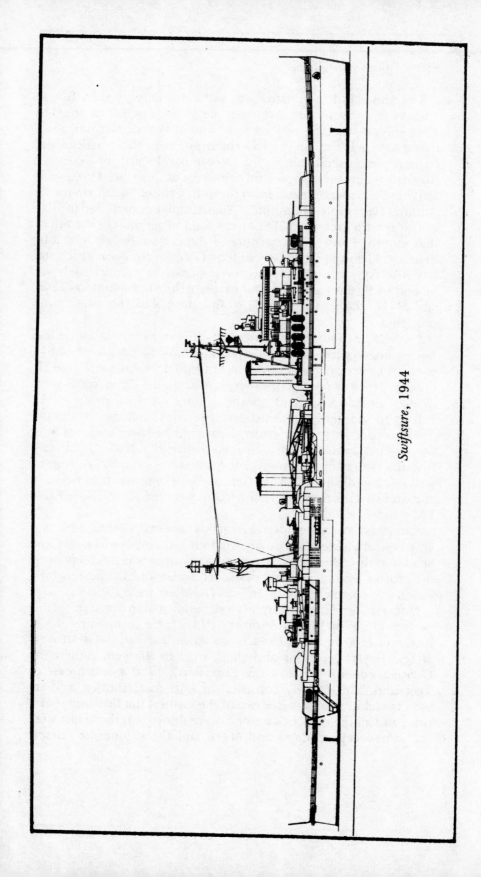

Swiftsure, 1944

The same kind of initiative was still being employed by British cruisers at the war's end. For example, in the English Channel in 1944 several hot little actions were fought against German units trying to reach the safety of German ports. In these actions the cruisers were usually employed as command ships for destroyer squadrons and most successful they were at this role. Three such Striking Forces were set up from the 10th Cruiser Squadron under Admiral Dalrymple-Hamilton in August and they patrolled the Bay of Biscay with great élan. They were soon in action. On the 6th of that month, Force 26, consisting of the cruiser *Bellona* and four destroyers fell upon a convoy of four German auxiliaries escorted by five warships. In a brief action every one of the enemy vessels was hit and badly damaged and four of them, the minesweepers *M263*, and *M486*, the patrol ship *V414* and store ship *Otto*, were sunk outright.

Force 28, the cruiser *Diadem* and destroyers *Onslow* and the Polish *Piorun*, intercepted the large naval auxiliary *Sperrbrecher 7* (7,078 tons) off La Rochelle and sank her. On 14th-15th August, Force 27, the cruiser *Mauritius* and destroyers *Ursa* and the Canadian *Iroquois* made a similar foray and caught another German group off La Pallice. In another hot little action the repair ship *Richthofen* and the minesweeper *M385* were badly damaged; the latter sank, and the destroyer *T24* was severely damaged by shellfire. Not content with this, the same ships operating off Audierne on 22nd/23rd August attacked a whole flotilla of five German minesweepers near Belleisle and quickly sank them all; their victims were the *V702*, *V717*, *V720*, *V729* and *V730*.

Similar activity was undertaken at this time in the Mediterranean. One typical incident took place on 15th September 1944 off Cape Spatha in the Aegean. Here a German convoy was intercepted by the cruiser *Royalist* and the destroyer *Teazer* and in the resulting action the enemy vessels *Erpel* and *Heidelberg* were sunk.

Nor were similar raids any less well conducted in the Arctic at this period. On 12th/13th November 1944 a force comprising the 8-inch cruiser *Kent*, the 5·25-inch cruiser *Bellona* and the destroyers *Myngs*, *Verulam*, *Zambesi* and the Canadian *Alonquin* caught the German convoy KS 357 off Listerfiord, to the south-east of Egersund. This convoy consisted of four mechantmen and six escorts and in a brief mêlée two of the former, the *Cornouailles* and *Greif*, and all the escorts, save one, were destroyed; those lost were the minesweepers *M427* and *M416* and the submarine chasers

UJ1221, UJ1223 and *UJ1713*.

The final action in these waters took place on the night of the 27th/28th when the German 4th Destroyer Flotilla, the big destroyers *Z31, Z34* and *Z38* under Captain von Wangenheim, were sighted at long range and in bright moonlight by the cruisers *Diadem* and *Mauritius*. The German destroyers fired torpedoes without effect and then were forced to turn back to the safety of Bergen. Although the two cruisers chased them at top speed and managed to score hits which badly damaged the *Z31* and slightly damaged the *Z38*, the enemy managed to gain the protection of the coastal batteries before they could be brought to book.

So much for the relative successes. However not all such operations were so well conducted or happy in their outcome as these, and there were some outright blunders as well. Let us examine a few of the less conclusive operations on our side to keep a sense of balance in our narrative. During the early years of the war, for example, strong German destroyer forces operated off the east and south Coasts of Britain, laying minefields and striking at coastal convoys and enjoyed almost complete immunity despite attempts by cruiser/destroyer striking forces to intercept them. Moreover, on the rare occasions they were caught they managed to inflict far greater damage on the British ships than they themselves suffered.

These forays have been almost completely ignored by naval historians. One typical incident took place on the night of 17th/18th October 1940. Two German destroyer flotillas were involved, with Commodore Bey and the large *Hans Lody, Friedrich Ihn, Karl Galster* and *Erich Steinbrinck* operating in the Bristol Channel with the small escort destroyers *Falke, Greif, Jaguar, Kondor, Seeadler* and *Wolf* in support; all ships were operating out of Brest. The 5th Destroyer Flotilla was based at Plymouth and carried out almost nightly patrols to intercept these ships, and were sometimes backed up by cruisers.

It was the *Newcastle* which intercepted the German flotilla on this occasion, at 1600 on a dark winter evening with light fading fast. She at once steered to engage them working up quickly to 32½ knots. Fire was opened off Land's End. The German ships quickly fired torpedoes at the cruiser and made off at their best speed but were unable to lose her initially in the prevailing weather conditions. The *Erich Steinbrinck* later claimed to have scored a torpedo hit on the *Newcastle*, a claim still repeated today yet completely untrue; even so the Germans made a clean escape without damage. The 5th Flotilla itself was in a good position to intercept them but failed to take any action.

> On one occasion gun-flashes from the enemy flotilla were sighted, reflected in the sky from behind the Lizard promontory. But in the absence of any report from naval headquarters they were taken for anti-aircraft fire by our own defences. The enemy slipped away and by daybreak was safe in his base.*

Little wonder then that these operations are completely unrecorded in British naval histories to date.

However the biggest disaster to overtake British forces in the Channel took place some three years later, when we should have learnt better. The frequent use of the Channel to escort their raiders and blockade runners to and from Germany had led in the summer and autumn of that year to regular destroyer sweeps up the enemy side of that stretch of water to intercept them. On some occasions available light cruisers from the Home Fleet were sent to work with them; the first time was early in October when the cruiser *Charybdis* (Captain G.A.W. Voelker) was used.

These sweeps had become a regular feature and were known as Operation Tunnel. The routine used was never varied and the German radar posts had had ample time to plot them and make detailed notes on exactly what took place each time. Despite this, and the fact that *Charybdis* had never before worked in this role, for her tasks hitherto had almost exclusively been AA defence with the fleet, the same plan was kept to. There was some dissension about this among the skippers of the destroyers taking part, and the captain of the *Limbourne* was not even at the briefing. Thus the British force consisted of ships of differing designs and capabilities which were completely unknown to each other as a fighting unit, while the enemy had a pretty good idea of our basic plan. It was a recipe for disaster and so it proved.†

The British force which sailed to carry out Tunnel again on the night of 22nd/23rd October 1943 consisted of the *Charybdis*, the two Fleet destroyers, *Grenville* and *Rocket* and four of the slower *Hunt*

---

* Rear-Admiral A.F. Pugsley, *Destroyer Man* (Weidenfeld & Nicolson, 1957).
† See the personal account of this operation of Roger Hill, *Destroyer Captain*, (William Kimber, 1975). He describes the *Hunts* as having no torpedoes, but, being of the group III type, they *all had* a twin 21-inch mounting each.

class escort destroyers *Limbourne, Stevenstone, Talybont* and *Wensleydale*. Their target was the German blockade runner *Munsterland* which had sailed from Brest the same afternoon with an escort of five escort destroyers, (each of which carried six torpedo tubes as well as gun power equal to our Fleets), together with eight smaller escorts. The German escort disposition were flexible, with the five destroyers placed ahead of the convoy but separate from it to enable them to act independently. Conversely the British dispositions were rigidly wrong: the *Charybdis* led the line, followed by the two Fleets and then the *Hunts* astern of them, with the second-in-command aboard *Limbourne*.

Soon after midnight the British force were some seven miles off Brittany and commenced to sweep west at thirteen knots. On their part, at around 0030, the waiting German radar operators picked them up as expected and carefully tracked them passing the word to the German ships at sea. These warnings were intercepted by the *Hunts* and by Plymouth Command, but *Charybdis*, if she received them did nothing to change the fixed plan. The *Munsterland* was turned back out of harm's way while five enemy destroyers prepared to deal with the Tunnel force as planned. *Charybdis* picked them up on her own radar at a range of 14,000 yards at 0130 and signalled the destroyers to increase speed, but only the rear destroyer, *Wensleydale*, picked up this signal and her overtaking the others ahead of her caused some confusion, which was compounded when the first German torpedoes arrived and friendly starshells illuminated the leading British ships instead of the enemy. *Charybdis* was hit by at least two of the torpedoes and the *Limbourne* by others and at 0146 both ships were sinking with heavy loss of life while the other destroyers had close shaves from collisions in the confusion. Although they later returned to pick up survivors the German destroyers contented themselves merely with watching them by radar and made no attempt to interfere. The *Munsterland* resumed her journey unscathed. The destroyers *T23* and *T27* claimed the hits that sank *Charybdis* and the *T22* the *Limbourne*. Only 150 survivors were found from *Charybdis'* crew of 668 and Captain Voelker was not among them. Altogether the loss of this fine ship was on a par with the sinking of the *Canberra* at Savo Island, which we have described, the exposing of the *Dorsetshire* and *Cornwall* to Japanese dive bombers unsupported, and anchoring *Spartan* off Anzio when radio-controlled bombs were being used regularly.

Other cruiser losses were not so obviously failures of technique; some were due to bad luck or due to the ships being placed in impossible positions. Perhaps the most unlucky loss was of the *Trinidad*, for it was largely brought about by the fact that one of her own torpedoes, fired against German destroyers during an Arctic convoy battle, faulted and circled round to hit the ship that had fired it! She was thus weakened and was finished off by air attacks a few days later. The loss of *Edinburgh* in those same waters to German destroyer attack also illustrated that these enemy ships were not so helpless as has been made out, although again the British cruiser had already been badly damaged by submarine torpedoes and could not manoeuvre to avoid further attacks.

The sinking of the *Curacoa* by the *Queen Mary* on 2nd October 1942, was due to navigational errors, which the House of Lords enquiry finally attributed to both parties, two-thirds to the Admiralty and one-third to Cunard-White Star Company. Whoever's fault it was some 338 men lost their lives as a result. The loss of the *Manchester* by scuttling after she had been damaged astern by E-boat torpedoes was the subject of a court martial which reached the conclusion that this action was 'premature', but examination of the records to find out why is still not encouraged.

The heavy losses suffered by British cruisers to enemy submarines were perhaps in the main inevitable. Cruisers were not meant to combat submarines and were not built to stand up to torpedo hits underwater as were battleships. Despite this, many cruisers took hits, even more than one hit, very well, survived to reach harbour and were repaired to fight again. The fact that every cruiser sunk by submarine was torpedoed in the Mediterranean save for one, may be one reason. The differing levels of water were found to affect adversely the workings of the Asdic detection device to a far greater degree than elsewhere rendering detection difficult. The loss of the *Galatea* might be put down to over-confidence; she was about to enter harbour at Alexandria when hit, and considered herself in safe waters thus relaxing her watertight integrity condition. The loss of the *Calypso*, which was closely screened by destroyers at the time, was simply skill on the part of the attacking U-boat, against which there was no defence in so small and old a vessel.

Some protection might be afforded by listening for approaching torpedoes on the ships' hydrophones, but this was only effective if there was sufficient time to take avoiding action. Some cruisers were fitted with Asdic and depth charges, but there is no record of any submarine being sunk, or even inconvenienced by cruiser attack, which is hardly surprising. Warships are built for specific functions and anti-submarine operations were never a serious consideration for cruisers.

The resilience of some cruisers to torpedo hits was astonishing. In the long list of cruisers damaged by submarine attacks were the *Hobart*, torpedoed by the Japanese submarine *I-11* of New Georgia in July 1943 and taking eighteen months to repair, *Arethusa, Liverpool, Argonaut, Cleopatra, Phoebe, Fiji, Kenya, Newfoundland* and *Nigeria*. The only cruisers to strike back against the underwater enemy with any success were the *Hermione*, which rammed and sank the Italian submarine *Tembien* off the south coast of Sicily on 2nd August 1941 and the *Dragon*, which shelled the Vichy submarine *Persée* off Dakar in September 1940, before destroyers finished her off.

Torpedoes fired by E-boats and similar light surface craft also caused some casualties; among them was the *York*, torpedoed by an explosive motor boat at Suda Bay, Crete, and she was finished off by dive bombing before enough repairs had been effected for her to sail to safety, *Leander*, torpedoed by Japanese destroyers in a night action in the Solomon Islands in the south-west Pacific in July 1943, and *Diadem* damaged by an explosive motor boat on 12th August 1944, and *Capetown* in April 1941.

Apart from the loss of the *Curacoa*, the natural hazard of collision, amplified many by the special conditions at sea during 1939-45 led to some accidents of this nature. The most serious of these resulted in the loss of the destroyers *Imogen*, rammed by the *Glasgow* off Duncansby Head, Scotland on 16th July 1940 and the *Fraser*, a Canadian ship, on 25th June off the Gironde estuary, by the *Calcutta*. Both incidents involved heavy loss of life. The *Delhi* was damaged in a collision with *Uganda* on 3rd September, 1943, in the Mediterranean and again by an explosive motor boat at Split, Yugoslavia towards the end of the war. The *Sheffield* was in a collision with the minesweeper *Cadmus* on 9th December, 1942 but happily the little ship survived this knock.

Mines took a heavy toll. The biggest disaster for British cruisers took place on the night of 18th/19th December 1941, when Force 'K' ran into a unreported minefield laid off Tripoli in deep water. At around 0106 on the morning of the 19th, the force had just crossed the 80 fathom line, considered to be safe from mines, had reduced speed to 24 knots and was commencing a turn to sweep along the coast in search of a reported convoy. This has been described in detail in an earlier book together with the poignant signals that accompanied it.*

Briefly the squadron was in line ahead in the order *Neptune*, *Aurora*, *Penelope* and four destroyers. The first indication of trouble was that there was an explosion on the *Neptune*'s port side and at once the *Aurora* hauled out of line to starboard whereupon six minutes later she detonated a second mine on her port side, abreast 'B' turret. At once she took on a heavy list to port and started to flood by the bows. Her port forward oil tanks and store rooms flooded at once and this slowly spread aft. The *Aurora* eventually heeled over eleven degrees but counterflooding corrected this. She was however badly damaged under water with her hull buckled for a length of 120 feet. The shell hoists of 'A' and 'B' turrets were jammed. Her speed was reduced to ten knots.

Penelope thought both her consorts had been torpedoed and likewise turned hard starboard, only to detonate a mine on her port side abreast the bridge. She was the only cruiser of the three to have manned her hydrophones and streamed her paravanes but this did not save her damage, although it minimised it; the mine exploded outboard of the hull which reduced the scale of her injuries. She remained structurally sound and in good fighting order.

Neptune had stopped, but while the destroyer *Lance* closed her another mine exploded under the cruiser's port quarter. This was at 0112 and thirteen minutes later yet a third mine was detonated by this unfortunate vessel, again under her stern, and these explosions blew off most of her quarterdeck structure. She was still afloat and, while the damaged *Aurora* limped off to Malta as best she could, the *Penelope* and the destroyers prepared to take *Neptune* in tow. This was being organised when the *Kandahar*, which had closed to take off survivors, was mined at 0304. While further attempts were being made to rescue both ships, the *Neptune* struck yet another mine amidship at around 0400, and this, coupled with her previous damage, proved too much for her. She rolled over quickly and sank with all but one of her crew.

Apart from the *Scylla*, mined off Normandy and subsequently never repaired, other British crews suffered varying degrees of damage from mines. The extent of the damage was considerably

* See Peter C. Smith & Edwin Walker, *Battles of the Malta Striking Forces* (Ian Allan, 1974).

more than had been anticipated before the war. The acoustic mines laid by the Germans were particularly virulent devices against which even the largest cruisers suffered badly.

One of the first major casualties was the *Belfast* which was damaged by one of these monsters on 21st November 1939 in the Firth of Forth. The power of the explosion was sufficient to break the cruiser's back and she was in dockyard hands undergoing an almost complete re-building for almost three years. Other cruisers which suffered damage from mining were the *Galatea*, twice, on 1st and 9th September 1940, the *Sheffield*, in a 'friendly' minefield off Iceland on 4th March 1942, was a particularly unfortunate ship, but she survived it.

Despite all this misfortune and damage, the British cruiser probably handed out more damage than she herself sustained throughout the war and Table 21 illustrates one aspect of this cost effectiveness. Armed Merchant Raiders are omitted.

* * *

Table 21
Enemy warships destroyed by British cruisers 1939-45 (Major units only)

A: German

Ship	Type	Date	Area	Killers
Hermann Schoemann	Destroyer	2-05-42	Arctic	*Jamaica & Sheffield*
Friedrich Eckoldt	Destroyer	31-12-42	Arctic	*Sheffield*
Z-26	Destroyer	29-03-42	Arctic	*Nigeria*
Z-27	Destroyer	28-12-43	Bay of Biscay	*Enterprise & Glasgow*
T-25	Destroyer	28-12-43	Bay of Biscay	*Enterprise & Glasgow*
T-26	Destroyer	28-12-43	Bay of Biscay	*Enterprise & Glasgow*
M-10	Minesweeper	14-03-44	off Lorient	*Bellona*
M-263	Minesweeper	6-08-44	Ile d'Yeu	*Bellona*
M-273	Minesweeper	12-01-45	off Egersund	*Bellona & Norfolk*
M-385	Minesweeper	15-08-44	Biscay	*Mauritius*
M-486	Minesweeper	6-08-44	off Ile d'Yeu	*Bellona*
Bremse	Minelayer	6-09-41	off Murmen	*Aurora & Nigeria*
Sperrbrecher 7	Minesweeper	12-08-44	off La Pallice	*Diadem*

B: Italian

Colleoni	Light Cruiser	19-07-40	off Crete	*Sydney*
Espero	Destroyer	28-06-40	Ionian Sea	*Sydney*

Artigliere	Destroyer	12-10-40	off Malta	*York*
Ariel	Destroyer	12-10-40	off Malta	*Ajax*
Airone	Destroyer	12-10-40	off Malta	*Ajax*
Nullo	Destroyer	21-10-40	Red Sea	*Leander*
Vega	Destroyer	10-01-41	off Malta	*Bonaventure*
Fulmine	Destroyer	9-11-41	Ionian Sea	*Aurora & Penelope*
Folgore	Destroyer	2-12-42	off Sicily	*Aurora, Sirius & Argona*
Tembien	Submarine	2-08-41	off Sicily	*Hermione*

* * *

With the end of the war the usual wholesale scrappings associated with the coming of peace took place and once more economy was the watchword. Naturally the old cruisers, many of which had been well past their allotted life-span *before* the war, were not expected to survive and so the surviving 'C', 'D', 'E' and 'Improved *Birmingham*' were quickly disposed of. Many of these ships had, in fact, been laid up as early as 1944 as accommodation and training units, and a few soldiered on in this role for a few years more.

Of the more modern ships, the *County* Class were approaching the end of their life spans also and, being too large for modern fleet requirements in terms of limited manpower, quickly followed the small cruisers to the breakers. A few, those which had received a large degree of modernisation in the war period, were retained as training ships or flagships on distant stations. The *Norfolk, Devonshire* and *Sussex*, along with *Cumberland*, which was fitted out as a trials' cruiser for the testing of new weapons at sea, fell into that class, and thus were retained until the 1950's. The *London* should have lasted much longer having been rebuilt in a far more complete manner and having benefited from the latest advances. Unfortunately her machinery had not been renewed and the cash was not available to allow this to be done. Moreover she would have remained an odd ship out as the only 8-inch cruiser in the Royal Navy, and so, after her exploits on the Yangtse in aid of the *Amethyst*, she too, sadly, was scrapped at the same time. All the early war plans for a large class of heavy cruisers with 8-inch guns foundered early on and so these, to be named after Admirals according to Manning and Walker, never came about.

Postwar there were good grounds to get quickly underway with at least one class of cruiser that embodied *all* the lessons of that

Birmingham was heavily ...aged by Stukas in the ...terranean in 1942, but ...merged as good as new ...went on to accept the sur-...er of what little remained ...e German surface fleet in ...

...orting the army during ... numerous amphibious ...ings in Europe between ... and 1945 became one ...e principal functions of ...ewer light cruisers with ... batteries of 6-inch guns. ... the *Mauritius* is seen in ...n at night firing salvoes ...st German troop con-...ations.

...famous *Arethusa* served ... great merit throughout ...var and this aerial view ...s her as she was in ...mber 1943. She sur-... the war despite con-...able more action and ...ge.

The much reduced post-war fleet saw few of the war veterans serving, but among them were *Cleopatra* (bottom) and the newer *Diadem* (top) both seen here with the Home Fleet in 1947.

conflict and a new form of 6-inch gun with a high rate of fire was under development, along with a new AA mounting, a twin 3-inch gun to replace both the Bofors and Oerlikons; these had been shown to be too small to stop Kamikazes and the like. This class reached fruition on the drawing boards in 1947 and were known as the *Minotaur* Class. They would have been 15,000 tonners, armed with twelve 6-inch guns in twin turrets, three forward and two aft, and no less than sixteen of the new 3-inch guns, a speed of 31 knots. They were never built, for funds continued to dwindle and the whole future and role of the conventional types of warship were under hesitant review. The closest that any nation came to construction of ships of similar size and layout was the American *Worcester* class of the same period.

What remained for the Royal Navy cruisers? It was decided that future requirements for that type of vessel should be set at a modest 25, far cry from the 70 considered essential scant years before. But even this modest figure proved to be pie-in-the-sky against the fierce parsimony that followed 1945. A plan to modernise the various ships was drawn up but even this fell through and only slight improvements were made to most vessels. The pre-war 'Town' class were getting long in the tooth by this time and only limited work was done on them before they were laid up. The *Didos* were far too small to take all the equipment needed to bring them up to standard and were mostly cocooned after limited service post-war. The exception was the *Royalist* one of the most modern of the type and was given an extensive facelift in the mid-50's. The *Colony* class were also modern but had been built to war-standard finish and consequently deteriorated more quickly. They lingered on until the 1960's, although many were sold abroad before then. The *Superb* and *Swiftsure* remained, along with the larger *Belfast*, and these were taken in hand for more comprehensive modernisation. But even this had to be abandoned in some cases, and the *Swiftsure* lingered, half re-built, for years in Chatham dockyard before the financial axe fell again and she was broken up.

The only bright spot was the completion of the *Lion*, *Tiger* and *Blake*, armed with the new guns, but what advantage there was in these weapons was thrown away by the decision to equip them with four instead of twelve main guns. They made a good show nonetheless but lasted in their conventional role for only a short time before being laid up or reduced to hideous and useless hybrids by being converted to 'Helicopter Cruisers'.

And so the conventional cruiser followed the other two types of warship around which the fleets of two world wars had been built, the battleship and the destroyer, into oblivion. Even the aircraft-carrier followed these in the late 1970's and now there are only a hotch-potch of hybrid types remaining, bearing the old designations that have absolutely no relevance to their previous functions. 'Through-Deck Cruisers' are really small, cheap aircraft carriers, 'Guided Missile Destroyers' are small cruisers equal in size to the *Didos*, 'Frigates' are a combination of the best qualities of the old destroyers and 3rd-class cruisers but the terms used are meaningless.

The lingering fate of the old type of British cruiser is best illustrated by the dates of their final departure from the Navy List contained in Table 22.

* * *

Table 22
The scrapping of the British Cruiser Fleet, 1945-70

Ship	Date	Disposal	Yearly Total
Vindictive	Feb 1946	Scrapped at Blyth	
Cardiff	Mar 1946	Scrapped Troon	
Caradoc	April 1946	Scrapped Briton Ferry	
Diomede	May 1946	Scrapped Dalmuir	1946-7
Enterprise	April 1946	Scrapped Newport	
Capetown	June 1946	Scrapped Preston	
Ceres	July 1946	Scrapped Blyth	
Hawkins	Dec 1947	Scrapped Dalmuir	1947-1
Kent	Jan 1948	Scrapped Troon	
Caledon	Feb 1948	Scrapped Dover	
Dauntless	Feb 1948	Scrapped Inverkeithing	
Danae	Mar 1948	Scrapped Barrow	
Aurora	May 1948	Sold to China	
Colombo	May 1948	Scrapped Newport	1948-12
Delhi	May 1948	Scrapped Newport	
Suffolk	June 1948	Scrapped Newport	
Achilles	July 1948	Sold to India	
Berwick	July 1948	Scrapped Blyth	

Emerald	July 1948	Scrapped Troon	
Despatch	Aug 1948	Scrapped Troon	
Carlisle	May 1949	Scrapped Alexandria	
Frobisher	May 1949	Scrapped Newport	
Despatch	Aug 1949	Scrapped Troon	1949-5
Orion	Aug 1949	Scrapped Troon	
Ajax	Nov 1949	Scrapped Newport	
Leander	Jan 1950	Scrapped Blyth	
London	Jan 1950	Scrapped Barrow	
Norfolk	Feb 1950	Scrapped Newport	1950-5
Scylla	May 1950	Scrapped Barrow	
Arethusa	Aug 1950	Scrapped Troon	
Devonshire	Dec 1954	Scrapped Newport	1954-1
Australia	Jan 1955	Scrapped Barrow	
Shropshire	Jan 1955	Scrapped Dalmuir	
Sussex	Jan 1955	Scrapped Dalmuir	1955-4
Argonaut	Nov 1955	Scrapped Newport	
Phoebe	Aug 1956	Scrapped Blyth	
Sirius	Oct 1956	Scrapped Blyth	1956-3
Royalist	Oct 1956	Sold to New Zealand	
Nigeria	Aug 1957	Sold to India	
Diadem	Sept 1957	Sold to Pakistan	1957-2
Dido	July 1958	Scrapped Barrow	
Glasgow	July 1958	Scrapped Blyth	
Liverpool	July 1958	Scrapped Bo'ness	1958-4
Cleopatra	Dec 1958	Scrapped Newport	
Bellona	Feb 1959	Scrapped Briton Ferry	
Euryalus	July 1959	Scrapped Blyth	
Newcastle	Sept 1959	Scrapped Faslane	
Cumberland	Nov 1959	Scrapped Newport	1959-5
Newfoundland	Dec 1959	Sold to Peru	
Ceylon	Feb 1960	Sold to Peru	

Superb	Aug 1960	Scrapped Dalmuir	
Birmingham	Sept 1960	Scrapped Inverkeithing	1960-4
Jamaica	Dec 1960	Scrapped Dalmuir	
Uganda	Feb 1961	Scrapped Osaka, Japan	1961-1
Black Prince	Aug 1962	Scrapped Osaka, Japan	
Kenya	Oct 1962	Scrapped Faslane	1962-3
Swiftsure	Oct 1962	Scrapped Inverkeithing	
Mauritius	Mar 1965	Scrapped Inverkeithing	1965-2
Bermuda	Aug 1965	Scrapped Briton Ferry	
			1966-0
Sheffield	Sept 1967	Scrapped Inverkeithing	1967-1
Gambia	1968	Sold for Scrapping	1968-1

*   *   *

Only *Belfast* remains in British waters, moored on the Thames as a Museum. She is not typical of Britain's cruisers of World War II, but she is the last. Go visit her.

Appendixes

Appendix One
British Cruiser Classes built and planned by 1939
(Tonnages and crews as originally built)

Kent Class. Heavy Cruisers. 9,750 to 9,870 tons. Six or eight 8-inch guns; eight 4-inch guns, eight 21-inch torpedoes. 31 knots. 679 Crew

Pendant	Name	Completion Date
84	Australia	24.4.28
65	Berwick	15.2.28
33	Canberra	10.7.28
56	Cornwall	8.5.28
57	Cumberland	23.2.28
54	Kent	25.6.28
55	Suffolk	31.5.28

London Class. Heavy cruisers. 9,830-9,850 tons. Eight 8-inch guns; eight 4-inch guns, eight 21-inch torpedoes. 32 knots. 650 crew.

39	Devonshire	18.3.29
69	London	31.1.29
73	Shropshire	12.9.29
96	Sussex	19.3.29

Norfolk Class. Heavy cruisers. 9,925 to 9,975 tons. Eight 8-inch guns; eight 4-inch guns; eight 21-inch torpedoes. 32 knots. 650 crew.

40	Dorsetshire	30.9.30
78	Norfolk	30.4.30

(Two others, *Northumberland* and *Surrey* cancelled January 1930 owing to Defence cuts)

York Class. Heavy cruisers. 8,250-8,390 tons. Six 8-inch guns; four 4-inch guns; six 21-inch torpedoes. 32 knots. 600 crew.

68	Exeter	23.7.31
90	York	1.5.30

Caledon Class. Light cruisers. 4,180 tons. Five 6-inch guns. two 3-inch guns; eight 21-inch torpedoes. 29 knots. 400 crew

53	Caledon	6.3.17
61	Calypso	21.6.17
60	Caradoc	15.6.17

(*Caledon* re-armed as AA cruiser 1942-43 with eight 4-inch guns)

Ceres Class. Light cruisers. 4,190 tons. Five 6-inch guns, two 3-inch guns, eight 21-inch torpedoes. 29 knots. 400 crew.

58	Cardiff	25.6.17	(*Ex-Caprice*)
59	Ceres	1.6.17	
62	Curacoa	18.2.18	
88	Capetown	14.10.22	

(*Curacoa* re-armed as AA cruiser 1940-41 with eight 4-inch guns)

Coventry Class. AA cruisers. 4,190 tons. Ten 4-inch guns, 16 2-pdr guns. 29 knots. 400 crew.

| 43 | Coventry | 21.2.18 | (*Ex-Corsair*) |
| 42 | Curlew | 14.12.17 | |

Colombo Class. AA cruisers. 4,290 tons. Eight 4-inch guns, 4 2pdr guns. 29 knots. 400 crew.

87	Cairo	14.10.19	
82	Calcutta	21.8.19	
67	Carlisle	16.11.18	
89	Colombo	18.6.19	(*Ex-Cawnpore*)

Dauntless Class. Light cruisers. 4,850 tons. Six 6-inch guns; three 4-inch guns, twelve 21-inch torpedoes. 29 knots. 450 crew.

44	Danae	22.6.18
45	Dauntless	2.12.18
74	Delhi	7.6.19
46	Dragon	16.8.18
93	Dunedin	10.19
99	Durban	31.10.21
30	Despatch	30.6.22
92	Diomede	22.4.22

(Four others, *Daedalus*, *Daring*, *Desperate* and *Dryad* cancelled) *Delhi* was re-armed as AA cruiser 1941-42 with five 5-inch guns, US model)

Effingham Class. Light cruisers. 9,550-9,860 tons. Seven 7·5-inch guns, five 4-inch guns, six 21-inch torpedoes. 30·5 knots. 712 crew.

36	Vindictive	21.9.18	(*Ex-Cavendish*)
98	Effingham	9.7.25	
81	Frobisher	20.9.24	
86	Hawkins	23.7.19	

(Note one other *Raleigh* was wrecked August 1922. *Effingham* re-armed with nine 6-inch guns, eight 4-inch guns. *Vindictive* used as Repair Ship)

Emerald Class. Light cruisers. 7,550-7,580 tons. Seven 6-inch guns, three 4-inch guns, sixteen 21-inch torpedoes. 33 knots. 572 crew.

| 66 | Emerald | 14.1.26 |
| 52 | Enterprise | 31.3.26 |

(One other, *Euphrates*, cancelled).

Leander Class. Light cruisers. 6,830-7,270 tons. Four or eight 6-inch guns, eight 4-inch guns; eight 21-inch torpedoes. 550 crew. 32 knots.

70	Achilles	6.10.33	
22	Ajax	21.4.35	
75	Leander	24.3.33	
20	Neptune	22.2.34	
85	Orion	18.1.34	
48	Sydney	24.9.35	(*Ex-Phaeton*)
29	Perth	6.7.37	(*Ex-Amphion*)
63	Hobart	13.1.36	(*Ex-Apollo*)

(Last three were a modified type, handed over to RAN)

Arethusa Class. Light cruisers. 5,220-5,270 tons. Six 6-inch guns, four or eight 4-inch guns, six 21-inch torpedoes. 450 crew. 32·5 knots

26	Arethusa	23.5.35
12	Aurora	12.11.37
71	Galatea	4.8.35
97	Penelope	13.11.36

Southampton Class. Light cruisers. 9,100-9,400 tons. Twelve 6-inch guns, eight 4-inch guns, six 21-inch torpedoes. 32 knots. 700 crew.

19	Birmingham	18.11.37	
21	Glasgow	8.9.37	
76	Newcastle	5.3.37	(*Ex-Minotaur*)
24	Sheffield	25.8.37	
19	Southampton	6.3.37	(*Ex-Polyphemus*)
62	Gloucester	27.1.39	
11	Liverpool	2.11.38	
15	Manchester	4.8.38	

Improved Southampton Class. Light cruisers, 10,000-11,500 tons. Twelve 6-inch guns; twelve 4-inch guns, six 21-inch torpedoes. 850 crew. 32 knots.

| 35 | Belfast | 3.8.39 |

16	*Edinburgh*	6.7.39

Dido Class. Light cruisers. 5,450-5,770 tons. Eight or ten 5.25-inch guns, six 21-inch torpedoes. 32 knots. 530 crew.

61	*Argonaut*	8.8.42
31	*Bonaventure*	24.5.40
33	*Cleopatra*	5.12.41
37	*Dido*	30.9.40
42	*Euryalus*	30.6.41
74	*Hermione*	25.3.41
93	*Naiad*	24.7.40
43	*Phoebe*	30.9.40
82	*Sirius*	6.5.42

Modified Dido Class. AA cruisers. 5,450 tons. Eight 4·5-inch guns, six 21-inch torpedoes. 520 crew. 32 knots.

88	*Charybdis*	3.12.41
98	*Scylla*	12.6.42

(Correct 5·25 inch armament was not ready in time for these ships and both were war casualties before they could be armed correctly)

Improved Dido Class. Light cruisers. 5,770 tons. Eight 5.25-inch guns, six 21-inch torpedoes. 32 knots. 535 crew.

63	*Bellona*	29.10.43
81	*Black Prince*	20.11.43
84	*Diadem*	6.1.44
89	*Royalist*	10.9.43
95	*Spartan*	10.8.43

Colony Class. Light cruisers. 8,000-8,800 tons. Twelve 6-inch guns: * (Only nine); eight 4-inch guns, six 21-inch torpedoes. 730 crew 33 knots.

52	*Bermuda*	21.8.42
30	*Ceylon**	13.7.43
58	*Fiji*	17.5.40
48	*Gambia*	21.2.42
44	*Jamaica*	29.6.42
14	*Kenya*	27.9.40
80	*Mauritius*	1.1.41
59	*Newfoundland**	20.1.43
60	*Nigeria*	23.9.40
46	*Trinidad*	14.10.41

| 66 | *Uganda** | 3.1.43 | (Became Canadian *Quebec* 1943) |

Minotaur Class. Light cruisers. 8,800-8,900 tons. Nine 6-inch guns, ten 4-inch guns, six 21-inch torpedoes. 31·5 knots. 730 crew.

53	*Minotaur*	25.5.45	(Became Canadian
08	*Swiftsure*	22.6.44	*Ontario* 1945)
25	*Superb*	16.11.45	

Appendix Two
British Cruiser Losses 1939-45

1939	Nil.		
1940	*Effingham*	18.5.40	Wrecked off Norway, Struck submerged rocks Vestiford.
	Curlew	26.5.40	Bombed German aircraft Norway.
	Calypso	12.6.40.	Torpedoed by Italian submarine *Bagnolini* south of Crete.
1941	*Southampton*	11.1.41	Bombed by Stukas east of Malta.
	York	26.3.41	Damaged by explosive boat Suda Bay, Crete. Finished off by German bombers on 22.5.41 while repairing.
	Bonaventure	31.3.41	Torpedoed by Italian submarine *Ambra* south of Crete.
	Fiji	22.5.41	Bombed by German aircraft south of Crete
	Gloucester	22.5.41	Bombed by German aircraft south of Crete
	Calcutta	1.6.41	Bombed by German Stukas off Egypt.
	Sydney (Ran)	19.11.41	Sunk by German raider *Kormoran* West of Australia.
	Dunedin	24.11.41	Torpedoed by German Submarine *U-124* central South Atlantic.
	Galatea	14.12.41	Torpedoed by German submarine *U-205* south of Crete.
	Neptune	19.12.41	Mined off Tripoli.
1942	*Perth (RAN)*	1.3.42	Sunk by Japanese cruisers in Java Sea.
	Exeter	1.3.42	Sunk by Japanese cruisers in Java Sea.
	Naiad	11.3.42	Torpedoed by German submarine *U-565* off

Egyptian coast.

	Dorsetshire	5.4.42	Sunk by Japanese Navy dive bombers SW of Ceylon.
	Cornwall	5.4.42	Sunk by Japanese Navy dive bombers SW of Ceylon.
	Edinburgh	2.5.42	Sunk by own forces after damage in action south German destroyers Barents Sea.
	Trinidad	15.5.42	Bombed by German aircraft in Barents Sea after damage in surface action.
	Hermione	16.6.42	Torpedoed by German submarine *U-205* south of Crete.
	Canberra (RAN)	9.8.42	Sunk by Japanese cruisers off Savo Island, Solomons.
	Cairo	12.8.42	Sunk by own forces after torpedoed by Italian submarine *Axum*
	Manchester	13.8.42	Scuttled by crew after torpedo damage from Italian E-boats, Sicilian Channel.
	Coventry	14.9.42	Bombed by German Stukas in eastern Mediterranean.
	Curacoa	2.10.42	Rammed and sunk by RMS *Queen Mary* in North Atlantic.
1943	*Carlisle*	9.10.43	Bombed by German Stukas south of Rhodes, Aegean. Never repaired.
	Charybdis	23.10.43	Sunk by German destroyers *T-23* and *T.27* in English Channel.
1944	*Spartan*	29.1.44	Sunk by German bombers off Anzio.
	Penelope	18.2.44	Torpedoed by German submarine *U-410* NW of Naples.
	Dragon	8.7.44	Sunk by German Marder unit off France.

Appendix Three

British Cruisers: Summary of Service. (September 1939-March 1946)

Australia (RAN)

Completed refit and trials Cockatoo Island 29th September 1939.

Australian Squadron October 1939-May 1940

Detached to South American Squadron May-July 1940.

1st Cruiser Squadron, Home Fleet, July-February 1941.

4th Cruiser Squadron, East Indies, March 1941-June 1941

Australian Squadron, July-August 1941

Attached East Indies, September-December 1941.

Australian Squadron, December 1941-July 1945.

Damaged by Kamikaze aircraft off Philippines 21st October 1944, 5th January 1945 and 8th Jaunary 1945.

Refit August-December 1945. Scrapped Barrow 1955.

Berwick

8th Cruiser Squadron America and West Indies, September-November 1939.

Refit November 1939.

1st Cruiser Squadron, Home Fleet, December 1939-October 1940.

Mediterranean, November 1940-February 1941. Spartivento November 1940.

Damaged by German cruiser *Hipper* on 25th December 1940.

March-July 1941, C.S.I. October-November 1941 Refitting. May-August 1942 Refitting. August-December 1942 Refitting. March 1941-June 1945 1st Cruiser Squadron, Home Fleet.

July 1945-February 1946, Portsmouth Command, Trooping.

Scrapped at Blyth July 1948.

Canberra (RAN)

Australia Squadron September 1939-February 1941.

4th Cruiser Squadron, East Indies, March 1941-June 1941.

Mediterranean Fleet July 1941.

East Indies, August 1941.

Australia Squadron September 1941-August 1942

Sunk by Japanese Cruisers at Battle of Savo Island 9th August 1942

Cornwall

5th Cruiser Squadron September 1939 (China).

Force 'I', Indian Ocean, October 1939-January 1940.

6th CS, South Atlantic, February 1940-June 1941.

Sank German raider *Pinguin* 8th May 1941 off Seychelles.
6th CS East Indies, July 1941-February 1942.
4th CS Far East Fleet, March-April 1942.
Sunk by Japanese Navy dive bombers south of Ceylon 5th April 1942.

Cumberland
South Atlantic Command, September 1939.
Force 'G' October 1939-January 1940.
South American Division February-March 1940.
6th CS South Atlantic, April 1940-July 1940.
South Atlantic Command, July 1940-July 1941.
1st CS Home Fleet, August 1941-December 1943.
Refitting September-October 1941. Refit March-April 1942. Refit August-1942-December 1943.
1st CS Home Fleet, February 1944.
4th CS Eastern Fleet, March 1944-December 1944.
5th CS Eastern Fleet, January-October 1945.
Plymouth Command, Trooping, November 1945-March 1946.
Scrapped Newport from November 1959 (Trials Ship post-war).

Kent
5th CS China Station, September-December 1939.
4th CS East Indies, December 1939-July 1940.
3rd CS, Mediterranean, September-November 1940.
Damaged by aerial torpedo off Bardia 17th September 1940. Temporary repairs Alexandria. Refitting Devonport. Bombed and damaged in Devonport dockyard 21st April 1941.
January-September Repairs and refitting.
September 1941-December 1944, 1st, CS Home Fleet.
Refitting July-September 1942. Refit October 1943.
Category 'B' Reserve Gareloch, January 1945.
Scrapped at Troon from January 1948.

Suffolk
September 1939 Refitting.
October 1939. 18th CS Home Fleet. (Refitting Mediterranean)
1st CS Mediterranean (For Home)
January 1940-April 1943 1st CS Home Fleet.
Damaged by German aircraft off Stavanger, Norway, 17th April 1940.
Repairs and refitting May 1940-March 1941.
Boiler and machinery refit April-July 1942.

4th CS Eastern Fleet, May 1943-June 1944.
5th CS January 1945-July 1945., East Indies Command.
August 1945-March 1946, Nore Command, Trooping.
Scrapped at Newport from June 1948.

Devonshire
September-November 1939. 1st CS Mediterranean Fleet.
1st CS Home Fleet, November 1939-October 1940.
South Atlantic Command, November 1940-February 1942.
Sank German raider *Atlantis* 23rd November 1941 off Ascension Island.
Refitting March-April 1941. Refitting February-March 1942.
4th CS Eastern Fleet, March 1942-August 1943.
Refitting and re-equipping May 1943-March 1944.
September 1943-June 1945, 1st CS Home Fleet.
July 1945-March 1946, Plymouth Command, Trooping.
Converted to Cadet Training Ship post-war.
Scrapped at Newport from December 1954.

London
Being completely re-built from September 1939-February 1941.
1st CS Home Fleet March 1941-March 1944.
Detached to West Africa June 1941.
Refitting January-April 1943.
4th CS, Eastern Fleet, March-June 1944.
5th CS, Eastern Fleet, June 1944-December 1944.
5th CS East Indies Command, January 1945-October 1945.
Refitting June-July 1945.
Nore Command, Trooping, November 1945-March 1946.
Damaged by shore batteries Yangtse River 1948.
Scrapped at Barrow from January 1950.

Shropshire
1st CS, Mediterranean Fleet,
Force 'H', October 1939-January 1940.
6th CS South Atlantic Command, February 1940-September 1940.
4th CS East Indies Command, October 1940.
Detached to Red Sea November 1940.
4th CS East Indies Command, December 1940-July 1941.
Refitting April 1941.
1st CS Home Fleet, August 1941-February 1942.
Refitting January-February 1942.

South Atlantic Command, March-August 1942.
Transferred to Royal Australian Navy September 1942 to replace *Canberra*.
Refit December 1942-May 1943.
Working up August-September 1943.
Australia Command, October 1943-March 1946.
Scrapped at Dalmuier and Troon from January 1955.

Sussex
1st CS Mediterranean Fleet, September 1939.
Force 'H', October-December 1939.
East Indies Squadron, January 1940.
4th CS East, Indies Command, February-March 1940.
1st CS Home Fleet, May 1940-February 1941.
Refitting May 1940.
Refitting September 1940 at Scotts. Bombed in dock, burnt out and sunk
on 18th September 1940. Salvaged and rebuilt October 1940-August
1942. (Nore Command March-August 1941, 1st CS, Home Fleet
September 1941-August 1942)
1st CS Home Fleet, September 1942-January 1943.
4th CS, Eastern Fleet, March 1943-May 1944.
Refitting June 1944-April 1945.
5th CS East Indies Command, June 1945-March 1946.
Scrapped at Dalmuir from January 1955.

Dorsetshire
5th CS, China, September 1939.
Force 'I', October 1939-February 1940.
6th CS, South Atlantic Command, March-July 1940.
South Atlantic Command, July 1940-June 1941.
Torpedoed *Bismarck* during final action 27th May 1941.
Refitting June-August 1941.
East Indies Command, Sept 1941-February 1942.
4th CS, Eastern Fleet, March-April 1942.
Sunk by Japanese Navy bombers in Indian Ocean 5th April 1942.

Norfolk
18th CS, Home Fleet, September 1939.
1st CS October 1939-December 1940.
Bombed and damaged Scapa Flow by German bombers 16th March 1940.
Repairs and refit April-July 1940.
Force 'K', South Atlantic, January-February 1941.

1st CS, Home Fleet, March 1941-July 1942.
Refitting July-September 1941. Refitting February-March 1942.
18th CS Home Fleet, August-September 1942.
1st CS, Home Fleet, October 1942-July 1945.
Refitting April-May 1943.
At sinking of *Scharnhorst,* North Cape, 26th December 1943. Damaged by
11-inch shell. Refitting and repairs February-October 1944.
5th CS, East Indies Command August 1945-March 1946.
Scrapped at Newport from February 1950.

Exeter
South American Division, September 1939.
Force 'G', October 1939-January 1940.
Heavily damaged at River Plate action 13th December 1939.
Refitting and repairs February-July 1940.
1st CS, Home Fleet, July 1940-June 1941.
East Indies Command, July 1941-January 1942.
4th CS, East Indies Command, February-March 1942.
Bomb damage by Japanese aircraft 25th February 1942.
Action damage by Japanese ships 27th February 1942.
Sunk by Japanese cruisers off Sumatra on 1st March 1942.

York
8th CS, America & West Indies, September 1939-December 1939.
1st CS, Home Fleet, January-April 1940.
18th CS, Home Fleet, May-July 1940.
3rd CS, Mediterranean Fleet, September 1940-April 1941.
Sank Italian destroyer *Artigliere* and helped sink Italian destroyer *Ariel* off
Sicily 12th October 1940.
Badly damaged by Italian explosive motor boat Suda Bay Crete, and
finally sunk by bombing Axis aircraft, 22nd May 1941, while repairing.

Caledon
7th CS, Northern Patrol, September November 1939.
3rd CS Mediterranean Fleet, December 1939-July 1940.
7th CS. Mediterranean Fleet, July 1940.
Red Sea Force, September-December 1940.
4th CS East Indies Command, January 1941.
Red Sea Force, February-October 1941.
Refitting September-October 1941.
East Indies Command, November 1941-February 1942.

5th CS East Indies Command, March-August 1942.
Coverted UK into an AA cruiser, September 1942-February 1944.
March 1944-April 1945, Mediterranean Fleet.
Reduced to Reserve, Category 'C', Falmouth from June 1945.
Scrapped at Dover from February 1948.

Calypso
7th CS, Northern Patrol, September-November 1939.
3rd CS, Mediteranean Fleet, December 1939-June 1940.
Torpedoed and sunk by Italian submarine *Bagnolini* off Tobruk on 12th June 1940.

Caradoc
Channel Force, September 1940.
8th CS, America & West Indies, October 1939-February 1940.
Refitting March-April 1940.
8th CS, America & West Indies, May 1940-March 1942.
Refit at New York, October 1941-March 1942.
Home Fleet, April-June 1942.
5th CS, Eastern Fleet, July 1942-July 1943.
South Atlantic Command, August 1943-April 1944.
Base Ship, Eastern Fleet, May 1944-December 1944.
Base Ship, East Indies Command, January-October 1945.
Reduced to reserve Devonport December 1945.
Category 'C' reserve, Falmouth February 1946.
Scrapped at Briton Ferry from April 1946.

Adventure
Attached Minelayer, Portsmouth Command, September 1939.
Attached Minelayer, Dover Command, November 1939.
Portsmouth Command, December 1939-July 1940.
Refitting December 1939-September 1940.
1st M/L Squadron, July-November 1940.
Western Approaches, December 1940-August 1941.
Refitting September 1941-December 1941.
1st M/L Squadron, September 1941-October 1943.
Refitting October 1943.
Plymouth Command, November 1943-March 1944.
Accommodation ship Portland and Portsmouth, March-October 1944.
Duty with ANCXF Portsmouth, November-1944-April 1945.
Reserve Portsmouth, May-September 1945.

Category 'C' Reserve Falmouth, September 1945-March 1946.
Scrapped Briton Ferry from July 1947.

Cardiff
12th CS, Northern Patrol, September 1939.
11th CS, Northern Patrol, October-November 1939.
11th CS, Home Fleet, December 1939.
8th CS, America & West Indies, January-February 1940.
Portsmouth Command, March-April 1940.
Gunnery Firing and experimental ship Portsmouth May 1940.
2nd CS at Dover, June-October 1940.
2nd CS Portsmouth Command, November 1940.
Western Approaches, December 1940-February 1941.
Gunnery Firing Cruiser, Western Approaches, March 1941-September
1945.
Category 'C' Reserve, Gareloch October 1945-March 1946.
Scrapped at Troon from March 1946.

Ceres
Channel Force, September 1939.
11th CS Northern Patrol, October-December 1939.
Designated Australia-on passage January-March 1940.
5th CS China Station (Singapore), April-May 1940.
4th CS, East Indies Fleet, May 1940-July 1941.
East Indies Fleet, August 1941-February 1942.
5th CS, Eastern Fleet, March 1942-October 1943.
Refitting September-October 1942.
Plymouth Command, November 1943.
Accommodation, Devonport, December 1943-August 1944.
Duty with ANCXF September 1944.
Reserve Fleet, Portsmouth, January 1945-March 1946.
Scrapped Blyth from July 1946.

Coventry
AA Cruiser, Home Fleet, November-December 1939.
Damaged by bomb Sullum Voe 1st January 1940.
20th CS Humber Force, January-April 1940. Refitting.
1st AAS, Humber Force, May-June 1940.
AA Cruiser, Home Fleet, July 1940.
Mediterranean Fleet, September 1940-August 1942.
Refitting January-March 1941. Refitting March-April 1942.

Torpedoed and sunk in Mediterranean by own forces after damage by dive bombers off Egypt 14th September 1942.

Curacoa

Converting to AA Cruiser, September-1939-February 1940.
20th CS, Humber, March-April 1940. Bomb damage Andalsnes 24.4.40
1st AAS, Humber Force, May-December 1940. (Refitting).
AA Cruiser, Home Fleet, November 1940-August 1942.
Refitting May-June 1942.
SEF, Western Approaches, September-October 1942.
Rammed and sunk by *Queen Mary* in Atlantic, 2nd October 1942.

Curlew

Refitting, September-1939-Feb 1940.
20th CS, Humber Force, March 1940.
Damaged May 1940. Temporary Repair.
Bombed and sunk Ofotfiord, Norway, 26th May 1940.

Cairo

AA Cruiser, Channel Force, September 1939.
1st AAS, Home Fleet, October-November 1939.
20th CS, Humber, December 1939.
1st AAS, Home Fleet, January-April 1940.
Bombed and damaged at Narvik, 28th May 1940.
Refitting and repairs May-July 1940.
1st AAS Home Fleet, Humber. July-September 1940.
Western Approaches, October 1940-March 1941.
AA Cruiser Home Fleet, April 1941.
Mediterranean Fleet, May-1941-August 1942.
Damaged by Italian cruisers in Mediterranean, 15th June 1942.
Torpedoed and sunk off Bizerta by own forces after damage by Italian submarine AXUM.

Calcutta

Attached AA cruiser Home Fleet, September-October 1939.
20th CS, Home Fleet, November 1939-April 1940.
1st AAS, Home Fleet, May 1940.
1st AAS, Dover Command, June 1940.
Rammed and sank Canadian destroyer *Fraser* off Gironde on 25th June 1940.
AA Cruiser Western Approaches, July 1940.

Attached AA Cruiser, Mediterranean Fleet, September 1940-June 1941.
Sunk by German bombers north-west of Alexandria, 1st June 1941.

Capetown
11th CS, North Atlantic Command, September-October 1939.
3rd CS, Mediterranean Fleet, November 1939-July 1940.
4th CS, East Indies Command, August 1940-July 1941.
Torpedoed by Italian E-Boat *MAS213* off Kuba, Eritrea, on 8th April 1941.
Refitting and repairs July 1941-July 1942.
Attached East Indies Command, August 1941-February 1942.
5th CS, Eastern Fleet, March 1942-September 1943.
October-November 1943, Devonport, reduced C & M.
Accommodation Ship Devonport, December 1943-August 1944.
ANCXF duties, September 1944.
Catergory 'C' Reserve, Falmouth, January 1945-March 1946.
Scrapped Preston from June 1946.

Carlisle
September 1939-January 1940, Converting to AA cruiser.
February-March 1940, Gibraltar.
20th CS, Humber Force, at Plymouth, April 1940.
1st AAS, Humber Force, at Namos, May 1940.
1st AAS, Red Sea Force, May 1940-March 1941.
Mediterranean Fleet, April-July 1941.
Damaged by bombing off Crete, 22nd May 1941.
Attached Mediterranean Fleet, August-December 1941.
Attached AA cruiser, Red Sea Force, January-March 1942.
Attached AA Cruiser, Mediterranean Fleet, April 1942-May 1943.
Refitting Freetown July 1942-January 1943.
15th CS, Mediterranean, July 1943.
Mediterranean Fleet, August-December 1943.
Bombed and heavily damaged by Stukas south of Rhodes,
Aegean, 9th October 1943.
Mediterranean Fleet, February-June 1944.
Escort Base Ship at Alexandria, August 1944-March 1946.
Disposed of at Alexandria in 1949.

Colombo
11th CS, North Atlantic Command, Gibraltar, September 1939.
11th CS, Northern Patrol, October 1939.
18th CS, Home Fleet, November 1939.

Designated for Australia, December 1939-February 1940.
On passage Mediterranean, March 1940.
5th CS, China Station, Singapore, April-May 1940.
4th CS, East Indies Command, May 1940-April 1941.
Refit February-April 1941.
Attached AA Cruiser, Red Sea Force, April-August 1941.
Attached AA Cruiser, East Indies Command, September 1941-February 1942.
5th CS, Eastern Fleet, March-July 1942.
Refitting July 1942-January 1943.
Unallocated Plymouth Command, August 1942-June 1943.
July 1943, Gibraltar.
12th CS, Mediterranean Fleet, August-December 1943.
Attached Cruiser, Mediterranean Fleet, December 1943-May 1945.
Reduced to reserve, Plymouth, June 1945.
Accommodation ship, Falmouth, August 1945-March 1946.
Scrapped at Newport from May 1948.

Danae
9th CS, South Atlantic Command, September 1939-January 1940.
5th CS, China Station, January 1940-December 1941.
5th CS, Eastern Fleet, January 1942-December 1943.
Refitting at Tyne, August 1942-September 1943. Re-armed.
4th CS, Eastern Fleet, February-April 1944.
1st CS, Home Fleet, May-June 1944.
Duty with ANCXF August-September 1944.
Handed over to Polish Navy as *Conrad*, October 1944-September 1946.
Attached Cruiser, Portsmouth Command, October 1944-March 1945.
10th CS, Home Fleet, April 1945-March 1946.
Refitting December 1944-January 1945.
Scrapped at Barrow from March 1948.

Dauntless
9th CS, South Atlantic Command, September December 1939.
5th CS, China Station, January 1940-December 1941.
5th CS, Eastern Fleet, January 1942-July 1943.
Refitting August-September 1943.
C.W. Training Cruiser, Rosyth Command, October 1943-February 1946.
Refitting February-March 1945.
Scrapped at Inverkeithing from February 1946.

Delhi
12th CS, Nothern Patrol, September-October 1939.
11th CS, Home Fleet, November 1939-February 1940.
Unallocated RA(D) Malta, March 1940.
Flag of C-in-C, Alexandria, April 1940.
Unallocated, Mediterranean Fleet, May-June 1940. Refit Gibraltar.
Attached Cruiser, South Atlantic Command, July 1940-February 1942.
Refitted and converted to AA cruiser at New York, June 1941-August 1942.
Unallocated Cruiser, Home Fleet, March-September 1942.
1 SEF, October 1942.
Attached Cruiser, Mediterranean Fleet, Algiers, November-December 1942.
Damaged by bombing Algiers, 20th November 1942.
At Gibraltar damaged December 1942-January 1943.
Refitted January-March 1943.
Unallocated Cruiser, Mediterranean Fleet April-May 1943 Refitting. Tyne and Devonport.
12th CS, Mediterranean Fleet, July-November 1943.
Attached AA Cruiser, Mediterranean Fleet, December 1943-March 1945.
Damaged in collision with *HMS Uganda*, 3rd September 1943.
Damaged by explosive motor boat at Split, Yugoslavia, 1945.
Reduced to reserve Sheerness, April 1945.
June Reserve Fleet, Chatham, May-June 1945.
Category 'C' Reserve, Dartmouth July 1945-March 1946.
Scrapped at Newport from May 1948.

Despatch
9th CS, South Atlantic Command, September 1939.
8th CS, America & West Indies, October 1939-January 1942.
Refit June-July 1940, Refit April-June 1941. Refit May-July 1942.

Unallocated Cruiser, South Atlantic Command, February 1942.
Unallocated Cruiser, Home Fleet, March-July 1942.
Attached Cruiser, Home Fleet, August-November 1942.
West Africa Command, December 1942-September 1943.
Attached Cruiser, Portsmouth Command. Refitting at Portsmouth, October 1943-May 1944.
Accommodation Ship, Chatham, June-August 1944.
Duty with ANCXF, September 1944.
Reserve Fleet, Falmouth, October-December 1944.

Accommodation Ship, Portsmouth, January 1945-March 1946.
Scrapped at Troon from August 1946.

Diomede
7th CS, Northern Patrol, September-December 1939.
8th CS, America & West Indies, January-February 1940.
Detached, SW and W coast, March-April 1940.
Commodore, Kingston, May 1940-June 1942.
Detached USN Atlantic Fleet, July 1942.
Unallocated Cruiser, South Atlantic Command, August-November 1942.
Attached Cruiser, West Africa Command, December 1942-May 1943.
Refitting August 1942-October 1943.
Unallocated Cruiser, Rosyth Command, August-October 1943.
CWCTS duty, November 1943-September 1945.
Reduced to reserve Rosyth, October 1945.
Reserve Plymouth, November 1945.
Category 'C' Reserve, Falmouth, December 1945-March 1946.
Scrapped at Dalmuir from May 1946.

Dragon
7th CS, Northern Patrol, September 1939-February 1940.
3rd CS, Mediterranean Fleet, March-May 1940.
4th CS, East Indies Command, May 1940.
Attached Cruiser, South Atlantic Command, June 1940-November 1941.
5th CS, Eastern Fleet, December 1941-January 1943.
Refitting September-October 1942, Refitting December 1942-1943.
5th CS, Eastern Fleet, January-December 1943.
Refit and work up Scapa/Greenock October-December 1943.
Unallocated Cruiser Home Fleet, February 1944.
10th CS, Home Fleet, March-June 1944.
Damaged by Marder unit at Normandy and expended as a blockship at Arromanches, 8th July 1944.

Dunedin
12th CS, Northern Patrol, September 1939.
8th CS, America & West Indies, October 1939-October 1940.
Temporary detached Portsmouth Command, November 1940-February 1941.
Attached Cruiser, South Atlantic Command, March 1941-April 1941.
Temporary detached North Atlantic Command, June November 1941.
Torpedoed and sunk by *U-124* in Atlantic, 24th November 1941.

Durban
9th CS, South Atlantic Command, September-December 1939.
5th CS, China Station, January 1940-December 1941.
5th CS, Eastern Fleet, January 1942-November 1943.
Bombed and damaged at Singapore, 11th February 1942.
Refitting New York, May-June 1942, Refit January-March 1943.
November 1943, Devonport.
Unallocated Cruiser, Portsmouth Command, December 1943-June 1944.
Expended as blockship at Arromanches 9th June 1944.

Emerald
12th CS, Northern Patrol, September 1939.
Attached Cruiser, Halifax Escort Force, October 1939-September 1940.
Refit March-April 1940.
Attached Cruiser, Western Approaches, October 1940-February 1941.
Refit, November-December 1940.
4th CS, East Indies Command, March-June 1941.
Attached Cruiser, East Indies Command, July 1941-March 1942.
4th CS, East Indies Fleet, April 1942-July 1943.
Refitting Portsmouth August 1942-April 1943.
5th CS, East Indies Fleet, August-December 1943.
4th CS, East Indies Fleet, December-April 1944.
10th CS, May-September 1944, Home Fleet. Damaged near miss bomb
6th Unallocated Cruiser, Rosyth Command, October-November 1944.
June 1944.
Refitting Rosyth August-September 1944.
Reduced to Reserve Rosyth, December 1944.
Category 'B' Reserve Rosyth, January-June 1945.
Category 'C' Reserve July 1945-March 1946.
Scrapped at Troon from July 1948.

Enterprise
12th CS, Northern Patrol, September 1939.
Attached Cruiser, Halifax Escort Force, October 1939-April 1940.
Refit Portsmouth, March-April 1940.
Attached Cruiser, Home Fleet, May 1940.
Unallocated Cruiser, Western Approaches, June 1940. Refitting.
Attached Cruiser, North Atlantic Command, July 1940.
Force 'H', July September 1940.
Attached Cruiser, South Atlantic Command, October 1940-February
1941.

4th CS, East Indies Command, March-April 1941.

Force 'T', April-June 1941.

Attached Cruiser, East Indies Command, July 1941-February 1942.

4th CS, Eastern Fleet, March 1942-November 1943.

Refitting Portsmouth and Clyde, January-October 1943.

Attached Cruiser, Plymouth Command, December 1943-May 1944.

Helped to sink German destroyers *Z27, T25* and *T26* in Bay of Biscay action on 28th December 1943.

Refit February-March 1944.

1st CS, Home Fleet, June-August 1944.

Duty with ANCXF September 1944.

Reduced to Reserve Rosyth, October-December 1944.

Category 'B' Reserve January-April 1945.

Portsmouth Command, Trooping Duties, May 1945-January 1946.

Reduced to Reserve Portsmouth December 1946.

Category 'C' Reserve February-March 1946, Rosyth.

Scrapped at Newport from April 1946.

Effingham

12th CS, Northern Patrol, September 1939.

Detached, October 1939, Home Fleet.

Attached Cruiser, Halifax Escort Force, November 1939-April 1940.

Refitting Portsmouth, April-May 1940.

Wrecked on first operation on uncharted rock in Vestiford, on 18th May 1940.

Frobisher

Refitting and re-arming September 1939-February 1942.

Western Approaches and Portsmouth Command allocation.

18th CS, Home Fleet, March 1942.

4th CS, East Indies Fleet, April 1942-January 1943.

4th CS, East Indies Command, January 1943-April 1944.

1st Cs, Home Fleet, May-August 1944.

Refitting June-August 1944. Damaged by torpedo 9th August 1944.

ANCFX duties, September 1944.

Unallocated Cruiser, Rosyth Command, October 1944-March 1945.

Refitting as Cadet Training Cruiser, Rosyth, October 1944-March 1945.

Cadet Training Cruiser, April 1945-September 1945, Rosyth.

Portsmouth Command, Cadet Training Cruiser, October 1945-March 1946.

Scrapped at Newport from May 1949.

268 Cruisers in Action

Hawkins
Reserve Fleet (Flag), September November 1939.
Attached Cruiser South Atlantic December 1939-January 1940.
Flag South Atlantic, February-July 1940.
Attached Cruiser, South Atlantic, July 1940-January 1941.
4th CS, East Indies Command, February-June 1941.
Refit Durban June-July 1941.
Attached Cruiser East Indies Command, August 1941-February 1942.
Refit Portsmouth, February-May 1942.
4th CS, Eastern Fleet, March August 1942.
5th CS, Eastern Fleet, September 1942-March 1944.
Refit July-August 1943, Refit December-January 1945.
1st CS, Home Fleet, March-August 1944.
Refitting as Training Cruiser, September 1944-May 1945.
Reduced to Reserve Clyde, June-September 1945.
Category 'C' Reserve Falmouth October 1945-March 1946.
Scrapped at Dalmuir from December 1947.

Vindictive
Converting to Training Ship and Repair Ship, September 1939-March 1940.
Repair Ship Duties, Home Fleet, May-July 1940.
Repair Ship Duties, South Atlantic Command, July 1940-November 1942.
West Africa Command, December 1942.
Detached to Western Mediterranean December 1942-January 1943.
Force 'H', March-July 1943.
Refitting at Bizerta, August 1943-October 1944. Base Ship Duties.
Home Fleet Destroyer Depot Ship, November 1944-June 1945.
Reserve Fleet, Sheerness, July 1945-September 1945.
Reserve Fleet, Chatham, October 1945-February 1946.
Scrapped at Blyth from February 1946.

Achilles
Manned by RNZN. Flag of South Atlantic Command, September-December 1939. River Plate Battle 13th December 1939. Damaged.
Arrived Auckland for repairs and refit 26th February 1940.
Refitting March-July 1940.
RNZN duties July 1940-June 1944.
Damaged by bombs off Guadalcanal 5th January 1943.
Repairing at Portsmouth, damaged by major fuel explosion aboard on

22nd June 1943. Refitting and repairing Portsmouth April-1943-May 1944.

Unallocated Cruiser, Home Fleet, June-August 1944.

4th CS, Eastern Fleet, September 1944-January 1945.

4th CS, British Pacific Fleet, January-August 1945.

2nd CS, British Pacific Fleet, September 1945-March 1946.

Sold to Indian Navy as *Delhi* on 5th July 1948.

Ajax

South Atlantic Command, September-December 1939.

River Plate Battle, 13th December 1939. Damaged.

Refitting and repairing Chatham, February-July 1940.

Unallocated Cruiser Home Fleet, July 1940.

4th CS, East Indies Command, Sierra Leone, September 1940.

Unallocated Cruiser, Mediterranean Fleet, September-October 1940.

Helped sink Italian destroyers *Artigliere* and *Ariel* off Malta on 12th October 1940.

7th CS, Mediterranean Fleet, November 1940-May 1942.

15th CS, Mediterranean Fleet, June-December 1942.

12th CS, Western Mediterranean January 1943.

Damaged by bombs and Bone on 1st January 1943.

Refitting and repairing USA/Gibraltar January 1943-February 1944.

15th CS, Mediterranean Fleet, March-May 1944.

10th CS, Home Fleet, June 1944. Refit Clyde.

15th CS, Mediterranean Fleet, August 1944-December 1945.

Refit October-December 1945.

South American Cruise January-March 1946.

Scrapped at Newport from November 1949.

Leander

Manned by RNZN until May 1944.

RNZN duties September 1939-May 1940.

7th CS, Mediterranean Fleet, June 1940.

Red Sea June 1940-January 1941.

Sank Italian raider *Ramb I* 27th February 1941.

4th CS, East Indies Command, February-April 1941.

15th CS, Mediterranean Fleet, June-August 1941.

RNZN duties September 1941-December 1943.

Torpedoed in night action in Solomon Islands, 13th July 1943.

Temporary repairs Australia August-November 1943.

Refitting and repairs Boston USA, December 1943-September 1945.

Non-operational in UK September 1945-March 1946.
Scrapped at Blyth from January 1950.

Neptune
6th CS, South Atlantic Command, September 1939-April 1940.
Flag, Mediterranean Fleet, May 1940. Helped sink Italian destroyer *Espero*
28th June 1940. 7th CS, Mediterranean Fleet, June-September 1940.
4th CS, East Indies Command, October-November 1940.
Attached Cruiser, South Atlantic Command, December 1940-January
1941.
Refitting Chatham, February-June 1941.
Damaged by bombs at Chatham on 9th February and 16th February 1941.
Attached Cruiser, South Atlantic Command, July-August 1941.
7th CS, Mediterranean Fleet, September-December 1941.
Sunk by mines off Tripoli on 19th December 1941.

Orion
8th CS, America & West Indies, September 1939-April 1940.
Flag RA(D), Mediterranean Fleet, May 1940.
7th CS (Flag), May-June 1940.
Flag Ra(D) Mediterranean Fleet, July 1940.
Flag VA(D) Mediterranean Fleet, September 1940.
7th CS, Mediterranean Fleet, October 1940-May 1942.
Helped sink Italian destroyer *Espero* on 28th June 1940.
Bombed and damaged off Crete 29th May 1941.
Refit and repairs USA, November 1941-March 1942.
15th CS, Mediterranean Fleet, June-July 1942.
South Atlantic Command, August 1942.
15th CS, Mediterranean Fleet, January-July 1943.
Force 'K', Mediterranean Fleet, August-December 1943.
Refit Portsmouth October-November 1943.
15th CS, Mediterranean Fleet, February-April 1944.
Unallocated cruiser Rosyth, May 1944.
10th CS, Home Fleet, June 1944.
15th CS, Mediterranean Fleet, August 1944-March 1946.
Scrapped at Troon from August 1949.

Hobart (RAN)
RAN September 1939 onward.
Australia Squadron September-October 1939.
4th CS, East Indies Command, November-December 1939.

Force 'M' and Force 'I', January-May 1940.
Attached Cruiser, Red Sea Force, May-December 1940.
Australia Squadron, January-July 1941.
7th CS, Mediterranean Fleet, August-November 1941.
Australian Squadron December 1941-March 1946.
Damaged by bombing on 25th February and 27th February 1942 Java Sea.
Torpedoed and damaged off East Coast of New Georgia on 20th July 1943
by Japanese submarine *I-11*.
Refitting and repairing Sydney September 1943-December 1944.
Sold for breaking up in September 1961.

Perth (RAN)
RAN September 1939 onward.
8th CS, America and West Indies, September 1939-February 1940.
Australia Squadron March-December 1940.
7th CS, Mediterranean Fleet, January-July 1941.
Bombed and damaged off Crete, 30th May 1941.
Refit and Repairs Sydney, September-November 1941.
Australia Squadron August 1941-February 1942.
Sunk by Japanese ships in Sundra Straits 1st March 1942.

Sydney (RAN)
RAN September 1939 onward.
Australia Squadron September 1939-May 1940.
7th CS, Mediterranean Fleet, May 1940-January 1941.
Helped to sink Italian destroyer *Espero* on 28th June 1940.
Helped to sink Italian cruiser *Colleoni* on 19th July 1940.
Australian Squadron February-October 1941.
Sank and sunk by German raider *Kormoran* 19th November 1941.

Arethusa
3rd CS, Mediterranean Fleet, September 1939-December 1939.
2nd CS, Home Fleet, January-May 1940.
Home Fleet, Nore and North Atlantic Commands, May-June 1940.
Force 'H', July 1940.
Attached Cruiser, North Atlantic Command, July 1940.
Refit and repair Chatham September-October 1940.
2nd CS, Home Fleet, November 1940-January 1942. Refit September-
November 1941.
Damaged by bombs off Lofoten Islands on 27th December 1941.
Refit and repair February-April 1942.

15th Cs, Mediterranean Fleet, February-September 1942.
Force 'A', October-November 1942.
Torpedoed and damaged 18th November 1942.
Repairs and refit December 1942-March 1944.
1st CS, Home Fleet, May-October 1944.
Damaged by bombs 24th and 25th June 1944.
Repairs and refitting June December 1944.
15th CS, Mediterranean Fleet, January October 1945.
Reduced to Reserve Sheerness November 1945.
Category 'B' Reserve Chatham, December 1945-March 1946.
Scrapped at Troon from May 1950.

Aurora
18th CS, Home Fleet, September 1939.
Humber Force, October 1939.
2nd CS, Home Fleet, November 1939-October 1941.
Damaged by bombs off Norway 18th May 1940.
Repairs May-June 1940. Helped sink German minelayer *Bremse* in Arctic.
6th September 1941. 15th CS, Mediterranean Fleet, November 1941-
November 1942.
Sank Italian destroyer *Fulmine* in Ionaian Sea 9th November 1941.
Damaged by mines off Tripoli on 19th December 1941.
Repairs and refitting January-July 1942.
12th CS, Western Mediterranean, December 1942-November 1943.
Damaged by shore batteries 8th November 1942.
Sank Vichy destroyer *Typhon* off Oran 19th November 1942.
Helped sink Italian destroyer *Folgore* off Sicily on 2nd December 1942.
Damaged by bombs in Aegean 20th October 1943.
Repairs and refit November 1943-March 1944.
15th CS, Mediterranean Fleet, April 1944-March 1946.
Refit August-October 1945.
Sold to China as *Chungking* May 1948.

Galatea
Flag RA(D) Mediterranean Fleet, September-December 1939.
2nd CS, Home Fleet, January-May 1940.
Sheerness May-June 1940.
Humber Force, July 1940.
Home Fleet, September 1940-June 1941.
Damaged by mines on 1 September and 9 September 1940.
Repairs and refit Chatham November-December 1940.

15th CS, Mediterranean, July-December 1941.
Torpedoed and sunk off Alexandria by *U-557* on 15th December 1941.

Penelope
3rd CS, Mediterranean Fleet, September-December 1939.
2nd CS, Home Fleet, January-July 1940.
Damaged by grounding 9th April, damaged by bombs 10th April, damaged by grounding 11th April 1940 off Norway.
Repairs and refitting, May 1940-June 1941.
April-November 1941, 2nd CS, Home Fleet.
15th CS, Mediterranean Fleet, December 1941-May 1942.
Damaged by bombing on 26th March, 4th April and 8th April at Malta, 1941.
Repairs and refit USA, June-September 1942.
Portsmouth working up October-December 1942.
12th CS, Western Mediterranean. January-July 1943.
Damaged by shell fire 1st June 1943. Force 'Q' and Force 'K' October-December 1943.
Damaged by unexploded bomb in Aegean 7th October 1943.
15th CS, Mediterranean Fleet, December 1943-February 1944.
Torpedoed and sunk by *U-410* off Anzio on 18th February 1944.

Birmingham
5th CS, China Station, September 1939-January 1940.
18th CS, Home Fleet, February May 1940.
Detached Immingham/Rosyth May-June 1940.
18th CS, Home Fleet, July 1940-August 1941.
Refit November-December 1940.
Attached Cruiser, Mediterranean Fleet, September 1941-February 1942.
4th CS, East Indies Command, March 1942-December 1943.
Damaged by bombing July 1942 Eastern Mediterranean.
Repair and refit April-September 1943.
Damaged by torpedo 28th November 1943.
Repair and refit 1943 1943-January 1945.
10th CS, Home Fleet, February 1945-March 1946.
Scrapped at Inverkeithing from September 1960.

Glasgow
2nd CS, Humber Force, September 1939.
2nd CS, Home Fleet, October 1939.
2nd CS, Humber Force, November-December 1939.

18th CS, Home Fleet, January-October 1940.
Rammed and sank *HMS Imogen* 16th July 1940.
3rd CS, Mediterranean Fleet, December 1940-February 1941.
Damaged by aircraft torpedoes Suda Bay, Crete, 3rd December 1940.
Refit January 1940.
4th CS, East Indies Command, March-July 1941.
Temporary attached Mediterranean Fleet, August 1941.
Attached Cruiser, East Indies Command, September 1941-January 1942.
4th CS, East Indies Command, February-August 1942.
Refitting USA May-October 1942.
10th CS, Home Fleet, November 1942-April 1943.
Damaged by grounding 22nd February 1943.
Unallocated, Plymouth Command, May 1943.
10th CS, Home Fleet, July 1943.
Unallocated, Plymouth Command, August 1943.
10th CS, Home Fleet, September 1943-February 1944.
Helped sink German destroyers *Z27, T25* and *T26* in Bay of Biscay on 28th
December 1943.
Attached Cruiser, Plymouth Command, March-May 1944.
10th CS, Home Fleet, June-November 1944.
Attached Cruiser, Home Fleet, December 1944-June 1945.
Damaged by shell fire 25th June 1944.
10th CS, Home Fleet, July 1945.
5th CS, East Indies Command, August 1945-March 1946.
Scrapped at Blyth from July 1958.

Newcastle
18th CS, Home Fleet, September 1939-June 1940.
Repairs April-May 1940.
Temporary detached Western Approaches, July September 1940.
18th CS, Home Fleet, May-November 1940.
Force 'H', December 1940.
Detached South Atlantic Command, January-February 1941.
Attached cruiser, South Atlantic Command, March 1941-February 1942.
Refit September 1941. Damaged by torpedo on 15th June 1942 in
Mediterranean.
4th CS, Eastern Fleet, March 1942-December 1944.
Refit USA, September-December 1942. Refit Durban January-April 1943.
Refit June-September 1944.
5th CS, East Indies Command, January-May 1945.
Unallocated Plymouth, June-July 1945.

Refitting August-September 1945.
Plymouth Command, Trooping duties October 1945-February 1946.
Refitting February-March 1946.
Scrapped at Faslane from August 1959.

Sheffield
18th CS, Home Fleet, September-December 1939.
18th CS, Home Fleet, January May 1940.
Temporary detached Immingham, May-July 1940.
18th CS, Home Fleet, July 1940.
Force 'H', September 1940-September 1941. Spartivento, Genoa bombardment, *Bismarck* action etc etc. Damaged by mine off Islay 17th March 1941.
10th CS, Gibraltar, October 1941. Damaged by bomb Mediterranean 30th March 1941.
18th CS, Home Fleet, November 1941-September 1942.
Damaged by mine off Iceland, 4th March 1942.
Damaged in collision *HMS Cadmus* 9th December 1942.
Heavy weather damage Arctic 17th February 1943.
Helped sink German destroyer *Z-7* in Arctic 25th May 1942.
Sank German destroyer *Z-16* off Bear Island 31st December 1942.
10th CS, Home Fleet, October 1942-July 1943.
Refit April-May 1943.
Attached Cruiser, Plymouth Command, August-September 1943.
Force 'K', October-December 1943.
10th CS, Home Fleet, December 1943-November 1944.
Refitting, Unallocated USA and Portsmouth, August 1944-March 1946.
Scrapped at Inverkeithing from September 1967.

Southampton
2nd CS, Humber Force, September 1939.
2nd Cs, Home Fleet, October 1939.
2nd CS, Humber Force, November 1939.
2nd CS, Home Fleet, December 1939-January 1940.
18th CS, Home Fleet, February 1940-January 1941.
Helped sink Italian destroyer *Vega* off Partelaria 10th January 1941.
Bombed and sunk by *Stukas* east of Malta 11th January 1941.

Gloucester
4th CS, East Indies Command, September 1939-April 1940.
Attached Cruiser, South Atlantic Command, May 1940.

7th CS, Mediterranean Fleet, May-July 1940.
Helped sink Italian destroyer *Espero* off Morea 28th June 1940.
3rd CS, Mediterranean Fleet, September 1940-May 1941.
Damaged by bombs 11th January 1941.
Sunk by bombing off Crete, 22nd May 1941.

Liverpool
4th CS, East Indies Command, September-November 1939.
5th CS, China Station, December 1939-April 1940.
4th CS, East Indies Command, May 1940.
SO. Aden, May 1940.
Unallocated cruiser, Mediterranean Fleet, June 1940.
7th CS, Mediterranean Fleet, July 1940.
3rd CS, Mediterranean Fleet, September-November 1940.
Helped sink Italian destroyer *Espero* off Morea 28th June 1940.
Damaged by aerial torpedo in Mediterranean 11th October 1940.
Repairing and refitting, Alexandria and USA, November 1940-March 1942.
18th CS, Home Fleet, April-August 1942.
Damaged by torpedo 14th June 1942 in Mediterranean.
Repairing and refitting UK ports September 1942-August 1945.
15th CS, Mediterranean Fleet, October 1945-March 1946.
Scrapped at Bo' ness from July 1958.

Manchester
4th CS, East Indies Command, September-December 1939.
18th CS, Home Fleet, January-May 1940.
Temporary detached Humber Force, May-July 1940.
18th CS, Home Fleet, July-October 1940. Unallocated cruiser Nore November 1940.
Refit January-February 1941.
18th CS, Home Fleet, March-July 1941.
Damaged by torpedo in Mediterranean 23rd July 1941.
Repairs and refit USA September 1941-June 1942.
18th CS, Home Fleet, June-August 1942.
Scuttled by own crew after torpedo damage in Central Mediterranean, 13th August 1942.

Belfast
18th CS, Home Fleet, September-October 1939.
2nd CS, Home Fleet, November 1939-July 1940.

Damaged by mines 21st November 1939.

Repairing and rebuilding Rosyth and Devonport, December 1939-October 1942.

1st CS, Home Fleet, November-December 1942.

10th CS, Home Fleet, January 1943-November 1944.

At *Scharnhorst* sinking, 31st December 1943.

Major refit and rebuilding August 1944-May 1945.

10th CS, Home Fleet, June 1945.

4th CS, British Pacific Fleet July-August 1945.

2nd CS, British Pacific Fleet, September 1945-March 1946.

Preserved as monument in Thames in London.

Edinburgh

18th CS, Home Fleet, September-October 1939.

2nd CS, Home Fleet, November 1939-February 1940.

19th CS, Home Fleet, March 1940-May 1942.

Major refit and replacement of armour March-October 1940.

Torpedoed and sunk by German destroyers in Arctic, 30th April 1942.

Argonaut

Unallocated cruiser, Home Fleet, August-October 1942.

10th CS, Home Fleet, November 1942.

12th CS, Western Mediterranean December 1942.

Helped sink Italian destroyer *Folgore* off Sicily 2nd December 1942.

Damaged by torpedo in Mediterranean 14th December 1942.

At Algiers damaged January February 1943.

At Gibraltar damaged March-April 1943.

Repair and refit USA, May-November 1943.

Refitting UK November-December 1943.

Attached Cruiser Rosyth Command, February-April 1944.

10th CS, Home Fleet, May-June 1944. Damaged unexploded shell 30th June 1944.

15th CS, Mediterranean Fleet, August 1944.

Misc cruiser, Home Fleet, September 1944.

15th CS, Mediterranean Fleet, October-November 1944.

4th CS, East Indies Command, December 1944.

4th CS, British Pacific Fleet, January-February 1945.

Task Force 57, BPF, March June 1945.

Refit Sydney, July 1945.

Task Group 111-3, BPF, September 1945.

4th CS, British Pacific Fleet, October 1945-March 1946.

Scrapped at Newport from November 1955.

Bonaventure
Attached Cruiser, Western Approaches, May-June 1940.
15th CS, Mediterranean Fleet, July 1940-January 1941.
Helped sink Italian destroyer *Vega* off Pantepleria 10th January 1941.
3rd CS, Mediterranean Fleet, February-March 1941.
Torpedoed and sunk by Italian submarine *Ambra* off Sollum 31st March 1941.

Cleopatra
Unallocated cruiser, Home Fleet, December 1941-January 1942.
15th CS, Mediterranean Fleet, February 1942-May 1943.
Damaged by bombing off Malta 11th February 1942.
Damaged by shell fire Battle of Sirte, 22nd March 1942.
Damaged by bombing 30th September 1942.
12th CS, Mediterranean Fleet, July December 1943.
Damaged by torpedo on 16th July 1943.
Repairs and refitting Gibraltar and USA August 1943-March 1945.
Unallocated cruiser, Mediterranean Fleet, April-May 1945.
5th CS, East Indies Command, June 1945-February 1946.
Portsmouth Command to refit, February 1946.
Scrapped Newport from December 1958.

Dido
15th CS, Mediterranean Fleet, November 1940-April 1941.
Damaged by bombing off Crete 29th May 1941.
Repair and refitting USA, July-December 1941.
15th CS, Mediterranean Fleet, August 1941-December 1942.
Gibraltar Command, January 1943.
12th CS, Mediterranean Fleet, January-December 1943.
Damaged by bombing 17th October 1943.
Refit May 1943.
Force 'K' December 1943.
15th CS, Mediterranean Fleet, February-June 1944.
Rammed by *LCT* February 1944.
10th CS, Home Fleet, August 1944-March 1946.
Scrapped at Barrow from July 1958.

Euryalus
Unallocated cruiser, Home Fleet, July-August 1941.

15th CS, Mediterranean Fleet, September 1941-July 1943.
12th CS, Mediterranean Fleet, August-October 1943.
Force 'K', November 1943.
Major refit November 1943-June 1944.
Unallocated cruiser, Home Fleet, December 1943-November 1944.
Temporary attached cruiser, Home Fleet, December 1944. The CS, East Indies, January 1944
4th CS, British Pacific Fleet, February-April 1945.
Task Force 57, BPF, June-August 1945.
4th CS, BPF, June-August 1945.
2nd CS, British Pacific Fleet, September 1945-March 1946.
Scrapped at Blyth from July 1959.

Hermione
Unallocated cruiser, Western Approaches, April-June 1941.
Force 'H', July 1941-May 1942. 15th CS, Mediterranean Fleet, June 1942.
Sank Italian submarine *Tembien* south-west of Sicily, 2nd August 1941.
Torpedoed and sunk by *U-205* off Sollum, 15th June 1942.

Naiad
15th CS, Mediterranean Fleet, July 1940-March 1942. Refit March-April 1941.
Damaged by bombing 22nd May 1941.
Damaged by bombing 19th January 1942.
Torpedoed and sunk by *U-565* south of Crete 11th March 1942.

Phoebe
15th CS, Mediterranean, November 1940-March 1941.
Unallocated cruiser, Mediterranean Fleet, April 1941.
7th CS, Mediterranean Fleet, April 1941.
15th CS, Mediterranean Fleet, June 1941-August 1942.
Damaged by aerial torpedo 27th August 1941.
Repairs and refit Alexandria and New York, September 1941-April 1942.
Attached cruiser, South Atlantic Command, September-November 1942.
15th CS, Mediterranean Fleet, December 1942-January 1943.
Damaged by submarine torpedo 23rd October 1942.
Repairs and refit New York January-July 1943.
Unallocated Cruiser, Home Fleet August-October 1943.
Force 'K', Mediterranean, November 1943.
15th CS, Mediterranean Fleet, December 1943-March 1944.
4th CS, Eastern Fleet, March-November 1944.

Refitting March-April 1944.
Force 61, East Indies Command, December 1944.
5th CS, East Indies Command, January-October 1945.
Unallocated cruiser, Nore Command October 1945.
Refitting November 1945-March 1946.
Scrapped at Blyth from August 1956.

Sirius
Unallocated cruiser, Home Fleet, May 1942.
15th CS, Mediterranean Fleet, June-August 1942.
Attached cruiser, South Atlantic Command, September-November 1942.
12th CS, Western Mediterranean, December 1942-January 1943.
Helped to sink Italian destroyer *Folgore* off Sicily 2nd December 1942.
12th CS, Mediterranean Fleet January-December 1943.
Damaged by bombing in Aegean, 7th October 1943.
Repair and refit Malta, November 1943-February 1944.
Force 'K', December 1943.
15th CS, Mediterranean Fleet, February-May 1944.
10th CS, Home Fleet, June 1944.
15th CS, Mediterranean Fleet, August 1944-March 1946.
Scrapped at Blyth from October 1956.

Charybdis
Unallocated cruiser, Home Fleet, December 1941-January 1942.
Unallocated cruiser, Home Fleet, North Atlantic Command, February-August 1942.
Attached Cruiser, North Atlantic Command, September-November 1942.
12th CS, Western Mediterranean December 1942.
Attached cruiser, Home Fleet, January-April 1943.
Attached cruiser, Plymouth Command, April-August 1943.
Temporary detached, Mediterranean Fleet, September 1943.
Torpedoed and sunk by German destroyers off Channel Islands on 23rd October 1943.

Scylla
Unallocated cruiser, Home Fleet, July-August 1942.
Rear (D), Home Fleet, September 1942. PQ18.
10th CS, Home Fleet, October 1942.
12th CS, Western Mediterranean, November 1942-January 1943.
Unallocated cruiser, Home Fleet, January-July 1943.
Refit, January-July 1943.

Attached Cruiser, Plymouth Command, July 1943-December 1943.
10th CS, Home Fleet, March-May 1944.
Attached cruiser, Plymouth and Portsmouth Commands. Refitting as Escort Carrier Flagship October 1943-April 1944.
Mined and damaged off Normandy 23rd June 1944. Constructive Total Loss but not so decided until post-war.
Reserve, refit estimation June 1944-March 1946.
Scrapped at Barrow, from May 1950.

Bellona
Unallocated Cruiser, October-December 1943, Home Fleet.
Attached Cruiser, Plymouth Command, February-May 1944.
10th CS, Home Fleet, June 1944-March 1946.
Lent RNZN 1948-1956.
Scrapped at Briton Ferry, from February 1959.

Black Prince
Unallocated cruiser, Home Fleet, October-December 1943.
Attached cruiser, Plymouth Command, February 1944.
Unallocated cruiser, Home Fleet, March 1944.
Attached Cruiser, Plymouth Command, March-May 1944.
10th CS, Home Fleet, June 1944.
15th CS, Mediterranean Fleet, August-November 1944.
4th CS, East Indies Command, December 1944.
4th CS, British Pacific Fleet, January-September 1945.
2nd CS, British Pacific Fleet, October 1945-March 1946.
Scrapped at Osaka, Japan from August 1962.

Diadem
Unallocated Cruiser, Home Fleet, February-March 1944.
10th CS, Home Fleet, March 1944-March 1946.
Refit December 1945-January 1946.
Damaged by German explosive torpedo 12th August 1944.
Sold to Pakistan Navy as *Babr* on 5th July 1957.

Royalist
Unallocated cruiser, Home Fleet, September-November 1943.
Refitted and modified as Escort Carrier Flagship, November-December 1943.
Escort Carrier Flagship Duties, Arctic convoys, March-June 1944.
Escort Carrier Flagship Duties, Mediterranean Fleet, August 1944-January 1945.

ACF, East Indies Command, February-April 1945.
21st AC Squadron, East Indies Command, May-October 1945.
5th CS, East Indies Command, November 1945-March 1946.
Given to RNZN in 1956.

Spartan
Unallocated cruiser, Home Fleet, August-November 1943.
Attached Cruiser, Plymouth Command, November 1943 (at Malta)
Force 'K', Mediterranean Fleet, December 1943.
Hit and sunk by glider bombs off Anzio 29th January 1944.

Bermuda
Unallocated Cruiser, Home Fleet, August-October 1942.
10th CS, Home Fleet, November 1942-May 1943.
Attached Cruiser, Plymouth Command, July 1943.
10th CS, Home Fleet, August 1943.
Attached Cruiser Plymouth Command, September 1943.
10th CS, Home Fleet, October 1943-November 1944.
Major refit and re-equipment July 1944-March 1945.
Attached Cruiser, Home Fleet, December 1944-March 1945.
Temporary attached cruiser, Mediterranean Fleet, April-May 1945.
4th CS, British Pacific Fleet, June 1945.
2nd CS, British Pacific Fleet, July 1945-March 1946.
Scrapped Briton Ferry from August 1965.

Ceylon
Unallocated cruiser, Home Fleet, August-November 1943.
4th CS, Eastern Fleet, December 1943-November 1944.
Refit Durban, October-December 1944.
4th CS, Eastern Fleet, December 1944.
4th CS, British Pacific Fleet, January 1945.
5th CS, East Indies Command, February-October 1945.
UK Refitting October 1945-March 1946.
Sold to Peruvian Navy as *Coronel Bolognesi* in February 1960.

Fiji
Portsmouth Command, April-July 1940.
18th CS, Home Fleet, July-October 1940.
Damaged by submarine torpedo on 1st September 1940.
Repair and refit October 1940-February 1941.
Attached Cruiser, Mediterranean Fleet, April-May 1941.

Bombed and sunk off Crete, 22nd May 1941.

Gambia
Unallocated cruiser, Home Fleet, March 1942.
18th CS, Home Fleet, April 1942.
4th CS, Eastern Fleet, May 1942-September 1943.
Unallocated cruiser, refit October 1943. Home Fleet.
Temporary attached cruiser, Plymouth Command, February 1944.
Transferred to RNZN at Trincomalee March 1944.
4th CS, Eastern Fleet, March-November 1944.
4th CS, East Indies Command, December 1944.
4th CS, British Pacific Fleet, January-August 1945.
Task Force 57, May 1945.
2nd CS, British Pacific Fleet, September 1945-March 1946.
Refit Australia November 1945-January 1946.
Sold for scrapping 1968.

Jamaica
Unallocated, Home Fleet, July 1942.
18th CS, Home Fleet, August-September 1942.
10th CS, Home Fleet, October 1942-November 1944.
Helped sink Vichy destroyer *Typhon* 19th November 1942.
At sinking of *Scharnhorst* 26th December 1943.
Helped sink German destroyer Z7 in Arctic 2nd May 1942.
Refitting Portsmouth October 1944-July 1945.
5th CS, East Indies Command, August 1945-March 1946.
Scrapped at Dalmuir from December 1960.

Kenya
Unallocated, Home Fleet, September 1940.
10th CS, Home Fleet, October 1940-March 1943.
Damaged in collision with HMS *Brighton* 25th June 1941.
Damaged by shelling on 27th December 1941.
Torpedoed and damaged by Italian submarine *Alagi* in Mediterranean, 12th August 1942.
Repairs and refitting September 1942-January 1943.
Unallocated Cruiser, Home Fleet, January-March 1943.
4th CS, Eastern Fleet, April 1943-November 1944.
Refit February-March 1944.
Force 61, East Indies Command, December 1944.
5th CS, East Indies Command, January-March 1945.

Refitting at Chatham June 1945-March 1946.
Scrapped at Faslane from October 1962.

Mauritius
Unallocated, Home Fleet, December 1940.
10th CS, Home Fleet, January-June 1941.
Attached Cruiser, Mediterranean Fleet, July 1941 (Mombasa)
Attached Cruiser, East Indies Command, August 1941-February 1942.
Attached Cruiser, Plymouth Command, March-April 1942.
4th CS, Eastern Fleet, May 1942-May 1943.
15th CS, Mediterranean Fleet, July 1943.
Force 'K', Mediterranean Fleet, August-December 1943.
15th CS, Mediterranean Fleet, December 1943-April 1944.
1st CS, Home Fleet, May 1944.
Unallocated cruiser, Home Fleet, June 1944.
ANCXF Duties, September 1944.
Attached Cruiser, Plymouth Command, October 1944.
Unallocated Cruiser, Home Fleet, November 1944.
10th CS, Home Fleet, December 1944-March 1945.
Refitting April 1945-March 1946.
Scrapped at Inverkeithing from March 1965.

Newfoundland
Unallocated cruiser, Home Fleet, January 1943-March 1943.
12th CS, Mediterranean Fleet, April 1943
15th CS, Mediterranean Fleet, May-July 1943.
Force 'K', Mediterranean Fleet, August-December 1943.
Damaged by torpedo from Italian submarine *Ascianghi* 23rd July 1943
Repairs and refitting Boston USA September 1943-November 1944.
4th CS, British Pacific Fleet, January 1945-March 1946.
Refit Sydney, November 1945-January 1946.
Sold to Peruvian Navy as *Almirante Grau* December 1959.

Nigeria
New Cruiser, Tyne, September 1940.
10th CS, Home Fleet, October 1940-December 1943.
Rammed submerged wreck November 1940. Rammed German *Bremse* 6th September 1941.
Repair and refit, November-December 1941.
Helped sink German destroyer *Z26* in Arctic 29th March 1942.

Damaged by Torpedo from Italian submarine *Axum* in Mediterranean 12th August 1942.
Repairs and refitting New York, September 1942-January 1943.
10th CS, Home Fleet, January-December 1943.
Refit USA January-December 1943.
4th CS, Eastern Indies Command, December 1944.
Force 61, East Indies Command, December 1944.
5th CS, East Indies Command, January-November 1945.
Refitting Chatham December 1945-March 1946.
Sold to Indian Navy as *Mysore* August 1957.

Trinidad
New Cruiser, Home Fleet, November 1941.
10th CS, Home Fleet, December 1941-May 1942.
Damaged by torpedo Arctic (torpedoed herself)
Sunk by bombing Arctic 15th March 1942.

Uganda
Unallocated cruiser, Home Fleet, January 1943-March 1943.
Temporary detached West Africa, April 1943.
Attached Cruiser, Plymouth Command, April-July 1943.
Force 'K', Mediterranean Fleet, August-December 1943.
Damaged in collision with *HMS Delhi* 3rd September 1943.
Damaged by Glider bomb 13th September 1943.
Repairs and Refit USA December 1943-October 1944.
Handed over to RCN 21st October 1944, as *Quebec*
Unallocated cruiser, November-December 1944, Home Fleet.
4th CS, British Pacific Fleet, January-August 1945.
Pacific Command, RCN, September 1945-March 1946.
Refitting September-December 1945.
Scrapped at Osaka, Japan from February 1961.

Ontario
(RCN ex *Minotaur*).
New Cruiser, Home Fleet, June 1945.
4th CS, British Pacific Fleet, August-October 1945.
Unallocated Cruiser, RCN October 1945-March 1946.
Scrapped at Osaka, Japan from November 1960.

Swiftsure
Unallocated Cruiser, Home Fleet, August-October 1944.
4th CS, Eastern Fleet, November 1944.
4th CS, East Indies Command, December 1944.
4th CS, British Pacific Fleet, January 1945-March 1946.
Task Force 57 May 1945.
Scrapped at Inverkeithing from October 1962.

Superb
Unallocated Cruiser, Nore Command, November-December 1945.
Unallocated Cruiser, Mediterranean Fleet, February-March 1946.
Scrapped at Dalmuir from August 1960.

Appendix Four
Typical British Cruiser Deployments

*Denotes ship under orders to or proceeding to another Station.

January 1940
Home Fleet

1st Cruiser Squadron:	*Devonshire* (Flag)	– Clyde
	Berwick	– Left Clyde 30th December
	Norfolk	– Left Belfast 24th December
	Suffolk	– Left Clyde 20th December
2nd Cruiser Squadron:	*Edinburgh* (Flag)	– Left Rosyth 30th December
	Southampton	– Tyne. Repairs, to complete 23rd January.
	Glasgow	– Left Rosyth 30th December.
18th Cruiser Squadron:	*Manchester* (Flag)	– Left Scapa Flow 26th December. Patrol
	Newcastle	– At Scapa Flow
	Sheffield	– At Scapa Flow
Attached Cruiser:	*York*	– At Liverpool. Repairs. To complete 10th February and join Home Fleet.
Destroyer Command:	*Aurora*	– Clyde. Flag R/Admiral (D) Flotillas.

Northern Patrol

7th Cruiser Squadron:	(Non-operational)	
	Diomede* (Cdre)	– Plymouth. Refitting to complete 10th January approx.
	Dragon*	– Chatham. Refitting, completion 6-8 weeks from 22nd December.
11th Cruiser Squadron:	*Colombo** (Cdre)	– Left Scapa Flow 30th December.

	*Ceres**	– Left Scapa Flow 28th December. Patrol.
	*Dunedin**	– To leave Scapa Flow 2nd January.
Non-operational:	*Cardiff*	– Plymouth. Repairs. To complete 10th January.
	*Delhi**	– Belfast. Docking and refit. To complete 8th January.

Portsmouth Command

Attached Cruisers:	*Hawkins**	– Portland. Working up.
	Frobisher	– Portsmouth. Demilitarised Training Ship. Work suspended. To be re-armed.

Nore Command

Attached Cruisers:	*London*	– Chatham. Large refit. Dockyard control. To complete autumn depending on other commitments.
	Curacoa	– Chatham. Docking, converting to AA cruiser. Dockyard control. Complete 22nd January.

Humber Force

Anti-aircraft Cruisers:	*Cairo*	– At Port 'A'
	Calcutta	– At Port 'A'
	Coventry	– At Port 'A'

Western Approaches Command

Cadet Training Cruiser:	*Vindictive*	– At Plymouth. Re-armament and refit. Dockyard control. Complete 15th February.
Attached Cruiser (Non-operational)	*Carlisle*	– At Plymouth. Converting to AA cruiser. Dockyard control. Completing 12th January.

Rosyth Command:

Attached Cruiser (Non-operational)	*Belfast*	– Rosyth. Damage repairs. Date uncertain. Paid off Care and Maintenance 4th January.

Mediterranean Fleet

3rd Cruiser Squadron:	*Capetown* (Flag)	– At Malta.
	*Caledon**	– Left Malta 31st December.
	*Calypso**	– At Malta.
	*Arethusa**	– Left Malta 31st December.
	*Penelope**	– At Malta.
Destroyer Command Cruiser:	*Galatea**	– Left Malta 29th December.

Halifax Escort Force

Attached Cruisers:	*Emerald*	– Left Halifax 20th December.
	Enterprise	– Portsmouth. To sail 4th January and arrive Halifax 10th January.

South Atlantic Command:

Attached Cruisers:	*Ajax* (Flag)	– Left Falkland Islands 29th December for River Plate.
	Achilles (RNZN)	– Left Falkland Islands 29th December for River Plate.
	Dorsetshire	– Left Falkland Islands 29th December for River Plate.
	Cumberland	– Left Falkland Islands 29th December for Simonstwon, to arrive 11th January.
	Cornwall	– At Simonstown.
	Neptune	– At Freetown.

| | Shropshire | – Left Rio de Janeiro 30th December. |
| Non-operational: | Exeter | – At Port Stanley, Falkland Islands. Damaged. To sail 21st January for UK and arrive 15th February. |

America and West Indies Command:

8th Cruiser Squadron:	Orion	– Kingston, Jamaica. To Bermuda for docking and refit.
Attached Cruisers:	Despatch (Cdre)	– Left Panama 1st November. Patrol.
	Effingham*	– Left Halifax 29th December. Escorting and for Portsmouth for 7 week refit.
	Perth* (RAN)	– Left Kingston, Jamaica 28th December.

East Indies Command:

4th Cruiser Squadron:	Sussex* (Flag)	– Arrived Mauritius 1st January.
	Gloucester	– Left Port Victoria 31st December for Colombo.
	Hobart (RAN)	– Left Colombo 30th December.
	Kent	– At Colombo.

China Station:

5th Cruiser Squadron:	Birmingham (Flag)	– At Hong Kong. Docked for repairs.
	Liverpool	– Left Hong Kong 21st December. Patrol.
9th Cruiser Squadron:	Danae	– Hong Kong. Repair, complete uncertain.
	Dauntless	– Singapore.
	Durban	– Singapore.
Royal Australian Navy:	Canberra (Flag)	– Sydney.

	Sydney	– Sydney.
	Australia	– Sydney.
	Adelaide	– Freemantle.
Royal New Zealand Navy:	*Leander* (Brd. Pdt.)	– Left Auckland 1st January for Wellington.

Royal Canadian Navy:

Attached Cruiser:	*Caradoc*	– Esquimalt. Repairs, complete unknown.
Other Cruisers:	*Curlew*	– At Invergordon. Repairs to R.F. Completion uncertain.
Cruiser-Minelayer:	*Adventure*	– Plymouth. Damage repairs, to complete May/June.

January 1941

Home Fleet:

2nd Cruiser Squadron:	*Arethusa* (Flag)	– Arrived Scapa Flow 1st January.
	Aurora	– Arrived Scapa Flow 1st January.
Non-operational:	*Galatea*	– Chatham. Repairs. Completion 8th Jan.
10th Cruiser Squadron:	*Kenya* (Flag)	– Left Plymouth 25th December.
	Nigeria	– Left Scapa Flow 25th December.
	Mauritius	– Arrived Greenock 29th December.
Non-operational:	*Fiji*	– Greenock. Repairs. Completes 31st Jan.
Attached Cruisers:	*Devonshire*	– Detached to South Atlantic Station.
	Suffolk	– Greenock. Refit, completion 31st Jan.
	Sussex	– Greenock. Repairs, completion after September.
	Australia	– Liverpool. Docked. To Clyde 7th Jan.

15th Cruiser Squadron:	*Naiad* (Flag)	– Arrived Scapa Flow 27th December.
	Bonaventure	– Arrived Gibraltar 29th December.
	Phoebe	– Arrived Oban 24th December.
Non-operational:	*Dido*	– Tyne. Repairs, completion 17th Jan.
18th Cruiser Squadron:	*Manchester* (Flag)	– Left Scapa Flow 26th December.
	Birmingham	– Arrived Scapa Flow 27th December.
	Edinburgh	– Left Scapa Flow 24th December.
Detached or off-station:	*Newcastle*	
	Southampton	
Attached Cruiser:	*Kent*	– Plymouth, Care & Maintenance. Repairs. Completion at least ten weeks after 30th December, 1940.
Anti-Aircraft Cruisers:	*Cairo*	– Under C-in-C Western Approaches.
	Curacoa	– Arrived Scapa Flow 31st December.

Portsmouth Command:

| Attached Cruiser: | *Penelope* | – Tyne. Repairs. Completion early June. |

Western Approaches Command:

Anti-aircraft Cruiser:	*Cairo*	– Tyne. Repairs, completion 21st Jan.
Attached Cruisers:	*Emerald*	– Plymouth.
	Cardiff	– Tyne. Repairs. Completion 17th Jan for Gunnery Firing duties.
	Frobisher	– Plymouth. Dockyard control. Re-arming completion mid-1941.
	Exeter	– Plymouth. Paid off.

| | Belfast | Repairs. To complete 7th March.
– Plymouth. Dockyard control. Care & Maintenance. Repairs. Date uncertain. |
| Cruiser-Minelayer: | Adventure | – Milford Haven. |

North Atlantic Command:

| Attached Cruiser: | Berwick | – Arrived Gibraltar 31st December. |
| Force 'H': | Sheffield | – Arrived Gibraltar 30th December. |

Mediterranean Fleet:

3rd Cruiser Squadron:	Gloucester (Flag)	– Left Piraeus 30th December.
	York	– Left Piraeus 30th December.
Non-operational:	Glasgow	– At Alexandria. Temporary repairs. Date uncertain. At least six weeks from 15th December 1940.
7th Cruiser Squadron:	Orion (V/Ad L/F)	– Arrived Alexandria 23rd December.
	Ajax	– Arrived Suda Bay 1st January.
	Perth	– Arrived Suda Bay 1st January.
	Sydney	– Malta.
Non-operational:	Liverpool	– Alexandria. Repairs. Date uncertain.
Attached cruiser:	Southampton	– Arrived Alexandria 30th December.
Anti-aircraft cruisers:	Calcutta	– Left Suda Bay 30th December.
	Coventry	– Alexandria. Damaged.

Red Sea Force:

| Attached Cruisers: | Caledon | – Left Aden 29th |

		December.
	Leander	– Left Bombay 27th December.
Anti-aircraft Cruiser:	*Carlisle*	– Arrived Aden 29th December.

East Indies Command:

Attached Cruisers:	*Capetown*	– Left Colombo 29th December.
	Ceres	– Leaves Mombasa 2nd January.
	Colombo	– Leaves Mombasa 2nd January. Patrol.
	Shropshire	– Arrived Mombasa 31st December.

China Station:

5th Cruiser Squadron:	*Dauntless*	– Arrived Penang 21st December.
	Durban	– Singapore.
Non-operational:	*Danae*	– Hong Kong. Docking, completion uncertain.

South Atlantic Command:

Force 'K':	*Norfolk*	– Left Scapa Flow 18th December.
	Dorsetshire	– Left Freetown 27th December.
Force 'L':	*Dragon*	– Left Freetown 3rd December. Patrolling.
Attached Cruisers:	*Cumberland**	– Left Freetown 1st December.
	Enterprise	– Left Montevideo 15th December.
	Cornwall	– Arrived Simonstown 28th December.
	Delhi	– Left Lagos 23rd December for Manoca.
	Devonshire	– Arrived Simonstown 26th December.
	Dunedin	– Left Gibraltar 29th

		December, for Freetown.
Hawkins		– Arrived Freetown 30th December.
Neptune		– Left Freetown 28th December.
Newcastle		– Left Freetown 10th December. On patrol.

America & West Indies Station:

8th Cruiser Squadron:	*Despatch*	– Arrived Nassau 30th December.
	Dunedin	– Temporarily detached South Atlantic Command
	Caradoc	– Temporarily detached. Arrived Bermuda 27th December.
	Diomede	– Left Kingston, Jamaica 20th December.
Royal Australian Navy:	*Canberra* (**Flag**)	– Arrived Sydney 19th December.
	Adelaide	– Arrived Noumea 29th December.
	Hobart	– Left Freemantle 29th December for Sydney.
Off Station:	*Australia*	– Liverpool. Docked.
	Perth	– Mediterranean Fleet (7th CS)
	Sydney	– Mediterranean Fleet (7th CS)
Royal New Zealand Navy:	*Achillies*	– Left Sydney 29th December for Auckland.
	Leander	– Off Station. Red Sea Force.
Other Cruiser:	*London*	– Chatham. Dockyard control. Due completion after re-build 17th February ex-trials.

January 1942

Home Fleet:

1st Cruiser Squadron:	*Norfolk* (Flag)	– Left Iceland 14th January.
	Berwick	– Left Iceland 9th January.
	Cumberland	– Left Murmansk 13th January.
	Kent	– Left Iceland 15th January.
	Suffolk	– Arrived Scapa Flow 15th January.
Non-operational:	*London*	– Tyne. Repairs. Completion 22-25th Jan.
	Shropshire	– Chatham. Refitting. Completion 7th Feb.
	Sussex	– Greenock. C & M Repairs. Completion 9th August.
2nd Cruiser Squadron:	*Arethusa*	– Arrived Scapa Flow 1st January.
10th Cruiser Squadron:	*Nigeria* (Flag)	– Arrived Scapa Flow 14th January.
	Kenya	– Arrived Scapa Flow 14th January.
	Trinidad	– Left Seidisfiord 10th January.
18th Cruiser Squadron:	*Edinburgh* (Flag)	– Arrived Tyne 15th January.
	Sheffield	– Arrived Scapa Flow 7th January.
Non-operational:	*Manchester*	– In USA, Refitting.
Attached Cruisers:	*Charybdis*	– Clyde. Trials and working up.
	Cleopatra	– Arrived Scapa Flow 10th December.
Detached Cruiser:	*Liverpool*	– Clyde. Repairs. Completion end January.

Rosyth Command:

AA Cruiser:	*Curacoa*	– Arrived Rosyth 17th January.

| Portsmouth Command: | Belfast | – Plymouth. Dockyard control. Completion end October. |
| | Frobisher | – Plymouth Dockyard control. Re-arming completes 13th February |

Western Approaches Command:
| Irish Sea Escort Force: | Cairo | – Plymouth. Refit completes 27th January. |
| Gunnery Firing Cruiser: | Cardiff | – Clyde. |

North Atlantic Command:
| Force 'H': | Hermione | – Arrived Gibraltar 14th January. |

Mediterranean Fleet:
7th Cruiser Squadron:	Ajax	– Arrived Alexandria 31st December.
Non-operational:	Orion	– USA, refitting.
15th Cruiser Squadron:	Naiad (Flag)	– Alexandria.
	Dido	– Alexandria.
	Euryalus	– Alexandria.
	Penelope	– Malta.
Non-operational:	Aurora	– Malta. Repairs, completion end February.
	Phoebe	– USA Refitting.
AA Cruiser:	Coventry	– Bombay. Refitting, completion mid-February

Red Sea Force:
| AA Cruiser: | Carlisle | – Alexandria. |

East Indies Command:
Attached Cruisers:	Caledon	– Left Colombo 14th January.
	Ceres	– Arrived Durban 8th January.
	Colombo	– Arrived Mombasa 10th January.

	Cornwall	– Arrived Bombay 6th January.
	Dorsetshire	– Left Durban 13th January for Aden 20th January.
	Emerald (C-in-C)	– Left Singapore 16th January.
	Enterprise	– Left Colombo 12th January.
	Exeter	– Left Singapore 14th January.
	Glasgow	– Left Colombo 12th January.
	Mauritius	– Left Colombo 2nd January.
Non-operational:	*Capetown*	– Bombay. Refitting, completion end April.
	Hawkins	– Portsmouth. Refitting, completion April.

Eastern Fleet:
5th Cruiser Squadron:

	Dauntless	– Left Bathurst 13th January.
	Danae	– Arrived Singapore 6th January.
	Dragon	– Arrived Batavia 6th January.
	Durban	– Arrived Singapore 13th January.

South Atlantic Command:
Attached Cruisers:

	Birmingham (Flag)	– Left Chile 10th January
	Devonshire	– Arrived Freetown 12th January.
Non-operational:	*Newcastle*	– Plymouth. Repairs. Completion 22nd January
	Vindictive	– Base Repair Ship.

America & West Indies Command:
8th Cruiser Squadron:

	Diomede (Commodore)	– Bermuda. For sea 19th January.

	Despatch	– Left Talara 13th January.
Non-operational:	Caradoc	– USA, Refitting.
Royal Australian Navy:	Australia (Flag)	– Arrived Noumea 7th January.
	Adelaide	– Arrived Sydney 17th January.
	Canberra	– Left Sydney 11th January
	Hobart	– Arrived Freemantle 11th January.
	Perth	– Arrived Noumea 7th January.
Royal New Zealand Navy:	Achillies	– Arrived Noumea 7th January.
	Leander	– Arrived Suva 17th January.
Refitting in USA:	Delhi	– New York 3rd May 1941. Completion Jan.
	Orion	– Arrived Mare Island 5th Sept. Completes Feb.
	Manchester	– Arrived Philadelphia 23rd Sept. Completes Feb.
	Caradoc	– Arrived New York 29 Oct. Completes Feb.
	Phoebe	– Arrived New York 21st Nov. Completes April.

January 1943

Home Fleet:

1st Cruiser Squadron:	Kent (Flag)	– Left Scapa Flow 31st December.
	Berwick	– Left Scapa Flow 31st December.
	Cumberland	– Left Hvalfiord 23rd December.
	Norfolk	– Left Hvalfiord 31st December.
	Sussex	– Tyne. To sail 5th January.

Non-operational:	London	– Tyne. Refitting, completion end April.
	Suffolk	– London. Refitting. Completion Feb.
10th Cruiser Squadron:	Belfast	– Scapa Flow.
	Bermuda	– Left Scapa Flow 31st December.
	Glasgow	– Arrived Scapa Flow 26th December.
	Jamaica	– Arrived Kola Inlet 24th December.
	Kenya	– Tyne.
	Sheffield	– Arrived Kola Inlet 25th December.
	Uganda	– Left Tyne 30th December.
Non-operational:	Liverpool	– Rosyth. Refitting. Completion uncertain.
	Nigeria	– USA. Refitting.
Attached Cruiser:	Charybdis	– Barrow. Radar repairs. Ready 20th Feb.
Minelaying Cruiser:	Adventure	– Plymouth. Ready 6th January.
Plymouth Command:	Colombo	– Plymouth. Paid-off. Re-arming. Completes mid-Feb.

Western Approaches Command:
Gunnery Firing Cruiser: *Cardiff*   – Clyde. Refitting. Completion 21st Jan.

Mediterranean Fleet:

15th Cruiser Squadron:	Cleopatra (Flag)	– Arrived Malta 14th December.
	Euryalus	– Arrived Malta 14th December.
	Orion	– Arrived Malta 21st December.
	Penelope	– Arrived Scapa Flow 2nd December.

| | *Phoebe* | – Arrived Trinidad 30th Dec for New York. |
| AA, Cruiser: | *Carlisle* | – Arrived Scapa Flow 7th December 1942. |

Western Mediterranean:
12th Cruiser Squadron:
Aurora (Flag)

Western Mediterranean:

12th Cruiser Squadron:	*Aurora (Flag)*	– Arrived Algiers 15th December.
	Ajax	– Bone.
	Scylla	– Left Gibraltar 30th December for Clyde.
	Sirius	– Arrived Algiers 1st January.
Non-operational:	*Argonaut*	– Algiers-damaged.

Inshore Squadron:

| AA Cruiser: | *Delhi* | – Gibraltar-damaged. |
| Fleet Repair Ship: | *Vindictive* | – Mers-el-Kebir. |

Eastern Fleet:

4th Cruiser Squadron:	*Birmingham* (Flag)	– Arrived Kilindini 5th December.
	Devonshire	– Arrived Aden 2nd January.
	Frobisher	– Arrived Durban 1st January.
	Gambia	– Arrived Durban 1st January.
	Mauritius	– Arrived Kilindini 30th December.
Non-operational:	*Emerald*	– Portsmouth. Modernisation. Completion mid-Feb.
	Enterprise	– Clyde. Refit and re-arm.
	Newcastle	– Plymouth. Repairing.
5th Cruiser Squadron:	*Capetown*	– Arrived Kilindini 21st December.

	Caradoc	– Arrived Bahrein 30th November.
	Ceres	– Left Aden 27th December.
	Durban	– Arrived Bombay 30th December.
	Hawkins	– Arrived Kilindini 27th December.
Non-operational:	Caledon	– Chatham Repairs. Completion June.
	Danae	– Tyne. Refit. Completion 30th April.
	Dauntless	– Simonstown. Refitting. Completion 25th January
	Dragon	– Liverpool. Refitting. C & M. Completion 30th April.

West Africa Command:

Attached Cruiser:	Despatch	– At Sea.
Non-operational:	Diomede	– Rosyth. Refitting. Under review.
Royal Australian Navy:	Australia (Flag)	– Left Brisbane 1st December.
	Adelaide	– Left Melbourne 15th December.
	Hobart	– Left Brisbane 11th November.
Non-operational:	Shropshire	– Chatham. Refitting for RAN. Completion mid-May.
Royal New Zealand Navy:	Achilles	– Melbourne.
	Leander	– Auckland.
Refitting in USA:	Nigeria	– Arrived Charleston 23rd October. Completion end May.

January 1944

Home Fleet:

| 1st Cruiser Squadron: | Kent (Flag) | – Scapa Flow. |

	Norfolk	– Left Kola Inlet 30th December.
Non-operational:	Devonshire	– Tyne. Modernisation. Completion Feb.
	London	– Rosyth. Repairs.
10th Cruiser Squadron:	Belfast (Flag)	– Left Kola Inlet 30th December.
	Bermuda	– Scapa Flow.
	Glasgow	– Arrived Plymouth 29th December.
	Jamaica	– Left Kola Inlet 28th December.
	Nigeria	– Chatham.
	Sheffield	– Kola Inlet.
Cruisers Working Up:	Bellona	– Scapa Flow. For Med.
	Berwick	– Scapa Flow.
	Black Prince	– Scapa Flow.
	Cumberland	– Scapa Flow.
	Diadem	– Tyne.
	Gambia (RNZN)	– Left Horta 27th December. For East.
	Euryalus	– Clyde. Refitting. Completion end Feb.
	Royalist	– Clyde. Repairs. Completion 8th Jan.

Rosyth Command:

Attached Cruiser:	Dauntless	– Rosyth.
Non-operational:	Liverpool	– Rosyth. Refitting. Completion 15th November 1944-Reduced complement.
C.W. Candidate Training Ship:	Diomede	– Rosyth.

Nore Command:

| Attached Cruiser: | Caledon | – Chatham. |

Portsmouth Command:

| Non-operational: | Despatch | – Portsmouth. Paid Off. Repairs. |

	Durban	– Portsmouth. Paid Off. C & M.

Plymouth Command:

Attached Cruisers:	*Scylla*	– Chatham. Repairs. Completion 10th March.
	Ceres	– Plymouth. (Tender to FOLIOT).
	Capetown	– Plymouth. (Tender to FOLIOT).
	Enterprise	– Plymouth.
Cruiser Minelayer:	*Adventure*	– Milford Haven.

Western Approaches Command:

Gunnery Firing Cruiser:	*Cardiff*	– Clyde.

Mediterranean Fleet:

AA Cruisers:	*Colombo*	– Left Tunis 28th December.
	Delhi	– Left Tunis 27th December.

Gibraltar Command:

Attached Cruiser:	*Ajax*	– Arrived Scapa Flow 28th December.
Non-operational:	*Argonaut*	– Tyne. Refitting. Completion end Feb.
Fleet Repair Ship:	*Vindictive*	– Bizerta.

Malta Command:

Force 'K' – 15th Cruiser Squadron:	*Penelope* (Flag)	– Left Gibraltar 26th December.
	Arethusa	– Arrived Norfolk, Va, 18th Dec.
	Dido	– Arrived Taranto, 24th December.
	Mauritius	– Left Gibraltar 28th December.
	Orion	– Left Malta 21st December.

	Phoebe	– Arrived Alexandria 28th Dec.
	Spartan	– Arrived Gibraltar 28th Dec.
Non-operational:	*Aurora*	– Taranto. Repairs.
	Cleopatra	– Refitting USA.
	Newfoundland	– Refitting USA.
	Sirius	– Massawa. Repairs. Completion mid-Feb.
	Uganda	– Refitting USA.

Levant Command:

AA Cruiser:	*Carlisle*	– Alexandria.

East Indies – Eastern Fleet.

4th Cruiser Squadron:	*Newcastle* (**Flag**)	– Trincomalee.
	Ceylon	– Left Bombay 6th December.
	Emerald	– Arrived Kilindini 7th Dec.
	Frobisher	– Arrived Durban 24th Dec.
	Kenya	– Left Kilindini 4th December.
	Suffolk	– Bombay.
	Sussex	– Left Kilindini 28th Dec.
Non-operational:	*Birmingham*	– Alexandria. Repairs.
	Hawkins	– Simonstown. Refitting. Completes 6th January.
5th Cruiser Squadron:	*Danae*	– Abadan.
	Dragon (**Polish**)	– Arrived Greenock 29th Dec.

South Atlantic Command:

Attached Cruiser:	*Caradoc*	– Durban.
Royal Australian Navy:	*Australia* (**Flag**)	– Left Milne Bay 21st November.
	Adelaide	– Freemantle.
	Shropshire	– Left Milne Bay 21st November.
Non-operational:	*Hobart*	– Sydney. Repairs.

		Completion April/May.
Royal New Zealand Navy:	Leander	– USA Refitting.
	Achillies	– Portsmouth. Refitting. Completion mid May. C & M.
Refitting in USA:	Newfoundland	– Boston. Repairs. Completion 28th February.
	Cleopatra	– Philadelphia. Repairs.
	Uganda	– Charleston. Refitting.
	Leander	– Boston. Repairs.

January 1945.

Home Fleet:

1st Cruiser Squadron:	Norfolk (Flag)	– Arrived Scapa Flow 23rd December.
	Berwick	– Left Scapa Flow 2nd January.
	Devonshire	– Left Scapa Flow 4th January.
10th Cruiser Squadron:	Diadem (Flag)	– Left Scapa Flow 31st December.
	Bellona	– Arrived Scapa Flow 18th December.
	Dido	– Arrived Scapa Flow 28th December.
	Mauritius	– Arrived Scapa Flow 23rd December.
Detached Cruisers:	Belfast	– Tyne. Refitting. Completion March.
	Bermuda	– Clyde. Refitting Completion March.
	Birmingham	– Portsmouth. Repairs. Completion Jan.
	Glasgow	– Tyne. Repairs. Completion April.
	Jamaica	– Portsmouth. Refit. Completion April.
	Sussex	– Chatham. Repairs. Completion Feb.

Rosyth Command:

C.W. Candidates Training *Dauntless*† – Rosyth.
Squadron:

Diomede† – Rosyth.
Unattached Cruisers: *Hawkins* – Clyde. Converting to C.W. Training Cruiser.

Frobisher – Rosyth. Repairs. To convert to C.W. Training Cruiser.

Liverpool – Rosyth. C & M. Refit. Completion mid-July.

Reserve Fleet: *Capetown* – Plymouth. Falmouth Category 'C'.

Despatch – Portsmouth Accommodation. Ship. Category 'C'.

Ceres – Portsmouth Accommodation Ship. Category 'C'.

Emerald – Rosyth. Category 'B'.
Enterprise – Rosyth. Category 'B'.
Caledon – Berth unallocated. Category 'C'.

Carlisle – Berth unallocated. Category 'C'.

Colombo – Berth unallocated. Category 'C'.

Dauntless – Berth unallocated. Category 'C'.†

Diomede – Berth unallocated. Category 'C'.†

Portsmouth Command: *Scylla* – Chatham. Damaged. Repairs.

Danae – CONRAD. Southampton. Refitting. Completion 10th Jan for Polish Navy.

Mediterranean Fleet:

15th Cruiser Squadron: *Ajax* (Flag) – Left Piraeus 3rd January.
Aurora – Salonika.

	Orion	– At sea.
	Sirius	– Khios.
	Arethusa	– Clyde.
AA Cruisers:	Caledon	– Kavalla. To reduce to Category 'C'.
	Colombo	– At sea. To reduce to Category 'C'.
	Delhi	– At sea.
	Carlisle	– Alexandria. Accommodation ship.

† To be relieved and placed in reserve.

Escort Cruiser Squadron:	Royalist	– Alexandria. Repairs. Completion Feb.
East Indies Command:	Euryalus (Flag)	– Left Suez 29th December.
	Kenya	– Trincomalee.
	London	– left Trincomalee 17th December.
	Newcastle	– Left Trincomalee 30th December.
	Nigeria	– Left Trincomalee 30th December.
	Phoebe	– Left Trincomalee 30th December.
	Suffolk	– Left Trincomalee 1st January.
	Cumberland	– At Simonstown. Refitting.
British Pacific Fleet:	Swiftsure (Flag)	– At Sydney.
	Achillies (RNZN)	– Left Freemantle 20th December.
	Argonaut	– Left Trincomalee 1st January.
	Black Prince	– Left Trincomalee 1st January.
	Ceylon	– Left Trincomalee 1st January.
	Gambia (RNZN)	– At Auckland.
	Newfoundland	– Arrived Alexandria 30th December.
	Uganda	– Left Clyde 1st January.

Royal Australian Navy:	*Australia* (Flag)	– At Manus.
	Hobart	– Arrived Melbourne 30th December.
	Shropshire	– At sea.
	Adelaide	– Freemantle. Reduced complement.
Royal New Zealand Navy:	*Leander*	– Boston. Repairs. Completion 30th April.
	Sheffield	– Boston. Refitting for RNZN.

Western Approaches Command:

Gunnery Firing Cruiser:	*Cardiff*	– Lamlash.
Non-operational:	*Cleopatra*	– Clyde. Refitting. Completion March.

January 1946

Home Fleet:

10th Cruiser Squadron:	*Dido* (Flag)	– Portland.
	Bellona	– Portland.
	Birmingham	– Portsmouth. Repairs. Completion Jan.
	Diadem	– Portsmouth. Repairs. Completion Jan.
Cruisers refitting:	*Leander* (RNZN)	– Tyne. Completion February.
(See below for commands)	*Mauritius*	– Birkenhead. Completion Feb.
	Sheffield	– Portsmouth. Completion March.
	Phoebe	– Plymouth. Completion March.
	Nigeria	– Plymouth. Completion March.
	Kenya	– Chatham. Completion April.
	Scylla	– Chatham.
	Ceylon	– Portsmouth.

Superb	– Arrived Portland 2nd Jan for 'Shake down' prior joining Fleet.

Cruisers in 'Trooping' Duties:
(See below for commands)

Berwick	– Due Freemantle 8th January.
Cumberland	– Due Malta 8th Jan.
Devonshire	– Left Colombo 3rd January.
Enterprise	– Left Freetown 6th January.
London	– Arrived Chatham 4th January.
Newcastle	– Due Malta 8th January.
Suffolk	– Arrived Chatham 16th November.

Rosyth Command:
C.W. Candidates Training Cruiser: *Dauntless* – Rosyth.

Nore Command:		
	Kenya	– Refitting.
	London	– Refitting.
	Nigeria	– Refitting.
	Phoebe	– Refitting.
	Suffolk	– Refitting.
	Superb	– Shaking down.

Portsmouth Command:

Cadet Training Cruiser:	*Frobisher*	– Arrived Gibraltar 7th January.
	Berwick	– Trooping.
	Enterprise	– Trooping.
	Scylla	– Repairs under review.
	Sheffield	– Refitting.
Accommodation Ships:	*Ceres*	– Portsmouth. Category 'C' Reserve.
	Despatch	– Portsmouth. Category 'C' Reserve.
Plymouth Command:	*Cumberland*	– Trooping.
	Devonshire	– Trooping.

| | Newcastle | – Trooping. |
| | Mauritius | – Refitting. |

Reserve Fleet:
Rosyth Area:

	Emerald	– Rosyth. Category 'C'.
	Kent	– Gareloch. Category 'B'.
	Cardiff	– Gareloch. Category 'B'.

Plymouth Area:

	Delhi	– Dartmouth. Category 'C'.
	Caledon	– Dartmouth. Category 'C'.
	Capetown	– Falmouth. Category 'C'.
	Diomede	– Falmouth. Category 'C'.
	Hawkins	– Falmouth. Category 'C'.

Cruisers Reducing to Reserve: Arethusa – Chatham. To Category 'B'.

| | Caradoc | – Devonport. To berth Falmouth, Category 'C'. |

Cruisers to be Paid Off into Reserve:

| | Carlisle | – Alexandria. Berth unallocated. Category 'C'. |
| | Dauntless | – Rosyth. Berth unallocated. Category 'C'. |

Mediterranean Fleet:
15th Cruiser Squadron:

	Orion (Flag)	– Malta.
	Aurora	– Arrived Patras 30th December.
	Liverpool	– Arrived Trieste 21st December.
	Sirius	– Arrived Haifa 23rd December.

Off Station: Ajax – Due Gibraltar 8th January for Freetown.

Escort Base Ship: Carlisle – Alexandria. For Category 'C'.

East Indies Command:
5th Cruiser Squadron:

| | Norfolk (Flag) | – Batavia. |
| | Glasgow | – Arrived Trincomalee 5th January. |

	Jamaica	– Left Singapore 4th January.
	Sussex	– Arrived Colombo 5th January.
On passage:	Cleopatra	– At Trincomalee.
	Royalist	– Left Aden 5th January.

British Pacific Fleet:

2nd Cruiser Squadron:	Belfast (Flag)	– Arrived Shanghai 21st December.
	Achilles	– Tokyo.
	Bermuda	– Due Darwin.
	Black Prince	– At Shanghai.
	Euryalus	– Hong Kong.
Non-operational:	Gambia	– Auckland.
4th Cruiser Squadron:	Swiftsure	– Sydney.
	Argonaut	– Hong Kong.
Non-operational:	Newfoundland	– Sydney. Refitting. Completion January.
Royal Australian Navy:	Hobart (Commodore)	– Arrived Tarakan 30th December.
	Adelaide	– Sydney.
	Shropshire	– Sydney.
On passage:	Australia	– Due Durban 9th January.
Royal Canadian Navy:	Ontario	– Esquimalt.
Non-operational:	Uganda	– Esquimalt. Refitting. Completion Jan.

Royal New Zealand Navy:

| 2nd Cruiser Squadron: (RN). | Achilles | – (See above). |
| | Gambia | – (See above). |

Index

1139605   9HO·545

SMITH, P. C., AND DOMINY, J. R.

CRUISERS IN ACTION, 1939-1945

944 545   18/08/82   £11.95

Please renew/return this item by the last date shown.

So that your telephone call is charged at local rate, please call the numbers as set out below:

	From Area codes 01923 or 0208:	From the rest of Herts:
Renewals:	01923 471373	01438 737373
Enquiries:	01923 471333	01438 737333
Minicom:	01923 471599	01438 737599

L32b

Hertfordshire
COUNTY COUNCIL
Community Information

0 8 JUN 2006

6/12

19 JUL 2005

25 SEP 1995

23 NOV 1994

2 8 NOV 1994

3 1 JAN 1995

2 4 AUG 1995

2 4 MAR 1997

-2 SEP 1997

-1 OCT 1997

1 2 MAY 1998

3 MAY 2001

L32a